The Art of Getting More Back in Diplomacy

The Art of Getting More
Back in Diplomacy

Negotiation Lessons from North Korea,
China, Libya, and the United Nations

Eric N. Richardson

University of Michigan Press
Ann Arbor

For questions or permissions, please contact um.press.perms@umich.edu

Published in the United States of America by the University of Michigan Press
Manufactured in the United States of America
Printed on acid-free paper
First published October 2021

A CIP catalog record for this book is available from the British Library.

Library of Congress Cataloging-in-Publication data has been applied for.

ISBN 978-0-472-07506-5 (hardcover: alk. paper)
ISBN 978-0-472-05506-7 (paper: alk. paper)
ISBN 978-0-472-12953-9 (e-book)

Contents

Part II: Multiparty International Negotiations and Structural Factors

Digital materials related to this title can be found on the Fulcrum platform via the following citable URL: https://doi.org/10.3998/mpub.11978420

Acknowledgments

This primer on the art and science of negotiations focuses on observations from the working-level and on negotiations I participated in personally. It could not have been produced without contributions from all those I negotiated with, negotiated against, and observed, studied, and consulted with during my career as a lawyer and diplomat. I had some formal training in negotiation with law professor J. J. White and diplomatic instructor Harold Saunders, but most of the lessons in this text come from learning by negotiating and learning by watching others negotiate.

In addition to those whose work is discussed in detail here, I feel indebted to the other negotiators, too many to name, who contributed to these lessons in very positive ways. These include diplomatic supervisors and mentors Jeffrey Feltman, Sung Kim, Peter Mulrean, Richard Roth, and Richard Erdman; U.S. diplomatic colleagues Mark Lambert, Susan Thornton, David Sullivan, Steven Townley, Valerie Ullrich, Paula Schriefer, Susan O'Sullivan, Scott Busby, and Christopher Klein; nongovernmental colleagues John Kamm, Biro Diawara, Simona Ross, Hans Hogrefe, and others at UNHR, and David Harland, and others at the Centre for Humanitarian Dialogue. Those who contributed to these lessons were also negotiators from other countries where we had shared positions, such as the late Ambassador Youssef Ismail Bari-Bari, the late Ebenezzer Appreku, Ian Duddy, Sami Bougacha, Harriet Berg, Barbara Fontana, Yaprak Alp, Mats Foyer, and countless diplomats whom I found on the opposite side of the table in Washington, the United Nations, and in various capitals, but from whom I learned just as much.

As this is my first published book, I especially appreciate the help of my editors and reviewers, including William Inboden, Joel Wit, Robert Einhorn, Ronald Nowak, and the team at University of Michigan Press. Finally, and most importantly, I have to thank my family members for their reviews of the text, patience, support, and confidence, specifically Maureen, Siena, Maya, Zac, Mom, Dad, and Uncle Jeff.

CHAPTER I

Introduction

How to Get More Back in Multiparty Negotiations

Multiparty international political negotiations are unique. Like any negotiation, there are basic tools you can use to do a better job—whether for your client, your institution, your country, or yourself. This book focuses on lessons you can use drawn from multiparty international political negotiations I participated in personally, and it tells the inside story: the good and the bad, whether about the United States or other nations that I dealt with in more than twenty years as a diplomat working on problems from North Korea to China, and from Libya to the United Nations. In the end, one lesson stands out above all others: international political negotiators who bring an exclusively corporate or litigation approach to political negotiations underperform and often fail. And when they engage in multiparty international political negotiations, they often fail spectacularly, with negative consequences that can last a long time for their country, their interests, or their clients.

Many tactics deployed in business and litigation settlement negotiations only make sense for people negotiating over money. For a real estate mogul, a corporate lawyer, or a drug dealer, when you are negotiating over money, certain tactics work because you are splitting a finite commodity. Negotiations over money are designed to be a zero-sum game. Win-lose. Get more than the other guy does. The amount of difference is quickly and easily measured and valued in dollars and cents. How to maximize the financial takeaway from a business deal is the underlying approach of *The Art of The Deal*, the book Donald Trump authored, and of his negotiating style before and during his presidency. It is also an approach I have seen deployed repeatedly by negotiators who come to international political negotiations from outside of government, especially private litigators and dealmakers.

Some dealmaking tactics from private business can be deployed in international political negotiations. You can press your opposite number. You can walk away from a deal until you get what you want. You can criticize the dealmaking process in public and in private and use pressure from actors outside of the negotiation itself. Some of these tactics work in international political negotiations and some of their successes will be demonstrated in the chapters that follow. Diplomats I have spoken with from North Korea to the European Union and from Cuba to China would agree that "Getting More Back" for your country is the ultimate goal of any negotiation.

But serious failure often arises for a government when a negotiator from a commercial setting fails to adjust to the reality of multiparty international political negotiations, where your behavior, your reactions and your willingness to spoil relationships over zero-sum outcomes are judged over the long-term. In an international environment like the United Nations, a party who is your opposite number today may hold the key vote you need for success tomorrow. The nature of sovereignty and the international political environment means that nations have to deal with nations time and again, whereas commercial partners or competitors can often avoid an interlocutor from a past deal if that previous negotiation turned ugly or if sharp tactics resulted in a feeling of unfairness and bad blood. For the purposes of this book and considering differences between the international political negotiating landscape and that of a commercial actor, the bottom line is this: when money is not the primary thing at stake, international political negotiations require more diplomatic tactics focused on maintaining relationships and negotiating pathways. Sometimes "getting more back" requires different tactics in a political negotiation than it does in a financial one. So certain tactics that might yield positive short-term outcomes in a settlement negotiation or a business deal become so toxic in the international political negotiating environment between states that they are of limited utility and can even be counterproductive. As we will see in several of the case studies that follow, a businessperson's or litigator's approach can be especially damaging in multilateral negotiations in ongoing venues like the United Nations, where a given negotiation is just one incident in a continuing set of relationships among states that will be carried out over several negotiations on different topics over the course of years.

Success in international political negotiations, especially those that take place in a multilateral venue like the United Nations, becomes much more likely for negotiators who can explore the range of interests to find or create win-win situations. In a business or litigation setting, where negotiations are mostly over money or financial compensation, it is not always possible to create value by looking for win-win outcomes. But international political negotiations almost always have multiple successful outcomes because the objectives of the parties are about more than dollars and cents. States want prestige, security, recognition for their leader, better relationships, and financial gain, and have multiple other objectives in a political negotiation. When multiple states are involved in an international political negotiation, the web of interlocking objectives becomes even more complex. Because of this, multiparty international political negotiations present many more options for creative solutions that satisfy part or all of the interests of the key players.

As this book analyzes these case studies in detail and considers how different negotiating tactics worked or did not work, it will take both a theoretical and a personal approach. On the theoretical side, it will look at negotiating tactics in the context and perspective of multiparty international political negotiations. Multilateral negotiations—like in the United Nations—are just one type of multiparty negotiations. A multiparty political negotiation is one in which there are at least three participating parties. As a result, multiparty negotiations can find a negotiator (or the state that the negotiator represents) in several different roles. One key to getting more back for your client or country requires understanding the roles of direct participant, indirect participant, mediator, observer, and guarantor.

Direct participants are those whose interests are so central to the negotiation that an agreement cannot be reached without addressing their concerns. In the Israeli-Palestinian conflict, for example, Israel and the Palestinian Authority are direct participants, but other parties, including the United States, have had significant roles in those negotiations, including the ones I participated in during the late 1990s under the Oslo Accords.

Indirect participants may also have interests important to the negotiation at hand. But the interests of indirect participants are not so central to the issue such that the indirect participants' interests must be resolved as part of the overall deal at the heart of the negotiations. Sometimes the interests of indirect participants could be resolved in a parallel forum or could even be ignored and still produce a durable resolution of the key issues of the direct participants. On discussions of the North Korean nuclear issue, for example, Japan might be considered an indirect participant. As a neighboring country and potential target of the North Korean nuclear and missile threat, Japan clearly has strong interests in resolving the North Korean issue. It also has interests in trade and in discovering the fate of its citizens abducted by North Korea over the past forty years. But the North Korean nuclear issue could be addressed without Japan's participation, making it an indirect participant, rather than a necessary direct one.

Observers are just that, parties outside the negotiation who are observing. Some observers are also **mediators** but not all play that role. In multilateral negotiations, such as in the United Nations, it is more common that a member state, or even a part of the United Nations itself, plays the role of mediator. Mediation has become a complex profession, in both the political and the commercial world, with its own litany of tools and tactics. While mediation is not the primary focus of this book, it will be useful to identify from the case studies addressed here when an observer is acting as a mediator, to determine whether the mediator is a truly neutral party or an interested party, and whether the tactics deployed from the commercial world also apply in the international political arena. In the case of Libya's dueling governments after the downfall of Moammar Qaddafi, Egypt attempted to act as a mediator. But as we will see in chapter 5, Egypt's role in Libya is not a neutral one; it wants to resolve Libya's political disputes on terms that will install its favored actors to political power in Libya, on terms that will protect its border region, and on terms that will allow Egyptian workers to have jobs and earn money in Libya.

Finally, we will look at a particularly important role for some negotiation participants in multiparty talks, the role of the guarantor. **Guarantors** are defined as parties whose participation in the negotiation is because of the real or perceived influence that the guarantor can bring over one of the direct participants. One of the key questions this book will analyze through the case studies considers when and how a guarantor exerts this real or perceived influence, and how other participants in the negotiation can influence the guarantor to exert that influence. Sometimes this results in multiparty negotiations becoming a negotiation within the negotiation.

Given these complexities, success as an international negotiator in these different roles requires flexibility, perspective, and situational management. The later chapters in this book will look at a few examples of multiparty negotiations from these different perspectives and analyze which tools work best for negotiators in each of the different roles of direct participant, indirect participant, mediator, and observer. Sometimes a state attempts to disguise the role it is playing in a negotiation, because hiding its role is in its interest. For example, several of Libya's neighboring states have attempted to put themselves forward as neutral mediators of the ongoing civil war in that country, when their goal in mediating or bringing parties together was actually to ensure that their own national interest was protected. Moreover, regardless of which role a country is playing, we find that negotiators who can consider the interests of multiple parties and "create value" by deploying creative solutions that satisfy part or all of the interests of the key players tend to be the most successful negotiators, and the ones in greatest demand.

Throughout, I offer my personal experience as an American diplomat participating at the working level from within each of these negotiations and observing the conflicts or issues that negotiations are trying to resolve. Sometimes the stories are colored by experiences outside the negotiating room. For example, I was the one who suffered expulsion from the Chinese Foreign Ministry when U.S.-China relations over human rights reached a boiling point. I had to work to maintain relationships when a political appointee's Washington-focused rhetoric threatened to blow-up key relationships or a UN meeting. And it will be my future working-level colleagues who will have to find a way back to the negotiating table with South Korean allies or adversaries like the North Koreans because President Trump failed to institutionalize the relationships and processes necessary to discuss, agree, and verify denuclearization on the Korean Peninsula. But the observations made here are based on some twenty-five years of being on the ground as a negotiator and diplomat, and they provide real fodder for practical and academic work to make politicians, businesspeople, and future diplomats better negotiators.

So which tactics from the private negotiating environment can be deployed in the public sector and which do not work in international negotiations? This book will explore some of those questions and provide case studies from international political negotiations that illustrate negotiating styles, good and bad, and provide perspectives that will help you answer these questions for yourself and determine which negotiating styles work best for you.

First, we will look at tactics that work in any negotiation: political, financial, or otherwise. Do not give something up unless you get something back. International political negotiators who give something away without getting something back are just like negotiators in a financial deal who leave money on the table. Every concession is worth something, even in a political negotiation. Sometimes what you get back for giving something away is good will. Sometimes it is prestige. Sometimes it is more tangible. But if you care about the end product of the negotiation, each little concession should be thought of as a mini-negotiation on the path to getting what you want at the end of the process.

Second, the positions of a negotiating partner must be tested. Of course, how you test those positions matters. You might prefer to test positions in a relatively safe way for your client or country, rather than in a way that will, for example, lead a counterpart like North Korea to respond by launching a nuclear-tipped missile at the United States or marching thousands of troops on Seoul. But if a counterpart says they will not do something that is of high value to your country (or your client), do not take no for an answer until you test the proposition. The negotiating style, and errors, of the Brazilian delegation in Geneva in advancing a resolution in 2014–2016 to create the first UN mechanism on LGBTI rights, a UN independent expert, will be our primary case study as detailed in chapter 6. The case study examines whether proponents of creating a UN Special Mechanism to look at sexual orientation and gender identity could have created the mechanism two years earlier in 2014, when the issue first had a majority of the UN Human Rights Council. Or alternatively, did negotiators "leave money on the table" in 2014 by not pressing for creation of the mechanism until two years later.[1]

Third, invent options for mutual gain. Fisher and Ury's seminal negotiations primer *Getting to Yes* emphasizes how win-win options are usually available. Creative solutions that benefit all parties are almost always advisable. In multiparty international negotiations, a negotiator who can understand the complex web of objectives of the many states involved and the possible concessions that can create value or produce win-win solutions will often be able to come up with solutions and overcome obstacles. As we will see in chapter 10, sometimes many more than two parties consider themselves crucial participants in the negotiation. And when as many as 193 member states of the United Nations consider themselves party to the negotiations, finding enough "win" to go around can be challenging indeed. Sometimes the win-win solutions involve looking beyond the immediate negotiation. For example, until July 2018, Ethiopia's primary consideration in the United Nations was opposition to and criticism of its neighbor and rival, Eritrea. In my time working at the UN in Geneva, I frequently used U.S. support for Ethiopia in its campaign against Eritrea as a negotiating tool and tradeoff to find areas of common interest with Ethiopia on UN resolutions and topics that had nothing to do with Eritrea. Other states appreciated that a negotiation with the United States in the UN was an opportunity to raise

---

1. In addition to the detailed discussion in chapter 6, compare media coverage of the two events in Adam Howard, October 15, 2014, "UN Passes Resolution on Behalf of LGBT Citizens Around the Globe," MSNBC, available at http://www.msnbc.com/msnbc/un-passes-resolution-behalf-lgbt-citizens-around-the-globe, with Carol Morello, June 30, 2016, "UN Council Creates Watchdog for LGBT Rights," *Washington Post*, available at https://www.washingtonpost.com/world/national-security/un-council-creates-watchdog-for-lgbt-rights/2016/06/30/54976de6-3eee-11e6-80bc-d06711fd2125_story.html?utm_term=.c2fa20c82b7a

their bilateral interests with the United States—be they for a political visit, bilateral aid, or just a request for a visa.

At the same time, a tactic or tool uniquely available to those participating in multiparty negotiations is the ability to empower other states to take on certain leadership roles in multiparty negotiations. Frequently, the best way to achieve one's goals in the UN is to work with and through others. We will also look at the unique roles that parties can take on in multiparty negotiations, including roles of direct participant, indirect participant, observer, mediator, and guarantor.

Fourth, we will learn from best (and worst) practices and typical arguments used by different types of negotiators. This will include a brief discussion of standard arguments I have observed in international negotiations, as well as ways to debunk many of them. Chapter 3 provides a range of examples.

Following that, we will examine specific case studies and their impact on key aspects of negotiation theory. We will start by looking at the importance of understanding each party's Best Alternative to a Negotiated Agreement, or BATNA. A classic tool in teaching negotiating theory, understanding the BATNA also requires understanding one's interests and the interests of a negotiating partner and then coming up with ways of changing, or even deceiving, a negotiating partner about your BATNA. The idea of deceiving other parties about your BATNA is an approach that seems to appeal to those executives turned negotiators who would follow the theory of *The Art of the Deal*. On the other hand, we will show how "logical strongmen" in international politics, such as in Libya and North Korea, often are good negotiators because of their clarity about their BATNA. Ironically, negotiating counterparts often describe these strongmen as crazy or irrational, and yet the "irrational" strongmen often out-maneuver negotiators seen as coming from democratic or reasonable governments. Operating within their constraints and alternatives, these "logical strongmen" are usually clear-minded about their path and their alternatives because they operate in a world of very stark choices.

After that, the next chapters will illustrate the limits of a businessperson's winner-take-all approach to negotiations over money. These case studies demonstrate why and how certain aspects of a business-style approach to negotiation (walking away from the table, pushing for every concession or every dollar, or threatening counterparts) can be counterproductive. This is especially true in an environment of negotiation among and between states, where the same negotiating parties are likely to have to work together again on the same or different topics once the negotiation is completed.

Imagine the challenges President Trump faced with European partners in NATO after his handling of the summer 2018 NATO Summit. Trump wanted NATO partners to commit to spending a higher percentage of their annual national budgets on defense spending. Aiming to reach a target for spending 4 percent of GDP, Trump used several of these tactics, including public bullying and threats of trade retaliation, to pressure the NATO partner countries to reach this threshold. When the NATO countries largely held their ground and stuck to a previous deal in which they would gradually increase spending, Trump took to the airways to declare victory. He inaccurately claimed that his negotiating strategy caused European NATO leaders to offer new concessions, and that they agreed to faster and higher defense spending in future years. The president sought to use the media and claim victory, but this tactic did not ultimately cover up the fact that no new concessions were actually reached, and that the European NATO members merely reverted to their previous agreements about gradual defense spending increases.

I have watched political appointees turned ambassador bring this tough, litigation style to the UN with poor results. One ambassador whom I worked for at the UN Human Rights Council was very rough in initial encounters with other ambassadors, especially those from countries that had a bad human rights record, such as Sudan addressed in chapter 8. This played poorly not only with the country being criticized but also with other more influential ambassadors who observed this behavior.[2] It was necessary for professional diplomats to shore up the damaged relationship because, in the one country/one vote system of the United Nations, the United States would need that relationship again. Working with such an egotistical personality made me feel a bit like a diner at an American restaurant where someone else picks up the bill but leaves a poor tip. Much as you might subtly supplement the tip with an extra $20 bill, I felt the need to work with those offended by the litigator-ambassador and compensate for his rough behavior, in the interest of longer-term relations and the interests of my country. In this way, working in a UN environment is much like living in a city of limited restaurant choices. Don't leave a bad tip at a restaurant you plan to revisit. Similarly, in the United Nations, you will have to return again and again to the same negotiating counterparts and, over time, brinksmanship-type behavior will undermine their willingness to work constructively with you and detract from your ability to Get More Back for your country.

---

2. See, e.g., Interview with former Ethiopian ambassador Minelik Getahun, September 2017.

I observed more than one litigator-turned-ambassador who did not understand that countries like the United States have a special card to play in international political negotiations: **Giving Respect.** Giving respect in an international negotiation costs the country conceding it little or nothing—in fact, the giving of respect sometimes increases the giving state's supply. But time and again, be it with the litigator-turned-ambassador, or the U.S. political approach to refuse to negotiate with states in an "axis of evil" until prerequisites are met, poor negotiators squander the special commodity of Giving Respect. Chapters 10–12 deploy examples from negotiations over human rights in China and the Israel-Palestinian peace accords to illustrate how overreaching may produce a positive short-term outcome but can often damage the prospects for long-term sustainable win-win results that would better achieve the parties' interests.

The final chapters of this book will return to China and North Korea in 2021. With China, we consider how the breakdown in dialogue between the United States and China as a result of their growing power conflict and competition has limited the opportunity to explore win-win possibilities. Failure to cooperate in addressing the coronavirus pandemic is the most obvious result of the failure of these two superpowers to have a successful negotiation, but we consider a range of additional factors about their relationship as a way of illustrating the tactics discussed throughout this text.

In the North Korea situation, repeated summitry between President Trump and North Korean chairman Kim Jong Un aimed at reducing the threat of North Korea's nuclear weapons has failed and, in 2020, prospects for peace on the Korean Peninsula seem distant. Despite his claims of North Korea as a foreign policy success, President Trump has squandered any potential breakthrough with North Korea by failing to turn his summit meetings into an agreement with sufficient detail to make Americans safer and ensure North Korea's denuclearization. Through bluffing, threats, and ego, President Trump has brought the United States closer to conflict with nuclear-armed nations like North Korea and potentially Iran, China, and Russia, than it has been since the Cuban Missile Crisis. As we will examine in chapter 13, the as-yet-unfinished story of his negotiations with North Korea may be one of the tipping points that could undermine America's position as a superpower. Even to the extent that summitry with North Korea appears successful, the occasional face-to-face negotiation between two strongmen does not necessarily translate into implementation of a multiparty peace agreement, which will be necessary to establish lasting security on the Korean Peninsula.

One of the strengths of President Trump's unorthodox style as a "different type of negotiator" was a willingness to meet with Kim Jong Un or other authoritarian leaders when others would not. But North Korea's resumption of its provocative weapons programs and destabilizing behavior suggest that President Trump squandered that opportunity, no matter how good a personal relationship he claims to have established in meetings with Kim, Chinese President Xi, Russian President Putin or others. Getting More Back for your country often is more complicated than getting more back for yourself. In failing to understand and be able to deploy this lesson, many businessmen-turned-diplomats find their tactics failing them in the art of multiparty international negotiation.

PART I

Deploying Negotiating Theory and Tactics in Select Case Studies

CHAPTER 2

Negotiation Theory Overview

Setting the Stage

Like any tactician, a good negotiator needs a toolkit. This kit may include her personal qualities, her relationships, her knowledge and experiences, but it also should include tactics to deploy in a negotiation. To ensure that you have all the tools of international negotiation at your disposal, this chapter aims to give negotiators the basic theoretical background for creating their negotiations toolkit, while chapter 3 aims to fill your negotiator's toolbox with specific tactics and responses to negotiating behaviors and ploys that are sometimes put forth based on these theories. Whether deployed in a single negotiation or as part analyzing a set of negotiation case studies as in this book, deployment and understanding of these principles is essential for success. Moreover, situational management requires having a plethora of theoretical approaches, strategies, and tactics available and choosing the appropriate one to deploy depending on the content and context of the negotiation at issue. Finally, reviewing these principles is important as background for subsequent chapters, which will look at the application of these and other tactics over the course of several case studies.

Understanding and Identifying Each Side's Interests

In order to understand any negotiation, a negotiator must be aware of his (or his client or state's) interests as well as the interests of his counterpart. As Harvard professors Fisher and Ury describe it, this means parties should focus their negotiation efforts on interests rather than positions.[1] Positions are usually conclusory statements put forward to explain the desired negotiation outcome, but they rarely offer principles, ideas, or knowledge about the reasons why a desired outcome is needed by one party or the other. Understanding those underlying reasons and motivations is necessary for a negotiator to move beyond a discussion of dueling positions into a more nuanced analysis of interests. Discussion of interests also increases the likelihood for creative solutions that can result in win-win outcomes.[2]

A good negotiator not only understands his own side's interests and motivation but also strives to understand the interests and motivation of the other side. This is valuable in searching for new alternatives or "win-win" solutions that create value. In addition, a negotiator who strives to understand his counterpart's interests and motivation is more likely to be able to estimate how valuable certain concessions are to his counterpart, and to extract the best deal in exchange for any concessions he or she makes. The businessperson's approach to "never leave money on the table" in a negotiation can also apply to international political negotiations. As we will see in several of the forthcoming examples, particularly chapter 6's discussion of negotiations to create the first UN mandate offering protection based on Sexual Orientation and Gender Identity (SOGI), participants in a multiparty international political negotiation sometimes have difficulty testing the positions and interests of their opposite number. This can produce suboptimal results, and as described in chapter 6, may have delayed UN action to systematically protect LGBTI individuals from discrimination.

Best Alternative to a Negotiated Agreement (BATNA)

The principle of BATNA is one of the most useful theoretical and tactical principles in negotiation theory. It helps negotiators understand why a counterpart might not strike a deal. It also creates a framework for influencing the relative positions and beliefs of a counterpart about his alternatives, so as to make reaching a deal on favorable terms more likely.[3]

---

1. R. Fisher and W. Ury. 2011. *Getting To Yes*. 2nd ed. New York: Penguin Books. Chapters 1 and 3.

2. See, e.g., Jeswald W. Salacuse. 2003. *The Global Negotiator*. New York: St. Martin's Press, p. 49, emphasizing the need to "search for the other side's needs and interests and don't be afraid to reveal yours." As Salacuse notes, revealing your own interests can be easier once work has been done to build a relationship and establish trust, as illustrated in more detail in chapter 8's example involving negotiations with Sudan.

3. Fisher and Ury, *Getting to Yes*, chapter 6.

An early example of influencing a BATNA in U.S. diplomatc history comes from an analysis of Benjamin Franklin's letters to the French government at the time of the American Revolution. Franklin was sent to France in 1776 to persuade the French to join the war on the side of the underdog American revolutionaries and against the British.[4] His French counterparts repeatedly rebuffed his entreaties and noted privately their fear that entering the war against Britain was a greater risk to France's political and commercial interests than joining sides with the sympathetic upstart American revolutionaries. With his knowledge of French officials and culture, Franklin wooed them to the U.S. side, comparing the undeveloped American colonies to a lover whom France could seduce. Less colorfully, Franklin's narrative and descriptions aimed to influence the French BATNA. He pointed out that France had a limited opportunity to secure its position and lucrative trade with the American colonies, now and in the future. He bluffed and cajoled, suggesting that France needed to aid the colonies in order to improve its trading position. In future, the dispute with Britain might be smoothed over such that American trade might remain monopolized by Britain, thus closing the French out of a lucrative market. In the end, his efforts paid off and France agreed to offer limited aid to the American revolutionaries, which ultimately developed into Lafayette's assistance and full French recognition of the colonies later in the war.

As we will see in the examples that follow, an expert negotiator is keenly aware of his counterpart's BATNA and tries to influence it in a range of situations. Perhaps less well known is the importance of also being aware of your counterpart's and your own WATNA (the Worst Alternative to a Negotiated Agreement). Even the best negotiator can fail if she uses excessive brinksmanship and spoils a deal, failing to account accurately for the lack of alternatives to striking a negotiated agreement that are available to her and her client.

Seeking Win-Win Solutions[5]

One important reason for understanding your counterpart's interests, motivations, positions, and BATNA is the opportunity to turn zero-sum negotiations into win-win solutions. Negotiators often refer to this as "creating

---

4. Stacy Schiff. 2005. *A Great Improvisation: Franklin, France and the Birth of America*; see also William Grimes. April 6, 2005. "Ben Franklin Took on France with Insouciant Diplomacy." *New York Times*, E6: "When the Battle of Saratoga gave America the momentum, he pressed his advantage, tormenting Vergennes with the possibility that America might find it advantageous to strike a deal with Britain."

5. Fisher and Ury, *Getting to Yes*, chapter 4; Salacuse, *The Global Negotiator* (outlining seven principles for global deal making, stressing "always create value").

value." Analysts of negotiation theory often distinguish between distributive negotiations, which are zero-sum negotiations like real-estate deals or financial settlements, and integrative negotiations, which allow for possible win-win outcomes.

In most negotiations, especially multiparty international political ones, it is possible to find elements of an integrative negotiation. Usually, concepts or issues exist within the context or confines of a negotiation that parties value but that do not necessarily have to be divided or distributed in order for the parties to reach a successful conclusion. For example, in negotiations over language in UN resolutions, there are often principles or issues that are not central to the theme of the resolution that a good negotiator can insert or address to accommodate interests of some parties and find opportunities for compromise. Even in negotiations that are not about language, there are usually additional interests that one or another party has that can produce the opportunity for win-win solutions that create value. These might include actions that create prestige, such as treating a smaller state with respect or including favorable mention of a particular leader's favorite ideology or past achievement into a public document. We will see many examples of win-win solutions in the case studies.

Recently, the term "win-win cooperation" has been associated in particular with the thought of Chinese President Xi Jinping. As outlined at the end of chapter 9, a resolution in the UN Human Rights Council (HRC) in 2018 sought to institutionalize into soft law the value of the idea of win-win cooperation. While the Chinese definition of win-win cooperation may have particular characteristics, it would be a mistake for negotiators from outside China to resist the win-win concept solely because of its appearance in Xi Jinping's thinking and speeches. To the contrary, acknowledging the term can offer value to Chinese interlocutors that can be exchanged for something else. At the same time, negotiators who come from a different perspective can expand on the contents of "win-win cooperation" so that it does not necessarily erode international human rights standards or otherwise take on a meaning at odds with principles of a state's responsibility for protection of individual rights.

Evaluating Based on Objective Criteria[6]

To avoid conflicts that arise in negotiations or to work around obstacles that may arise, it is helpful if the parties can agree to evaluate a situation based

---

6. Fisher and Ury, *Getting to Yes*, chapter 5; Salacuse, *The Global Negotiator*, p. 53.

on objective criteria. Facts are usually a helpful arbiter for working around problems. If parties can agree on the facts of a situation, one can often find a way of characterizing those facts that will acceptably allow a negotiation to move forward.

When facts are in dispute, parties can often find the space to move forward by referring to factual assessments or previous studies to address different parties' positions related to past events. If there is dispute, for example, on who is at fault for a particular past action, it may be possible to refer to a UN or other international assessment of the situation as an objective criteria. Reasonable parties can rarely disagree that X or Y report described the facts in a certain way, even if they dispute the report itself.

In some cases, exploration of the facts will reveal that the dispute does not necessarily center on the facts but focuses on how to characterize those facts. Sometimes a party objects to certain embarrassing events being acknowledged in a public document but can agree to the facts themselves. This was the case, for example, in negotiations that will be discussed in chapter 8 with the government of Sudan over past human rights violations. When we hit a wall, I often returned to an agreement that we made early in the discussion to focus on the facts: for example, that in April 2016 unarmed student protestors were killed in a university protest. By relying on objective facts—that the students died—rather than emphasizing that it was security forces who did the killing, it became relatively easy to agree to describe the facts in the negotiated agreement, and we narrowed our dispute to how to refer to which parties were at fault. In other cases with Sudan where it was necessary to state which parties were at fault for an action, it was helpful to be somewhat vague and refer to outside criteria. For example, Sudanese counterparts could agree to take note that certain human rights violations were committed by "parties mentioned in the Independent Expert's report on page 72" instead of having to publicly restate the responsibility of certain security force actors.

Strategic Patience/Synchronizing Time Horizons

Having a reasonable time horizon for striking an agreement and a common understanding of your and your negotiating partner's relative time horizon for reaching agreement is an essential part of longer-term international political negotiations. Traditionally, American negotiators are impatient, seeking immediate results and tied to certain domestic political considerations, while Chinese negotiators often take the longer term view of political developments. The term "strategic patience" has been used to describe U.S. policy related to some examples in this book: on North Korea, it showed the change from a hurry to negotiate denuclearization steps under Special Envoy Christopher Hill to a willingness to negotiate but only under certain conditions, as pursued by Hill's successor, Special Envoy Stephen Bosworth. Ultimately the phrase was used to characterize the lack of activity on North Korea during the late Obama and early Biden administrations. Similarly, on Libya, the United States advocated a shift from the pressure for a unification deal in late 2016 under outgoing Special Envoy Jonathan Winer to a more measured approach, which hoped to bring the parties together but recognized that, as long as terrorism was being defeated in Libya, the United States could exercise more patience, an approach advocated in 2017 by U.S. Ambassador to Libya Peter Bodde. Different U.S. administrations feel differently about the concept of strategic patience and the concept has been heavily criticized. Generally, however, American negotiators are impatient and press to move faster than necessary to reach deals, and sometimes faster than merited by their own national interests. Other countries have learned this characteristic about U.S. negotiators. They sometimes use this impatience against the United States by withholding negotiating sessions or negotiating slowly, so that the concession of actually having a meeting becomes more important than the substance of the negotiation. In 2020–21, North Korea has used this tactic with the United States in withholding agreement to meet at the working level to follow up on agreements reached in summit meetings between President Trump and Chairman Kim.

Moving the Goalposts

One of the most frustrating experiences I had as an American negotiator occurred when officials at the U.S. State Department headquarters in Washington, D.C. would change their minds about what was and was not acceptable in an agreement; to use an analogy from American football, they were moving the goalposts. In UN negotiations, we found this happened often. In chapter 9, I describe how Washington authorized the U.S. delegation to the UN Human Rights Council in Geneva to raise the issue of Chinese human rights and to host a side event with Nobel Peace Prize laureates, including the Dalai Lama, under the condition that at least one of a traditional group of cosponsors joined in cohosting the event. After further domestic discussion and pressure from the Chinese government, the number of states that the State Department wanted to join with us in cohosting the event with the

Dalai Lama constantly changed. Washington's demand increased to "more than one," then six and then other, often inexact numbers of cosponsors that were required to commit to joining the United States before the China human rights situation could be raised in the UN. More disturbing, folding to a call from Chinese officials to the UN Secretary General, our government said we could not host an event with the Dalai Lama on UN grounds under any circumstances. (The event was eventually held at Geneva's Graduate Institute, next door to the UN, with the Deputy High Commissioner for Human Rights acting as moderator). This is just one of chapter 9's many examples of moving goalposts.

Moving the goalposts could be a tactic aimed at gaining more concessions. Over time, parties who have invested in a negotiation process with the belief that they will reach an agreement may become so invested that they are willing to continue to offer concessions—even more significant concessions than when the negotiation began and no deal was in sight—in order to reach the goal of an agreement. Often public expectations have been created that a deal will be reached (for example, Trump's North Korea summitry) or a negotiator will have promised her capital that she can bring home an agreement, so the prospect of loss of the potential agreement could cause the negotiator to concede more than was originally anticipated. In this way, shifting goalposts can be a positive tool when deployed carefully and selectively.

Unfortunately, the practice of moving the goalposts was common in the U.S. government while I was serving as a diplomat, but it was rarely used as an intentional tactic. Rather because our government is so large and the clearance process so cumbersome, the highest-level officials are often consulted only at the latest stages of an international negotiation. An opinion by a cabinet-level official or White House advisor that differs from the strategy pursued up until the point of their clearance can cause others to perceive the United States as moving the goalposts. And because of the lack of transparency of the inner workings of government decision-making, it can appear to other negotiating countries that the United States is moving its goalposts for tactical or malevolent reasons or to extract concessions, rather than as a result of such a cumbersome clearance process.

For example, in early 2017 while I was serving in the U.S. Libya External Office, the United States had advocated for a particular candidate to become the lead UN official handling Libya. Within the span of days, the White House reversed that position after a senior advisor who had not previously been consulted considered the question and vetoed the candidate that the United States had been supporting. Officials across the U.S. government had to explain that the candidate we pressed for in advocacy at levels as high as UN Ambassador Nikki Haley was now the candidate the United States opposed.

The shifting of goalposts can be especially challenging if it takes place after other government(s) reached an agreement with the United States on a path forward and brought their own domestic agencies to an agreement only to find out that the U.S. requirements, for whatever reason, had been changed. One such case was the negotiation over a resolution on China at the UN in 2004 and the release of Uighur businesswoman Rebiya Kadeer, As discussed in chapter 9, China agreed in 2004 to release Ms. Kadeer as part of an exchange in which the United States agreed to forego sponsoring a resolution about China's human rights at the UN Commission on Human Rights. However, the United States moved the goalposts and decided to go ahead with the resolution anyhow at the last minute, leaving Ms. Kadeer to another year in prison until her release was successfully negotiated. I accompanied her as she was released and arrived in exile in the United States in March 2005.[7]

Working with and through Others

There are many aspects of and benefits from working with and through others, but the lesson that I wish to emphasize here is the value that can accrue, especially in the United Nations, when large countries like the United States offer support for a principle or a resolution but avoid taking the lead. Favorable reaction to an idea proposed in a negotiation sometimes is a reaction to the idea itself. But it can also signify positive or negative reaction to the party or, in the UN context, to the UN member state that proposes the idea. Given a general tendency in the UN to seek consensus agreements, the idea of having a small state, a state from the developing world, or a state that holds a particular position—such as chair of a regional group, or vice-chair of the Human Rights Council—propose an idea can often get others to view the idea's merits more favorably. By contrast, when the United States raises an issue in the UN, a handful of states are likely to respond with immediate suspicion, including members of the so-called Like Minded Group, including China, Russia, Cuba, and Egypt.

---

7. "China Releases Political Prisoner Ahead of Visit by Rice." March 17, 2005. *New York Times*, available at https://www.nytimes.com/2005/03/17/international/asia/china-releases-political-prisoner-ahead-of-visit-by-rice.html

In multiparty negotiations, especially those in the United Nations, it is especially important to empower other partners and give them greater responsibility for the success of your project. This can be done at multiple levels in a multiparty negotiation; concrete illustrations from the HRC are conveyed in chapter 7. Sometimes empowering others occurs, for example, by having a smaller state member of a core group announce an initiative, such as in an organizational meeting for the HRC. Sometimes empowerment is demonstrated by having them lead the communications or send out an email announcing a particular meeting. In other cases, it involves having another party chair a meeting or lead a discussion. Empowering others in the UN context of negotiating resolutions can be as simple as being one of the last speakers on a topic and merely saying, "I agree with what the delegate from X country already said." You will see in the discussion of UN resolutions about privacy in the digital age and those on South Sudan the importance in the UN that core groups play in the formulation of policy and distributing information and responsibility for issues. It also can be useful for the United States to step back from a public leadership role on certain issues, as the U.S. position brings great strength but also political baggage. Sometimes U.S. leadership can even be a reason that other states will target an issue to be defeated, when the same issue might pass without controversy if it was led by a less politically powerful, and polarizing, sponsor.

Preparing Well before and during a Negotiation

As in any professional endeavor, preparation for your negotiation is crucial. Thinking through each of the elements of negotiation theory outlined above, when you might deploy them and how you would handle them, is an essential part of a toolkit. Sometimes a cheat sheet of interests and tactics can be readied in advance to help a negotiator anticipate what the positions, tactics, and interests of an opposing party will be, what external factors can be brought to bear to influence his sense of alternatives, and even to map the various interests on the other side or sides of a negotiation. Preparation may also include preliminary discussions to set the stage for leaders to close the gap on final issues or to reach a written agreement. As we will see in chapter 13, the failure to prepare for the Hanoi Summit between North Korea and the United States led to a breakdown and embarrassment for both Kim Jong Un and President Trump.[8]

---

8. See John R. Bolton. 2020. *The Room Where It Happened.* New York: Simon & Schuster.

For multiparty political negotiations, an elaborate series of negotiations is often required with the same issue often discussed multiple times at each level. Typically, experts take a first stab at reaching consensus on a draft agreement. Then ambassadors, foreign ministers, and finally heads of state may be consulted in turn to approve the same agreement or to settle differences. When issues or language are agreed upon at the expert or working level, the agreement often holds at other, higher levels. But when disagreements arise on a particular aspect of the agreement at any level, the custom is to "elevate" disagreements to higher-level decision-makers in protocol order, hoping that the higher-level officials can find agreement where experts could not. Sometimes higher-level decision-makers change and undo work done by experts or others if they disagree with an aspect of a draft decision. As you will read in chapter 8 on Sudan, I was typically empowered by the State Department to negotiate the terms of resolutions relating to human rights in Sudan. I assumed that my counterparts were similarly authorized, a question that was put to the test when one of Omar al-Bashir's ministers visited Geneva and tried to undo weeks of preliminary work on an agreement because it had been "elevated" to his level.

In larger or more extensive negotiations, it is advisable to have a team work together and take on different roles to help with the preparations and keeping track of interests, positions, and motivations of a counterpart. In my diplomatic experience, most multiparty political negotiators are concerned about who will speak during the negotiations and what they are going to say. In large countries like the United States, this often means a significant domestic negotiation over what the "instructions" for the negotiator will say and how much flexibility he or she will be given. Bottom-line instructions are, of course, important, but an excessive focus on them may leave to the side opportunities to prepare one's tactics and strategies for gathering information and analysis by those in a negotiating team who are not speaking, as well as for ensuring that a full range of tasks are undertaken.

One possible set of roles for a delegation and team members in a negotiation might include the following:

- Head of delegation: This is the main speaker, protocol leader of the delegation, and the one who makes decisions in the absence of instructions from the capital or headquarters.
- Deputy head of delegation: This person is usually also empowered to speak during the negotiation and may have organizational

chapter 11.

responsibilities, as well as backing up the head of delegation on all issues of his responsibility.

- Chief of staff: This person typically organizes the delegation for the head of delegation and communicates logistical and substantive information to the other team members.
- Note taker: One or more people on the delegation should be tasked with keeping a permanent record of what was said by all parties. In particularly sensitive or important negotiations, the capital or headquarters may want frequent updates to be sent by the note takers or even a verbatim transcript. In other cases, it is adequate to have merely a generalized set of notes for the record. Where negotiations are lengthy or where there is appetite for rapid or verbatim readouts of the negotiating sessions, it is helpful for notetaking to be handled by a team of drafters working in rotation with their output approved by the head of delegation.
- Interpreter: An essential role when multiple languages are at play, but American negotiators often underestimate the value of the interpreter. In Asia, many former interpreters have risen to be their country's foreign minister as a result of their ability to not only translate the words of important meetings but also to interpret the positions and interests that underlie those words. In North Korea, for example, the interpreter for the DPRK delegation during the Six-Party Talks is now first vice minister and arguably Kim Jong Un's most important foreign affairs interlocutor for the United States.
- Writer of agreement: If the negotiation aims to conclude with a written agreement, it is useful to have a lawyer on the delegation who can take part in the drafting process. The person writing the agreement should have a keen sense of the relative political and legal goals of the document. Sometimes a lawyer will be too comprehensive or try to specify in too much detail issues where it remains necessary to have some intentional ambiguity.

Given the use of computers, drafting often takes place with several participants gathered around a laptop or computer monitor. In such cases, "control of the pen" suggests that it is valuable for the writer also to be a fast typist. In putting down a set of words, the typist can give initial phrasing to an idea and can offer written formulations without conversation. This means the person controlling the pen or keyboard can input their ideas without signaling to other negotiators standing around the computer screen the full motivation behind his or her chosen words. In her memoirs, Condoleezza Rice relates a story about the 2006 G8 Summit, when a Hezbollah attack on Israel created the need to draft a joint statement on the fly. Recalling that her "mother had insisted on typing lessons 'just in case,'" Rice describes how she was able to type and negotiate, within and outside the U.S. government. a quick draft statement presented to the leaders.[9]

- Document or evidence expert: Many negotiations rely on past agreements or documents. Especially in negotiations that aim to produce legally binding agreements, it is often helpful for one member of the delegation to be the evidence expert and to hold original copies, where needed, of past agreements or other important resources.

- Observer of nonverbal communications and power dynamics: Sometimes the focus on what you should say causes a negotiator to miss cues given off by opposing parties. This can be especially true of nonverbal communication. A member of the other delegation may, for example, exhibit disapproval or displeasure of a position taken or a concession made by his own head of delegation but not say anything aloud. Similarly, there may be differences in power among the various participants in the other delegation. For example, in countries with a Communist Party structure, the highest-ranking party member is not always the one doing the talking. A keen observer of nonverbal cues, especially someone with language and cultural familiarity of the counterpart country, can be a key to learning valuable insights omitted by the note taker's rendition of what happened.

- Experts: Most negotiations have areas where expert knowledge is important, be they on trade issues, budget, scientific, or technical areas. It is important to have the right mix of experts on a negotiating team. Nevertheless, it is often sufficient to have experts in specific subject matters nearby, without them having to be constantly present in the negotiation room. In many of the Iran negotiations I supported while in Geneva, for example, a team of nuclear and missile experts was waiting in backrooms,

---

9. See Condoleezza Rice. 2011. *No Higher Honor*. New York: Broadway Books. Chapter 35. I am also a fast typist, having used a manual typewriter in my first paid job as a newspaper reporter while in high school in Michigan. As with Secretary Rice, these typing skills gave me a chance to have a hand—or at least several fingers—in the drafting of a range of agreements.

but they were not needed in the small negotiation sessions among the direct participants.[10] Still an adequate system needs to be in place for conveying information between the negotiators and their experts, usually headed by the chief of staff or deputy head of delegation.

Finally, we emphasize preparation for negotiations as a tool because it helps heighten awareness of all the pieces of your negotiation toolkit. Preparation can remind the negotiator of those tools and to plan when and how to best deploy them. In preparing this book, I reviewed the memoirs of most secretaries of state I worked for during my professional career—from Madeleine Albright to Hillary Clinton—and was surprised at how little they wrote about their negotiation toolkits. As with other senior diplomats, they focused on the instructions which articulate the positions that the United States would take. Often they focused in retrospect on justifying positions taken. They also focused on the question of when or whether the United States should be "willing" to negotiate with bad actors, like Iran or North Korea. Thus their memoirs are rife with examples of refusals to negotiate and of the bottom-line goals that they sought to achieve when negotiating, mostly in the Middle East or with North Korea.[11] Nevertheless, with all this focus on instructions and outcomes, they rarely shared detailed discussions of the actual tactics they deployed, or should have deployed, in preparing and conducting negotiations.

---

10. In negotiations that ultimately contributed to the Iran nuclear deal, the "backroom" experts passed the time by imagining which actors and actresses they would like to play their roles and the roles of their principals in an imaginary future Hollywood blockbuster entitled "P5 plus 1." Such banter, which can help to break the ice between and among delegation members, has been lost during the COVID-19 pandemic when negotiations have largely been forced to take place online, a topic we expand on in chapter 11.

11. See, e.g., Rice, *No Higher Honor*. For example chapter 3 of Rice's memoirs discusses the Bush administration's bottom-line positions on negotiations with North Korea, the EP-3 incident with China, and the Kyoto Protocol but offers little appreciation for the tactics one would have to deploy to reach the goals she outlines. One observation Rice does offer from a tactical point of view is to compliment Tony Blair on his use of humor in his first meeting with President George W. Bush. Reading prepared talking points about a trade dispute with which President Bush was clearly unfamiliar, Blair finished by saying: "And I have now just said everything that I know about this issue," which she assessed as a positive way of reading a counterpart and encouraging camaraderie. Similarly, where Secretary Clinton's book *What Happened* discussed foreign policy, it reframes description of major incidents to justify positions she took in the past, largely without detailing the negotiation tactics or approaches needed to reach those outcomes. Hillary Rodham Clinton. 2017. *What Happened*. New York: Simon & Schuster.

Among the memoirs I reviewed, Madeleine Albright's *Madam Secretary* is the best in this regard, particularly in outlining her role in using negotiation tactics to bring together participants in an effort to prevent, and then end, the war in Kosovo.[12] Albright is particularly insightful in describing how she used tactics with her Russian counterparts, and how they used or tried to use similar tactics against her. Nevertheless, for most others, their memoirs contain relatively little about how they consciously put negotiation tools to the service of diplomacy to achieve their goal and focus instead on the bottom-line positions. They appear to have underestimated in their memoirs the value of negotiation tactics to diplomacy. Perhaps these diplomats avoided discussion of their tactics and strategy because they wanted to keep them secret. Perhaps they observed and deployed them less often because they arrived only to close a deal, with good preparatory work having been conducted by others. Whatever the reason, my review of their memoirs suggests that senior statesmen and women failed to make full use of their toolkits for multiparty international negotiations.[13] This chapter and the subsequent one focus on the importance of having an overview of the available tools and tactics, because we do not want you to make the same mistake of overlooking them in your negotiations.

---

12. Madeleine Korbel Albright. 2003, *Madam Secretary*. New York: Miramax Books. Chapters 24 and 25.

13. Rice, *No Higher Honor*, chapter 3 (criticizing the Clinton administration approach to North Korea). Hopefully, these respected senior negotiators effectively deployed negotiation tactics but felt compelled to withhold the details of those discussions.

Oft Used Negotiation Tactics and Diplomatic Responses for Your Negotiation Toolkit

In addition to the general strategic tools provided in chapter 2, it is also important for a good negotiator to review the menu of tools and tactics that others may use with or against you in negotiations, and some possible responses. This is by no means an exhaustive list of negotiating tools or perspectives, but rather are those I came across frequently in my career, found deployed often by others, and whose use the case studies in subsequent chapters will discuss. First, we will look at tactics that are specifically applicable to negotiations that focus on wording—negotiations about UN resolutions or other agreements are the classic examples, but many business negotiations also revolve around the wording of a contract or other written document, which aims to have some level of legal enforceability. Second, we will look at some tactics often used in longer negotiations, especially those in the United Nations, and some possible responses that one can use if these tactics are deployed against you.

Tactics Specific to Negotiations about Wording

UN resolutions, like contracts, declarations, public and private statements, and most legal documents, are all about wording. In the United Nations in particular, negotiations about serious political and foreign policy concerns are usually resolved by finding the appropriate wording to capture a real-life situation with politically acceptable language. A good negotiator who understands her interests and those of the other parties can usually, in good faith, find a compromise in the language that is acceptable to all sides. That is, of course, if the other sides are also operating in good faith.

The following are tactics that I have often seen deployed in negotiations in the United Nations and some tips for how to work around them. They provide a negotiator in such a setting a quick toolkit of terms and phrases to use, even if the objective is sometimes markedly different from what the words appear to mean.

I. Avoid the Nasty Words but Get the Content Addressed

In negotiations with several states on human rights, it was clear that there were certain words that were offensive to a country accused of committing abuses. Concepts like "monitoring," for example, offended states as a potential restriction of their sovereignty. So if it was more acceptable to say that a resolution would create a mandate for documenting and assessing, why is it necessary to press for a more offensive term?

In other cases, a state might be willing to admit that a certain event and its difficult or painful consequences happened, but it may be reluctant to place blame. One technique I often used to break that deadlock was to refer to a report or other neutral document that outlined the allegation. Rather than to say, "Sudan's security services shot innocent protesters," we agreed in one negotiation, for example, to deplore "the incident documented in paragraph 68 of the recent report by the Independent Expert." What was the deplorable incident being discussed? The shooting of peaceful protesters on the campus of Khartoum University participating in a protest.. This indirect form of referencing was often a useful way of breaking an impasse. This tactic could also be very useful if an accused country or party was concerned about publicity; often domestic publicity concerns government officials much more than publicity that does not focus on their own citizens and remains read by a largely international or UN audience. Insertion of phrases such as "reports indicate" prior to statements about abuses also was a way of allowing an accused state to save face and it could claim, at least domestically, that the reports were just wrong. As I would often tell foreign counterparts and U.S. officials alike, once there was agreement on the key mechanisms and underlying principles of a resolution, good negotiators should always be able to find words to break a deadlock. This is especially true if they have fully explored options with their counterparts and are following a path of good faith, interest-based negotiations.

2. "We need to update/streamline the language"

Good negotiators often deploy two marvelous catchphrases, "update" and "streamline," which are often followed by "just a little" to hide major changes. Updating often is a surrogate for saying a party wants to add new concepts, while "streamlining" usually means the party involved wants to delete key language. When a negotiator asks to update or streamline language, he often does not want to be transparent about the reasons for doing so. I was surprised how often calls for updating or streamlining went unquestioned in my UN experience.

But won't you look silly if you challenge someone who is just seeking to update or streamline a document? Of course not. Rather than challenge another negotiator directly, an oft-used tactic is to ask targeted questions. A simple yet diplomatically phrased question about the updated or streamlined language can often help to expose the real motivation behind the party seeking to make this change in language. Moreover, if the question is posed in a public setting, like a UN negotiation, it can also serve to highlight for all negotiation participants the potential significance of the addition or deletion.

3. The Problem or Issue Being Addressed Does Not Exist in Our Country

Delegates from a UN member state who objected to or did not want to deal with a particular phenomenon would often say that the issue does not apply in their specific cultural context. When a state was uncomfortable discussing an issue, be it about human rights defenders, LGBTI persons, domestic violence, or other sensitive issues or vulnerable groups, it was common for a state to claim in a UN negotiation or related setting that the issue or problem did not exist.

A corollary to this denial was the approach that "there is no word for that" in our language. Egyptian delegates at the UN Human Rights Council often used this tactic to try to deflect or reformulate the core principles of a resolution that the Egyptian government did not like. Among words that Egyptian diplomats claimed were impossible to translate into Arabic were "human rights defenders," "reprisal," or other concepts they did not want to have resolutions discuss. Online research tools like Google can often help to rebut these specious arguments, but I found the most useful way to address this point was to sit next to another Arabic speaking diplomat during the negotiations and ask him or her. For example, when the Egyptians claimed that something was not translatable into Arabic, I would do a quick Google translate, and often ask the Tunisian diplomat seated nearby if this was the correct word in Arabic. Armed with the correct translation, I would try to offer it in rebuttal but sometimes found that the native Arabic speaker I consulted would jump in first and propose the appropriate Arabic word to the Egyptian detractor.

In addition, a list of tactics that a negotiator can use or should be aware of more generally in any negotiation follows. You can deploy these approaches in almost any situation, not just negotiations about wording. As with the other tactics we have discussed, they require testing based on the situation and response of a counterpart. A good negotiator keeps all of these negotiating approaches in his/her toolkit but deploys them as appropriate to the context and counterpart(s). They include:

1. <u>Be nice to people while differing on the substance:</u> This may be the most significant difference between the business-litigation model of negotiation and the United Nations model. Repeated interactions in multiparty political negotiations require that UN negotiators try to maintain positive relationships. Negotiators often have significant discretion to help counterparts whom they like and to block counterparts whom they dislike. By maintaining good relations with all, one can often find a compromise solution. Moreover, if one can disagree without being disagreeable, it builds respect and makes a friendly opposing party more interested in, and willing to find, a compromise or be helpful in the next interaction.

2. <u>"We know you are a friend":</u> Chinese diplomats were fond of trying to split individual negotiators from the U.S. position using this approach. Through complements, speaking Chinese, or using the prized "we know you are a friend of China," they would often attempt flattery to gain information about the status of positions in Washington and to help them determine which pressure points to push in Beijing, Washington, or other foreign capitals. Any government can do this, but I was surprised to the extent at which Chinese negotiators did this, including with me directly. A good negotiator can use this idea of flattering the other side as more reasonable or more favorable to his advantage. For example, I often used the tactic to elicit further information about Chinese positions so long as I was careful not to reveal more about U.S. positions than planned or authorized.

   In a negotiation environment where the negotiators claim to have a special bond of friendship or trust, it is also possible to use

your "favored" status to feed misinformation to an opposing negotiator. Feeding of misinformation can cause the opposing party to
waste time and energy on an unproductive route or disorient them
from the key issues of dispute. But like many of the Trumpian
tactics criticized here, feeding of misinformation is a tactic that
one cannot use very often, because it is likely to be discovered
eventually and undermine the very situation of trust that created
the opportunity for deploying the misinformation tactic in the
first place.

3. Be helpful internationally to distract from repression at home:
    Some of the best negotiators I worked with at the UN Human
    Rights Council were from states with their own human rights
    challenges. Diplomats from the Maldives, Rwanda, Ethiopia, Tur-
    key, and other states with blemished human rights records often
    went the extra mile to be helpful to the United States and other
    Western countries. The more difficult the topic, the more help-
    ful some of these diplomats and their delegations would be. Their
    help made it more likely that the United States would value coop-
    eration with the state and not wish to jeopardize it by criticizing its
    human rights practices. In the period from 2012 to 2015, Turkey
    was a particularly adept player in using this tool. The Turks joined
    the United States as a partner in more "core groups"[1] at the HRC
    than any other country, making it harder for the United States to
    criticize Turkish repression of Kurds, its limitations on free expres-
    sion, and other human rights foibles. For example, Turkey was a
    member of the core group with the United States, Sweden, Tu-
    nisia, Nigeria, and others on the discussion of Internet freedom.
    Such a position ensured that Turkey's practices related to Internet
    shutdowns were not singled out for criticism. Of interest, this type
    of cooperation in the HRC continued into the Trump administra-
    tion, even after Trump's withdrawal from the HRC and his falling
    out with President Erdogan. It is likely Turkey continued to coop-
    erate with the United States because the cooperation served its in-
    terests and succeeded in shielding Turkey from some international
    criticism.

---

1. A "core group" is a group of states, usually representing several of the five United
Nations regions, who band together to introduce a resolution or to advance a particular thematic position. Among the issues on which Turkey and the United States shared a core group
in 2013–2016 were Internet freedom, Syria, and countering violent extremism.

4. "Credibility of the institution requires it": This is an HRC-specific variation on the Fisher and Ury recommendation that parties identify objective criteria by which to evaluate the terms in their negotiations. I frequently used this argument in the Human Rights Council to differentiate between criticizing a delegation and criticizing a situation of human rights abuse in the country. This arguably neutral standard takes the personality out of the discussion and just suggests that the credibility of the institution demands a strong or specific response to human rights violations on the ground. A negotiator using this tactic might ask, "What kind of voice on human rights can the United Nations have if its Human Rights Council does not condemn the massive violations going on in _____?"

   This tactic can help states to justify a position that they want to take, or that they think is right. For example, a regional group often rallies behind other members of its regional group to prevent criticism of the state in the HRC. But diplomats from the same region as a country facing such criticism could agree to criticize the state at issue because "the credibility of the HRC requires it." In many cases, African states preferred to address themselves serious human rights violations by an African state and propose a resolution of their own, rather than have the resolution on a human rights challenge in Africa be tabled by those from another region. This desire to "police one's own human rights situations" was a significant trend during my years at the HRC, especially in Africa as a result of an African Union that was increasingly active on difficult human rights situations on the continent.

5. "Lawyer it up": A signature manifestation of this tactic is using legal references and citations to confuse or obfuscate a situation so that others do not understand or are embarrassed to admit they do not understand the underlying legal points. In discussions of economic rights, a variation of this tactic involves using economists to obscure debate or intimidate noneconomists from objecting. In fact, any specialist can be used in this way in negotiations. In my experience at the United Nations, the United States and other P5 countries are the only delegations with a panoply of lawyers analyzing the implications of resolutions, and their legal analysis is often too much for the handful of attorneys who are deployed across the rest of the UN landscape. Similarly, the opportunity to make a topic so complex that people lose sight of the issue being

debated and tend to defer or doubt a single expert is one of the reasons for the proliferation of expert witnesses in tort litigation cases in the United States.

6. <u>When parties are talking, they usually are not fighting:</u> In a business negotiation, it often pays to walk out of negotiations or cut them short if they seem not to be bearing fruit. However, in my experience with international political actors, most countries that are seriously engaged in negotiations do not exacerbate or intensify aggressive behavior outside the negotiation room while they are pursuing a negotiated agreement in good faith. It is true that in the Syria negotiations I observed, the war continued regardless of talks in Geneva. And negotiations are frequently a stalling tactic. But it is rare that a party initiates new conflict while at the negotiating table. Even the North Koreans, who may have used negotiations as a way to stall for time to improve their nuclear programs, did not initiate conflict during any round of the Six-Party Talks. Rather, they often used missile launches or threats of conflict as a bargaining chip to give them something to negotiate away. Similarly, Libyan expansionist General Khalifa Haftar has not initiated a new attack while engaged in negotiations (although he did launch his first attack on the Oil Crescent in September 2016 immediately after military talks between his forces and Western generals).

7. <u>Walking out of a negotiation:</u> Walking away from a deal is always possible but to walk away from a negotiation risks that you will not get back to a deal originally contemplated. When the cost of not getting back to a deal is just money, it is possible to pursue greater brinksmanship and targets of opportunity. In international political negotiations, walking away from a negotiation is far riskier and in general not recommended. One can certainly pause a negotiation for strategic or substantive impact. I have walked out of particular negotiation sessions, especially as a way of expressing that the position taken by your negotiating counterpart is unreasonable, sometimes with excellent results. Like a buyer in a market, this is one way of illustrating your bottom-line position. Moreover, in commercial negotiations this is a useful tactic—there are usually other parties who can substitute for a current negotiation partner to procure the items sought or to engage in the business transaction under discussion. But the structure of the international system and the unique prerogatives of states and their sovereignty indicate that when a door is shut entirely to negotia-

tions with a given state, the cost and opportunity to reopen it may be very high and the losses as a result of not negotiating can be catastrophic.

But for the many reasons mentioned elsewhere, it is unwise to walk away from an international political negotiation altogether. The approach, stated frequently by Trump National Security Advisor John Bolton, that negotiations with the United States are a reward for good behavior is a dangerous approach, employed with negative results in case studies from Iran to North Korea. As noted above, while recalcitrant actors are engaged in talks, they rarely expand their dangerous activities and often reel back aggressive activities.. At the same time, failure to be engaged in discussions deprives the United States of valuable information and communication channels. Of course, it is reasonable to withhold higher and higher levels of negotiators until groundwork is laid or as a "reward" for good behavior, but to terminate all channels for negotiation is, in my experience, an unwise and counterproductive negotiation approach on the public international stage.

Now that we have outlined some key theories, tools, and tactics likely to be deployed in multiparty international negotiations, let us look at how these tools have been used in practice based on a range of case studies from North Korea to Libya and the United Nations.

CHAPTER 4

DPRK, Denuclearization Discussions, and BATNAs (Best Alternative to a Negotiated Agreement)

In negotiating with North Korea about its nuclear program, the parties faced complex questions about the others' goals, motivations, and alternatives. The negotiation process that became known as the Six-Party Talks on the North Korean nuclear issue lasted for six formal rounds, from 2003 to 2009. I was a participant in these talks, both as a note taker while at the U.S. Embassy Beijing and later as an advisor while working for the North Korea Unit in the U.S. Department of State in Washington, D.C. The Six-Party Talks provide an excellent example of international, multiparty political negotiation, particularly an interest-based negotiation where negotiators need to explore mutual interest in an effort to overcome distrust and find mutual benefit. They also provide an important background to the ongoing threat of nuclear conflict with the DPRK, which is one of the most important current security situations and which will be discussed in detail in chapter 13.

A Case Study in Interest-Based Negotiations

Looking at the Six-Party Talks as an interest-based negotiation of the kind Fisher and Ury speak about, we can begin by analyzing the goals, or interests, that the United States, North Korea, and the many other parties with interests in the North Korean nuclear issue had related to the outcome of those talks. North Korea's goals included:

- Security guarantees that it would not be invaded or attacked by the United States, South Korea, or any other country;
- Survival of its totalitarian regime and its leaders' way of life built on the country's people and resources;
- International respect and legitimacy, especially from the United States;
- Normalization of relations with the United States and the international community;
- Economic enrichment of the regime and its elite followers;
- Economic development of the country and improvement of the standard of living of its people.

In addition to these goals related to the outcome of talks, the DPRK also had goals related to the process of the talks, which included:

- Developing channels to speak directly to the United States as an equal;
- Appearing on the world stage as a "normal" international actor, rather than the pariah state that the DPRK was often portrayed to be; and
- Delaying the international community's inspection of DPRK nuclear programs until it could further refine its nuclear weapons and delivery systems.

With respect to this last point, it is not clear if that was a goal of the DPRK throughout the six-year process of the Six-Party Talks or if it only became a goal at a later stage in the negotiations.

The goals of the United States were far narrower than the DPRK's and focused almost entirely on security concerns for the United States and its allies related to North Korea not advancing or using its nuclear or missile program. Among its goals were:

- Security from nuclear weapons (for itself, its allies, and the world);
- Security from attack on its allies (South Korea and Japan) using missiles or conventional weapons;
- Preventing the proliferation of nuclear weapons, technology, and material;
- Humanitarian concerns related to the safety of its own citizens, the treatment of North Koreans, and, especially for Japan, safety and accountability for Japanese citizens abducted by the DPRK.

Finally, in 2008 as now, negotiations over North Korea's threats to its neighbors and the world were a significant playground in which regional and global powers exercised authority and battled for influence on the world stage. Countries like China wanted to demonstrate their leadership and their ability to host major political negotiations. Russia and Japan wanted to demonstrate their relevance and ability to influence the direction of security in Northeast Asia. Many in the United States, China, and Russia saw the North Korean nuclear issue as one match in a game of triangular power politics that featured varying partnerships and alliance of interests, as these three powers tried to determine whether the shape of the post-Cold War world would involve cooperation between them or competition. In addition, South Korea wanted to orchestrate a future on the Korean Peninsula that would leave it safe, prosperous, and able to exploit the low-cost labor and development needs in the DPRK to enhance its economic and political power. During the Six-Party Talks, South Korea's government rested in conservative hands, leaving it more likely to follow the lead of the United States, its alliance partner. But today, as we will see in chapter 13, the rise of progressive president Moon Jae-In and a return of "sunshine" policies toward the DPRK has the Republic of Korea pursuing peace with the DPRK more aggressively and with a much greater degree of independence from the United States than was apparent in the Six-Party Talks period.

Invent Options for Mutual Gain

In the face of clarity about these interests and their importance, the United States and its partners sought a basic deal from the DPRK based on a win-win premise: North Korea could be persuaded to denuclearize in exchange for a range of economic benefits and security guarantees. The United States first tried to deploy this perceived option for mutual gain during the Agreed Framework period of 1994–2002. Under the Agreed Framework, the United States, Japan, and South Korea agreed to provide certain economic incentives to the DPRK, in exchange for its adherence to safeguards and inspections of the International Atomic Energy Agency (IAEA). Specific terms of the pact and consequent agreements required that the DPRK shut down its nuclear reactor at Yongbyon, abandon construction of other nuclear plants, and seal under safeguards by the IAEA all spent fuel that could have been reprocessed to make plutonium for a nuclear weapon. Through the Korean Peninsula

Economic Development Administration (KEDO, whose first director Stephen Bosworth was the second North Korea envoy under whom I served as a U.S. diplomat), the DPRK was scheduled to receive two light-water nuclear reactors capable of providing vast quantities of the country's electrical needs, at a value of nearly $4 billion. In the interim while the reactors were being built, North Korea was to receive 500,000 tons of heavy fuel oil per year, essentially for free. This deal broke down when, in 2002 on a trip to Beijing, U.S. Assistant Secretary of State for East Asian and Pacific Affairs James Kelly learned that the DPRK had been cheating on its agreement and was attempting to enrich uranium for a nuclear weapon.[1] The United States abandoned the KEDO deal and rhetoric and sanctions escalated on both sides.

It was in this context that Ambassador Christopher Hill replaced Kelly as U.S. Assistant Secretary of State for East Asian and Pacific Affairs and as the lead envoy on North Korea. Hill became the U.S. chair for the Six-Party Talks and immediately began working on a new deal to try to dismantle North Korea's nuclear programs. It was also at this time that I began to be involved in the talks. Under Hill as under Kelly, the underlying perceived win-win tradeoff remained the same: the United States and other countries hoped that a combination of economic engagement, sanctions relief, and security guarantees would persuade the DPRK to abandon its nuclear programs. However, the political environment in which Hill operated differed significantly from that in which Kelly and his team confronted the DPRK over its hidden uranium enrichment program. Kelly came into office early in the George W. Bush administration. In 2001 and early 2002, the war against terror, in response to the September 11, 2001, attacks, was the defining political paradigm for U.S. foreign policy. In early 2002, President Bush had labeled North Korea, along with Iran and Iraq, part of an "axis of evil." Vice President Cheney was among a group of leading conservative advisors who advanced that policy, with many similarities to the "maximum pressure" campaign of the Trump administration. In this environment, Secretary of State Colin Powell was largely excluded from key U.S. decision-making on North Korea. In one famous incident, Powell announced plans to have talks with North Korea, only to find himself contradicted by the president and forced to issue his own reversal during a visit to Washington by ROK President Kim Dae Jung in March 2001.[2]

---

1. Rice, *No Higher Honor*, chapter 11, Kindle location 2862 of 12657.
2. "Bush Tells Seoul Talks with North Korea Won't Resume Now," *New York Times*, March 8, 2001.

By 2003, the political situation had begun to change. Powell was more firmly in control of foreign policy issues in the administration and National Security Adviser Condoleezza Rice had come around to the view that negotiating with the North Koreans was an advisable course of action.[3] Cheney continued to criticize and sometimes attempt to undermine the talks.[4] In general, Ambassador Hill was placed firmly in charge of the delegation and the negotiation strategy, with a remit from National Security Adviser Rice and Secretary of State Powell to work with the Chinese and try to negotiate the denuclearization of North Korea. When Rice took over as secretary of state in 2004, Hill's remit strengthened. She authorized him to talk to the North Koreans, used U.S. power to get the Chinese and Russians to support multilateral diplomacy aimed at denuclearization, and helped persuade President Bush to favor negotiations over regime change.[5]

Under Hill's lead, North Korea took significant steps to reverse and curtail its nuclear activities over the course of the 2007 to 2008 period, in exchange for a range of economic and prestige-related benefits. Among them, in 2007, the IAEA confirmed that a 5-megawatt nuclear reactor at Yongbyon had been shut down and sealed and North Korea committed not to transfer nuclear technology or know how to other parties. North Korea also dismantled other Yongbyon nuclear facilities, permitted inspection of those facilities and destroyed, in April 2008, the cooling tower for its Yongbyon nuclear reactor. North Korea did not test a nuclear device after October 2006 until talks had broken down, when it conducted its second nuclear test in May 2009. North Korea ultimately reversed its dismantlement of nuclear facilities,[6] but the denuclearization undertaken during the

---

3. Rice, *No Higher Honor*, chapter 23, Kindle location 5850 of 12657.

4. See the discussion of Powell and Rice in Cheney's autobiography, Richard B. Cheney and Liz Cheney. 2011. *In My Time*. New York: Simon & Schuster. See also Glenn Kessler, August 30, 2011, "Colin Powell versus Dick Cheney," *Washington Post*, available at https://www. washingtonpost.com/blogs/fact-checker/post/colin-powell-versus-dick-cheney/2011/08/30/ gIQAwYydqJ_blog.html?utm_term=.0011455f829d

5. Rice, *No Higher Honor*, chapters 38 and 55.

6. Denuclearization experts admit that nuclear dismantlement is almost never irreversible and, in fact, the North Koreans later restored the Yongbyon compound to produce plutonium after denuclearization talks broke down. See, e.g., Simon Denyer, February 22, 2019, "North Korea's Yongbyon Nuclear Complex at the Heart of Trump-Kim Summit," *Washington Post*, available at https://www.washingtonpost.com/world/asia_pacific/north-koreas-yongbyon-nuclear-complex-at-the-heart-of-trump-kim-summit/2019/02/22/ee99269a-352d-11e9-8375-e3dcf6b68558_story.html?utm_term=.fae3451e5989; *Ploughshares Fund. 2019. "Begun Is Half Done."* https://www.ploughshares.org/sites/default/files/resources/Begun-is-Half-Done-2019.pdf

peak of negotiation of the Six-Party Talks at least delayed development of the North's nuclear and missile programs and retarded its ability to pose a threat to the United States and its allies.

At the same time, North Korea began receiving some concrete development assistance and sanctions relief. Beginning after the September 2005 Joint Statement, the other five parties agreed to provide the DPRK with one million tons of heavy fuel oil, and the United States removed the DPRK from its State Sponsors of Terrorism list with corresponding symbolic sanctions relief. During this same period of time, North Korea also received significant food aid from the United States, although some U.S. officials insisted that the food aid was humanitarian in nature and not linked to the political deal on denuclearization.[7]

Under an interest-based theory of negotiations that seeks win-win solutions, the parties' interests should have made a deal possible that advanced both denuclearization of North Korea and its reintegration into the international community. North Korea did not require nuclear weapons or long-range missiles to protect itself from invasion or the survival of its regime as long as the United States had no intention of attacking the DPRK. If North Korea could be convinced that its nuclear program was not really a "deterrent,"[8] protecting it from attack by the United States, it could shift its focus and effort to other areas, including possible economic development.

As a result, the U.S. denuclearization goal in the Six-Party Talks of CVID—the Complete Verifiable and Irreversible Dismantlement of North Korea's nuclear program—was never really attainable. But the dismantlement and freezing of North Korean nuclear and missile programs were significant steps that at least delayed the day when the DPRK could miniaturize a nuclear device for delivery into U.S. territories or even the mainland, as discussed in chapter 13.

7. The United States has not provided food aid to the DPRK since the April 2009 collapse of the Six-Party Talks on the nuclear issue, despite varying levels of humanitarian need in the country and corresponding calls for increased response to the UN and others' appeals. See Andrew Natsios, March 7, 2012, "Op/Ed: U.S. Food Aid to North Korea Sends the Wrong Message," *Washington Post*, available at https://www.washingtonpost.com/opinions/us-food-aid-to-n-korea-sends-the-wrong-messages/2012/03/07/gIQA6MM1zR_story.html?um_term=.e1d0d197a1ab

8. North Korea has often argued that its nuclear program was a necessary deterrent and a measure of ensuring its security. But I observed repeatedly how this position collapsed under questioning. North Korea's massive conventional force in close proximity of Seoul was the major deterrent preventing the United States from launching a preemptive strike against the DPRK in the period from 2003 to 2008. Even if North Korea had possessed a nuclear weapon capable of being delivered to the United States, an attempt to use it would have relegated the entire country to an ash heap (see discussion of Hill-Kim Kye Gwan conversation, at end of this chapter).

Moreover, from an interest-based perspective, the international community could "afford" to give up the sanctions relief, international attention, and limited economic assistance in the form of food aid or fuel oil provided to the DPRK. Most importantly, economic development provided a win-win opportunity. The outside world would be only too happy to provide economic development that could transform North Korea. Under this notion, North Korea could progress from its status as a state with few development or employment opportunities, no consumer economy, and a lack of electricity that left the country embarrassingly dark on nighttime maps of the globe. Instead it would turn into a developing state with the opportunity for investment, and policies and development programs that would improve the economic standing of the regime and the daily lives of its citizens. Trade benefits also awaited most of the others in the Six-Party Talks—certainly South Korea, China, and Russia, if not Japan and the United States—should North Korea open its economy to foreign businesses and development.

Mistaken Assumptions, Misunderstanding of Interests, and BATNAs

So why did the negotiations break down? Several factors are responsible. First, there was an "ideological interference" in the process of negotiation, which kept the parties from finding a win-win outcome. Second, there were some basic misunderstandings by each side of all the interests of the other and an unwillingness to communicate about the most important issue of conflict between the parties: survival or destruction of the North Korean regime and ruling system. Finally, and relatedly, the parties did not fully understand each other's Best Alternative to a Negotiated Agreement, or BATNA, and Worst Alternative to a Negotiated Agreement, or WATNA. Thus they repeatedly tried to induce deals that were fatally flawed from the perspective and logic of the negotiating counterpart.

What does ideological interference mean? Unlike in a market-based negotiation, for the United States and Japan, in particular, there was an ideological opposition to dealing with North Korea that defied a search for win-win solutions. In the mindset of officials in the early phase of the Bush administration, North Korea was part of an axis of evil. According to this way of thinking, no amount of mutual benefit could make a truly patriotic American negotiate or, indeed, give concessions to the evil North Korean regime. As a result, the United States did not even talk with North Korea about its nuclear and weapons programs for several periods preceding and even between rounds of the Six-Party Talks. In many corridors of Washington government agencies, merely allowing North Koreans to conduct direct negotiations with America was seen as a reward unworthy of the DPRK police state. Some Japanese politicians may have had a similar abhorrence to negotiating with the DPRK, especially politicians focused on the case of abduction of Japanese citizens by North Koreans in the period 1977 to 1983. Ambassador Hill in particular became a target of some of those who were ideologically opposed to a deal with the North Koreans, in both the United States and Japan.

On the North Korean side, there was doubtless also an ideological discomfort among some of the regime's greatest hardliners about negotiating with South Korea, with Japan, and with the United States. Nonetheless, under Kim Jong-Il, the regime's relative economic weakness and perhaps a surprising pragmatism seemed to overcome this ideological interference on the North Korean side. Ideological concerns about not dealing with or rewarding the DPRK for its pariah state behavior seemed a stronger interfering factor in the negotiations for some in Japan and the United States than in the DPRK. Generally put, this is one example of how domestic political considerations can bias a political negotiation in ways that money cannot anticipate or adequately address.

Second, U.S. officials overestimated the value to the DPRK of economic benefits. Of course, in an underdeveloped state with few natural resources, little developed industry, and almost no trade except for with China, economic development was important. The main resources available to the DPRK were from export of its laborers to neighboring countries, illicit activities such as counterfeiting and smuggling, and even more dangerous exports, such as the sale of weapons and even nuclear technologies. Unlike in many countries, the DPRK was not interested in financial resources to expand the standard of living of its population or to boost its overall GDP. Rather, financial resources were, and largely still are, a tool of political power in the DPRK, enabling the leadership to reward the military, government, and technical elites needed for running the country and maintaining control. So exactly while the Six-Party Talks, like the KEDO project before them, were negotiating to provide the North Koreans with resources to enhance electricity production or other aspects of a domestic economy, the DPRK was engaged in bringing in resources through illicit means. One of the most damning elements of North Korean proliferation was made public in April 2008, when the CIA released images of a Syrian reactor facility the Israelis had destroyed some six months earlier, which looked strikingly similar to the North Korean facilities at Yongbyon. Those who opposed any dealings with North Korea, much less giving the DPRK economic incentives to denuclearize, found their hand significantly strengthened by evidence that the North was proliferating, and profiting from proliferation, in the midst of negotiations.

Third, many on the U.S. side, and likely some other delegation members in the Six-Party Talks, misunderstood how fragile the North Korean regime saw itself, and therefore how important one of its interests was, above and beyond all others. For North Korea, survival of its regime and its leaders' way of life was its highest priority. In this ranking, there was no close second place. The North Korean leaders knew that a "Trojan horse" connected with development would be the opening up of their society to information. They feared that the new information and new opportunities would pose a risk to their way of life. For this very reason, DVDs of South Korean soap operas were banned in the North, as they might raise doubts in the minds of the North Korean population about the deprivation the population was undergoing to protect the regime from imminent threat by South Korea and its allies. Doubtless, the regime was concerned also that information about the outside world such as on ROK television might show its citizens how advanced the economy of Seoul is, raising questions that the regime was not prepared to address. No North Korean official or leader wanted the mass of North Korean workers, farmers, and students to ask whether the ongoing sacrifice that had been required by North Korea's "juche" philosophy of self-reliance was worth it. Even a small risk of information crossing into the DPRK that raised such questions was unacceptable to North Korean leaders and caused the seemingly "logical" appeal of an offer of economic assistance to be less persuasive than those Western diplomats who were offering it realized.

This logic and focus on survival over economic development made perfect sense to the DPRK but was more difficult for the United States and its allies to understand. According to the DPRK's own logic, it made a correct judgment to forego economic benefits that it could not control, despite the avoidable hardship this caused for its people. After all, under the North Korean logic, it had succeeded in developing nuclear technology even though no one thought it would be able to do so. Why wasn't it also possible to produce its own economic breakthroughs at a later point in development?

One illustration of the North's correct focus on controlling information came when I was doing a rotation at the North Korean nuclear facility at Yongbyon in 2008–2009. At the time, local cellphones were becoming available for the first time in North Korea, connected on North Korea's internal phone system. Workers were scurrying to determine if they could afford to buy the phones, and how they would aid in communication with family and friends, including with those who lived abroad. The DPRK regime was careful so that, even when these cellphones were being made available, the network did not allow for communication outside the DPRK and did not include features such as Internet availability.[9] Some would say that this was a case of the regime's bizarre logic preventing it from enjoying a win-win solution in terms of economic development. Rather, I think the Kim Jong Il regime understood better than did its outside counterparts the fragile basis on which its regime was established.

In addition, security interests were not seen in the same way in the West and in the DPRK. For the North Korean leaders, maintaining their way of life required security. Nevertheless, even security of the territory of North Korea was only a vehicle toward maintaining the regime's way of life, not an end in and of itself. Security protected the territory the regime relied on. Enhancing security protected the interest of key defense and military officials who also supported the regime. While the Kim regime, especially certain elites, wanted respect and international legitimacy, it did not require those things for its survival. In addition, it was quite willing to trade off economic interests and the well-being of its own people, including their rights, food, and safety, so long as shortages in any of these areas never became so dire that they affected the stability and survivability of the regime.

Given the apparently mutually exchangeable set of interests that could result in a deal on denuclearization in exchange for development, why was it not possible for the parties to find a match that would lead to a denuclearization deal in the Six-Party Talks? Negotiators explored many aspects in an interest-based style much as Fisher and Ury would recommend.[10] However, the interests also did not match up over another dimension: timing. U.S. provision of economic benefits, sanctions relief, and conferral of international participation or prestige was a finite good that could be conferred on North Korea, consumed by it and then exhausted. On the other hand, U.S. security goals would only be truly achieved through the irreversible dismantlement of North Korean nuclear and missile facilities. And therein lay the rub. Irreversible was almost impossible to truly produce. Rather, as long as the technical expertise for constructing nuclear reactors or uranium enrichment remained in the minds of North Korean scientists and officials, they

---

9. Even today, North Korean officials who travel abroad often rush to get temporary telephones and SIM cards so that they can take advantage of access to Internet communication as a way to get information, photos, and social news from family and friends abroad.

10. Fisher and Ury, *Getting to Yes*, chapter 6.

could always rebuild the facilities and infrastructure needed to restart a nuclear program. For the DPRK, nothing it had given up was irreversible. It was only a matter of time before it was recouped.

U.S. officials handling the DPRK nuclear file had a different perspective on the period of negotiations and its impact. They understood much about the North Koreans' goals and logic. However, at the same time, they hoped for a change in DPRK thinking, in part because of pressure from and exposure to the international community. Ambassador Hill correctly noted that every day, week, month, or year that went by without any incident of North Korean aggression or proliferation was, in fact, a success for the United States and its partners. As a result, he based his negotiation style on the presumption that, if North Korean efforts were devoted to finding a solution at the negotiation table, they would not be devoting those efforts to their nuclear and missile programs. Ambassador Hill made a judgment, and a gamble backed by National Security Adviser and later Secretary of State Rice, that for a small country with limited resources, it would be challenging for North Korea to focus on multiple areas at once. Cheating was possible, but unlikely, this theory postulated, so long as the DPRK seriously thought negotiations could bring it toward its goals. Even more importantly, Hill judged that China and Russia would help to guarantee DPRK compliance and to discourage cheating. Supported by Secretary Rice and ultimately President Bush, the United States did, in fact, establish a solidarity of purpose in this regard with the Chinese hosts of the Six-Party Talks. Together, they believed that the process of engagement in the Six-Party Talks could, over time, build trust that ultimately could allow the North Koreans to make a longer-term commitment to irreversible dismantlement of their nuclear programs. They also hoped that the DPRK would find a new more prosperous, confident, and respected future in the international community so attractive that it would not feel a need to require nuclear weapons as a security guarantor.

Where did these negotiations fall apart then? I believe this was not a failure of exploring interest-based negotiation. Based on broad delegated authority, U.S. negotiators looked for, and when permitted to speak with the DPRK, explored, a broad range of possible win-win solutions across the range of bilateral and multilateral interests. Rather, even though the interests were understood, the talks were ultimately doomed by a failure to understand the other party's BATNA. North Korea had almost limitless alternatives to a negotiated agreement, and it knew so. It was valuable for North Korea to get any measure of enhanced international status, such as that provided by participation in international negotiations and bilateral meetings with the United States. It was also valuable for North Korea to get any amount of consumable economic and humanitarian assistance, be it fuel aid delivered as a direct outcome of the Six-Party Talks or food aid delivered on the margins in parallel with the Six-Party Talks but for humanitarian reasons. Moreover, the status quo for the past fifty-plus years had been for North Korea to live under constant security threat from South Korea, the United States, and its allies. Maintaining the status quo, therefore, remained a very good alternative for North Korea to the negotiated agreement. In effect, it was this alternative (or BATNA) that made it possible for DPRK negotiators to always reject concessions they deemed threatening to regime security, because they suffered little to no loss from failure to reach a deal. They had a very acceptable BATNA if they did absolutely nothing. And perhaps the North Koreans also calculated that they were continuing to develop their nuclear and missile programs in secret, particularly through uranium enrichment. As such, the North Koreans knew that the denuclearization steps they were agreeing to undertake were "reversible" and their nuclear deterrent could be restored in relatively short order if desired. In sum, North Korea had every incentive to try for a deal that fully satisfied its security demands, which meant not just confidence that the United States would not attack it but that the Kim family regime would remain secure in its leadership of North Korea. But if such a deal could not be reached, the DPRK leadership was fine—in its own unique way of thinking—with continuing its isolated struggle with the outside world and allowing the elite to consume most of the country's resources while the masses lived in economic and technological deprivation.

Moreover, because of its nuclear tests and steadily advancing nuclear technology, the DPRK's position under the status quo was growing stronger day by day. Whatever weaknesses the DPRK's nuclear capabilities involved—and they no doubt were numerous—the country had succeeded in developing a capable nuclear device. This was true despite isolation, despite sanctions, and despite pressure. The "cherished sword," as North Korean propaganda outlets called the nuclear program, was seen as a valuable deterrent against U.S. and South Korean aggression. Whereas North Korean negotiators during the Agreed Framework period felt that diplomacy was their primary tool for resolving conflicts, after the country's 2006 nuclear test, the DPRK felt that it had options other than diplomacy to compel, coerce, or fall back on. The existence of a nuclear deterrent, rudimentary as it was, also expanded the DPRK's sense of alternatives to a negotiated agreement and made diplomacy a tool, but not the only tool, in the DPRK toolkit. It is not clear that American negotiators in the period between 2006 and 2009 fully appreciated this change in North Korean thinking or the country's sense that it had reasonable options other than negotiating an agreement with the United States. In fact, it may not have been until 2017 when President Trump threatened fire and fury on North Korea, that the country again really reassessed its alternatives to a negotiated agreement.

The United States, on the other hand, had few alternatives to a negotiated agreement if it was to live up to its stated policy of not allowing the DPRK to become a nuclear state. In theory, it could ignore the DPRK's nuclear test or accept it as a nuclear state and begin to negotiate limits on its fissile material or delivery systems using an arms control paradigm. However, this was politically unpalatable. The United States had publicly stated a bottom line that it could neither achieve nor retreat from: it was insisting on rolling back the DPRK nuclear program and compliance with the Non Proliferation Treaty. At the same time, the United States could prevent the DPRK from becoming a nuclear state only by taking away its ability to make nuclear weapons through negotiation or by disarming the country through military attack and invasion. Participants in the Six-Party Talks did not doubt that the United States could reduce North Korean nuclear facilities to rubble if push came to shove. I recalled one particularly tense negotiation with the North Koreans in 2008. The U.S. and Chinese delegations had just completed a bilateral negotiation. After Chinese lead negotiator Wu Dawei, a chain smoker, left the room, the DPRK's Kim Kye Gwan came into the same room for a bilateral meeting, occupying the same chair in the Diaoyutai State Guesthouse in Beijing, which the chain-smoking Wu had just vacated. The DPRK's Kim began with a long diatribe about the DPRK's need for nuclear weapons as a deterrent against America aggression. Ambassador Hill interrupted Kim with a question: "So how exactly does this weapon make you safer? If you ever use it against the United States or its allies, what will be left of your capital is this," Hill said, illustrating by pouring the contents of Wu Dawei's ashtray onto the table in front of the DPRK negotiator. "You could," Kim calmly replied about the threat to reduce Pyongyang to ashes, "but you won't." Kim clearly understood that there was not a true nuclear deterrent to North Korea's devices. But he also understood that the United States, and indeed the world, was unlikely to allow a war to break out again on the Korean Peninsula as part of an effort to denuclearize the DPRK. He knew that his BATNA would let him walk away from the Six-Party Talks much sooner than Hill and the other parties ever would be able to abandon their mission to denuclearize North Korea.

Did the Paramount Nature of Security and Regime Survivability Mean There Was No Deal to Be Had?

Another possibility why the Six-Party Talks failed is that the interests and bottom lines of the parties were mutually incompatible in this negotiation. The United States' interest in the negotiations focused on North Korea giving up its nuclear technology, facilities, fuel, and the potential for creating nuclear weapons and long-range missiles that could strike the United States or its allies. The U.S. goal was a different kind of security. In the U.S thinking, security was achieved by making the United States and its allies safe from North Korean threats. Since nuclear issues were at the core of the Six-Party Talks, security for the United States and its allies meant denuclearization, sometimes identified as the complete, verifiable, irreversible dismantlement (CVID) of North Korea's nuclear programs. CVID could conceivably make the United States, and its Japanese and South Korean allies, safe from a DPRK nuclear threat. But, in fact, for South Korea it did nothing to remove the North Korean conventional threat, which was in some ways larger and more immediate with Seoul situated so close to the DMZ and DPRK border. For those in the United States, Japan, and South Korea who sought promises from the DPRK that would result in their total security, denuclearization was only a first step. For many, nothing short of disarmament would truly bring security. And for others, especially those neoconservatives who continued to see an interconnected global communist threat from the Cold War surviving in North Korea, only regime change would bring true security. To a large extent, I believe the North Koreans recognized this truth as much as, or more than, the United States negotiators did. And it meant, from a negotiation theory perspective, that the paramount nature of survival as an indispensable goal of the DPRK regime inevitably clashed with the paramount importance that the United States placed on security. Viewing these interests honestly and candidly, perhaps there never was a deal to be had.

Another factor working against a deal involved domestic interests in each country focused on demonizing the other. Dictatorships are less subject to public opinion or the different interagency viewpoints that are common political considerations in the United States. Because a dictatorship rarely can tolerate differing viewpoints, interagency differences are also reduced or eliminated, making it easier to settle on a single cohesive national position. But in the United States, a full range of views was present in the interagency and in the composition of the Six-Party Talks delegations I would manage. Within the United States, particularly strong suspicions of North Korea emanated from the offices of Vice President Dick Cheney and Secretary of

Defense Donald Rumsfeld.[11] Some negotiation experts consider domestic interests a wild card that can skew the outcome of an international negotiation. But I would maintain that domestic interests, just like other interests in a negotiation, are elements and factors that must be considered in international negotiations. Ambassador Hill was a particularly active, and candid, user of the media during his travels for the Six-Party Talks. Some officials on his own delegation represented the harder line viewpoint epitomized by the vice president and the Pentagon, and would report back to Washington through their own channels faster than official cables from the negotiating team. To address this back channeling, Hill used the media as a tool to convey his own report immediately after negotiations concluded and directly to policymakers, so long as they owned a TV.[12] In the long term, the public attention Ambassador Hill's media profile generated caused resentment in some parts of the Pentagon and the vice president's office, even reinforcing interagency efforts to undermine denuclearization talks.[13] In the United States, North Korea formed a kind of threat that was easy to demonize and easy to make into an enemy, whether real or in the Hollywood versions.[14] These examples of domestic difference of opinion in the United States illustrate the importance of taking differing viewpoints within a country into account, especially in a democracy. Among the tools in a political negotiator's toolkit, the media is sometimes an underutilized one.[15]

In conclusion, the discussions of the Six-Party Talks were a missed opportunity. The United States and its allies predicted that economic incentives

---

11. See Rice, *No Higher Honor*, chapter 11, Kindle location 2802 of 12657.

12. Nigel Quinney and Richard Solomon. 2010. *American Negotiating Behavior: Wheeler-Dealers, Legal Eagles, Bullies, and Preachers*. Washington, DC: U.S. Institutes of Peace, pp. 108–9 (Christopher Hill) and p. 123, chapter 5 on domestic politics.

13. Rice, *No Higher Honor*, Kindle, location 12087 of 12657 (Secretary Rice, in discussing negotiations to seek a verification protocol from the DPRK at the end of the Six-Party Talks process noted that Ambassador Hill's popularity with the media, and a disdain for repeated interagency meetings with groups suspicious of him made it challenging for her to give him the broad discretion needed to explore win-win negotiating opportunities with the North Koreans. "There was a tendency too in the Washington press corps to attribute every breakthrough exclusively to Chris [Hill's] negotiating skill, which would only reinforce the misguided notion that State was somehow winning a bureaucratic battle against other agencies that opposed the course we were on").

14. *Team America: World Police* of 2004 and *The Interview* of 2014 are classic examples of the North Korean bad guy as depicted in American culture and cinema.

15. At least, using the media was an underused tool for diplomats to report back to policymakers until President Trump's penchant for watching Fox News made officials in his own administration use the media to relay messages that previous administrations would have received in private.

could convince the DPRK to leave its isolation and abandon its "futile" nuclear deterrent in exchange for greater international respect, statements of security guarantees, and a more prosperous future for its citizens. While this calculation of a win-win outcome was logical from the U.S. negotiators' perspective, it missed elements of the DPRK's logic, including elements that caused the DPRK to be suspicious of economic development as a Trojan horse to destabilization. As Hill predicted, while North Korea was seriously engaged at the bargaining table, it was not launching missiles on Seoul or spreading its nuclear technology to others, especially at this key time in the war on terror. But in a preview of nuclear conflicts to come in the Trump administration, North Korean scientists were continuing to develop a covert nuclear and missile capacity, including uranium enrichment that the DPRK repeatedly denied until it was revealed to Stanford professor Sigfried Hecker during Hecker's 2010 visit to the country.[16] The DPRK likely did not pursue this covert nuclear and missile capacity any more broadly or aggressively during the years of Six-Party Talks than it would have done had there been no Six-Party denuclearization discussions underway. But it remains clear that what the international community was offering, in terms of economic and other benefits, was not enough to overcome the existential security concerns of the DPRK. What it wanted, and what it continued to press the Trump administration for, was a new kind of security relationship with the United States that would move past the Korean War and into a new era where the DPRK regime was seen as a permanent fixture controlling its country. The Kim family regime also wanted to be viewed as an equal to the United States and all other members of the international community.

---

16. Sigfried Hecker. Winter 2010. "Lessons Learned from the North Korea Nuclear Crisis." *Daedalus.*

CHAPTER 5

Libya and the Negotiation for a Unity Government

Local Power Outlasts the Ivory Tower

In 2016–2017 discussions on unifying Libya's government, Libyan strongman General Khalifa Haftar should have been an easy negotiating counterpart for the United States. A Libyan general under dictator Moammar Qaddhafi, Haftar later fell out of favor with Qaddhafi and was exiled to Chad and the Congo, where he was reportedly rescued by the United States. He later moved to the United States, where he and his family lived for twenty-five years. The United States and Haftar seemed to have a range of common points that would make negotiation easy: shared experience in the United States, a joint focus on counterterrorism (a commonality that increased drastically in importance after the 2016 election of Donald Trump to the presidency), frustration over the lack of governance in post-Qaddhafi Libya, and mutual suspicion of the Muslim Brotherhood.

On the other side of this negotiation to support Libya's Government of National Accord led by Prime Minister Fayez Sarraj was a coalition of Western governments and negotiators, including the United Nations itself. The United Kingdom, United States, France, Germany, Italy, and the UN Special Representative for Libya Martin Kobler repeatedly attempted to exclude Haftar from the political realm and establish the GNA's Sarraj as the sole power in Libya. Haftar remained undeterred by this effort and proceeded step-by-step to combat terrorists and take territory and political power until the Western and UN-backed parties sought to include him in direct negotiations. Even after they decided to engage, it took several months for the United States and Haftar to find a structure for direct negotiations. In a series of actions between 2016 and 2018, Haftar apparently and repeatedly came out on top in negotiations and in his actions on the ground. His success can largely be attributed to his clarity about his BATNA, juxtaposed against the failure by Western officials to see the logic of Haftar's position, viewed from his perspective and objectives and in light of his view of the alternatives.

The idea that an uneducated general like Haftar out-negotiated a team of United Nations interlocutors including envoys from many member states like the United States shows that you do not have to be the smartest, most educated, or most experienced person in a deal or negotiation to come out on top. Haftar's goals were simple: he wanted as much control as he could get of Libya at the lowest cost in military effort. Haftar initially despised politicians and negotiations, preferring instead to take power through military force. One reason Haftar was able to progress patiently from military isolation to his goal to be seen as a candidate to lead Libya politically was his clarity about his BATNA. Haftar learned that he could and should try to achieve his goals through political negotiation first because it was far less costly in blood and treasure than a pure military assault.

As a result, Haftar worked hard to win over tribal leaders in places where he wanted to advance. Starting in the east of Libya, Haftar in February 2014 called for the overthrow of Libya's Islamist linked Government of National Congress as a way for him to return from exile to national attention.[1] He used the international focus on defeating terrorists to slowly take territory under Operation Dignity, which he announced in May 2014. Throughout 2015 and 2016, Haftar established military governance in the areas that his Libyan National Army (LNA) occupied. In a lengthy assault of Libya's second-largest city, Benghazi, Haftar moved step-by-step and neighborhood-by-neighborhood until they had pushed out groups associated with terrorism, as well as other Islamist groups linked to Haftar's political enemies in February 2016. In September 2016, Haftar launched an attack on the Oil Crescent region, located between east and west, where most of Libya's oil exited from pipelines and was loaded on board tankers bound for Europe or refined for sale on the international market. Haftar took the facilities from a group known as the Petroleum Forces Guard, whose leader was widely seen as corrupt. Rather than keep the oil terminals under LNA control, he returned them and their wealth to Libya's National Oil Company. In 2017, Haftar similarly repelled an assault to retake the Oil Crescent but again

---

1. "Khalifa Haftar: The Libyan General with Big Ambitions." April 8, 2019. *BBC News*, available at https://www.bbc.com/news/world-africa-27492354

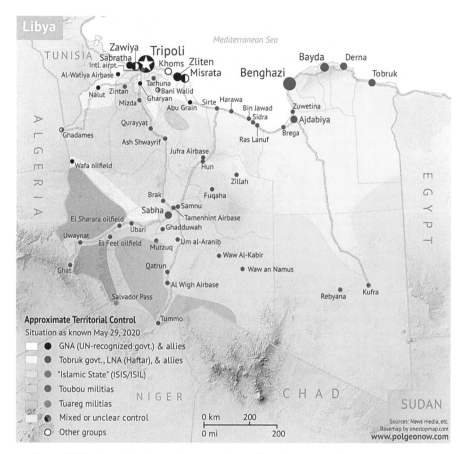

Figure 1. This is a political map depicting the conflict for territorial control that accompanied the political negotiations to establish a unified Libyan government in the period after the revolution to overthrow Qaddhafi. It depicts the military state of play and control in 2020 when there was a relative stalemate between the UN-backed Government of National Accord and the eastern-backed Libyan National Army of General Haftar and the House of Representatives.

scored political points by leaving Libya's economic lifeblood—oil—in the hands of National Oil Company technocrats. Bolstered politically and with further support of the House of Representatives, located in the east of the country, Haftar then moved against other cities where terrorists had established bases, including Derna, a city of 125,000 that fell to LNA control in June 2018. At the same time, Haftar's forces moved across Libya's desert and ungoverned south into Jufra and the area near Sebha. Throughout this move, Haftar took territory militarily when he had to, but he preferred to advance by striking agreements with the local tribes and officials who welcomed his forces as military governors.[2]

Haftar's cautious, step-by-step advance was replicated in his political bargaining with the international community, especially with the United States, in the period between 2014 and 2018. At the end of the Obama administration and the first few months of the Trump administration, Haftar refused to meet GNA Prime Minister Fayez Sarraj. American officials were frustrated by this, even arguing that it was evidence of why the United States could not trust the renegade general. But in fact, Haftar was reacting as a logical bargainer from his perspective. Haftar's patience, his timeline and his practical sense of his alternatives illustrate why his negotiation position was logical and why U.S. expectations that he drastically modify his behavior were not.

First, Haftar was, at age seventy-four, a patient negotiator as the international community, including the United Nations, the United States, and others, urged him to consider joining a civilian government or at least to work in a unified government structure under civilian control. Rather than react quickly to those who pressed him to consider joining a unified government, Haftar took his time. In part, he was waiting in late 2016 for information from the incoming Trump administration in order to calculate his next move. Advisers on both sides of the Atlantic (and in Cairo, Riyadh, and Abu Dhabi)[3] told Haftar that he would get full-throated support from the Trump administration. Motivated by a concern for counterterrorism above all, Haftar was led to believe that he might soon be anointed with U.S. support from the Trump administration. If the United States switched sides from support for the international government to him, Haftar thought there was little to stand in his way on a march to Tripoli. And if not, he was in no worse a position vis-à-vis the GNA and the international community than if he moved ahead with political negotiations in late 2016. In this case, uncertainty about the future U.S. position worked in Haftar's favor.

Haftar's U.S. interlocutor, Special Envoy for Libya Jonathan Winer, had

---

2. "Khalifa Haftar, Libya's Strongest Warlord, Makes a Push for Tripoli." April 20, 2019. *Economist*. Jonathan Tossell. January 2020. "Libya's Haftar and the Fezzan: One Year On." CRU Policy Brief. Clingendael Institute. https://www.clingendael.org/sites/default/files/2020-01/Policy_Brief_Libyas_Haftar_and_the_Fezzan_Jan_2020.pdf

3. Walid Phares was one of those positioning himself as a Trump envoy to Libya in the early days of the administration, among others. President Trump's April 2019 telephone call to Haftar appears to have fulfilled some of their promises and given Hafter the "green light" he was looking for to march on Tripoli and try to end the civil war by force. This aspect will be analyzed in more detail in chapter 12. See also "Trump Praises Libyan General as His Troops March on U.S. Backed Government in Tripoli," April 19, 2019, CNN News, available at https://edition.cnn.com/2019/04/19/politics/us-libya-praise-haftar/index.html

the opposite interest and was pressing for a quick agreement. Winer was one of the most active policy figures I have ever seen. Tirelessly, Winer would go through eighteen-hour days during his visits to Libya or elsewhere in the region, meeting with every Libyan official on a full range of topics in an effort to better understand the possibilities for unifying Libya under a productive and democratic government. But Winer was bound to a political timetable related to the U.S. election in November 2016 and transition in January 2017, and that made him and other U.S. policymakers impatient.[4] Winer knew that his position would likely expire after the transition. Even if Democratic candidate Hillary Clinton had won, Winer owed his position to his long political connection with Secretary of State John Kerry and he could not expect to wield the same level of influence over Libya policy after the election, no matter who prevailed. So when I arrived on the Libya account in 2016, Winer was interested in quick results and his impatience showed in the lack of chemistry with Haftar in their meetings. Given his alternatives to a negotiated agreement, Haftar judged he was better off waiting to hear the position of a future Hillary Clinton or Trump administration before acting on any inclination to join, or consider joining, a civilian government with GNA Prime Minister Sarraj. Once Trump won the election, Haftar's incentive to act before the January change of administrations was almost nonexistent.

Second, Haftar had good alternatives to negotiating an agreement. Haftar knew that he always had a great PLAN B or a great alternative to a negotiated agreement: he could revert to his military comfort zone and try to take by force what he did not succeed in getting at the bargaining table. This led Haftar to pursue a piecemeal approach. Where political negotiations were useful to his efforts to expand his territory and authority, he employed them, but always with the fall back option (and threat) of taking what he wanted by force. Where he could convince local leaders to support him, he did so peacefully, and then moved in without opposition. For example, in the Oil Crescent in the fall of 2016, Haftar's forces took control with minimal conflict and continued to provide the valuable oil resources under the control of Libya's National Oil Company. Similarly, in the area around Jufra and the three airbases at Tamenhint, Brak-al-Shati, and Jufra, Haftar slowly convinced the local tribes to support his forces rather than those affiliated

---

4. Quinney, *American Negotiating Behavior*, chapter 3 emphasized that U.S. negotiators "have a shorter term perspective and are usually driven by domestic considerations to press ahead rapidly before perceived windows of opportunity close: their sense of urgency manifests itself in numerous self-imposed deadlines" (p. 12).

with either the Benghazi Defense Brigades (BDB) or Misrata. He took the three airbases in May-June of 2017. The territorial gain was not cost free: dozens of lives were lost when the BDB and GNA Defense Minister Bargathi launched a sneak attack on the Brak al Shati airbase resulting in dozens of casualties among Haftar's LNA. But the brutal nature of the attack swung momentum from local tribes in Haftar's favor and he took the bases shortly thereafter with very little resistance. He also allowed the fleeing BDB and Misratan forces to leave with minimal loss of life, rather than pursue them and trigger a greater fight. This was again because Haftar realized that he had great alternatives to fighting. . . . He could take territory with little resistance by co-opting the locals. And both they and he knew that he always had the option of force, even to deploy force to pursue fleeing troops, but in most cases he chose not to use it.

Ultimately, the general learned to play the politician, both domestically and with the international community. For example, in May 2018 French President Macron convened Haftar and Sarraj in Paris—one of many power-broker meetings convened on Libya, which will be analyzed further in Part II. In the Macron-hosted session, Sarraj and Haftar announced elections would take place on December 10, 2018, in Libya.[5] Months later, the proposed December 2018 elections remain indefinitely postponed and the leadership deadlock between Haftar and Sarraj continues.[6] No U.S., UK, UN, or Western official has been able to break the deadlock. But Haftar remains as a leader and his LNA now controls the east and the south and has essentially surrounded the capital Tripoli, although an attempt to take Tripoli by force in 2020 was rebuffed In reaching this point, Haftar's clarity about his alternatives to a negotiated agreement helped him seize power at minimal cost and still transform his position from that of military strongman to politician with the possibility of leading Libya, either through elections or, if necessary, through occupation and force.

---

5. "Libyan Factions Agree to Hold Elections on 10 December," May 29, 2018, *The Guardian*, available at https://www.theguardian.com/world/2018/may/29/macron-hosts-libyan-factions-in-paris-in-push-to-secure-elections; "Emmanuel Macron Plans Crunch Summit to Push for Libyan Elections," May 23, 2018, *The Guardian*, available at https://www.theguard-ian.com/world/2018/may/23/emmanuel-macron-plans-summit-to-push-for-libyan-elections

6. In February 2021, the Libyan Political Dialogue Forum met in Geneva to select a new interim Prime Minister and Presidency Council to replace Sarraj with a goal of elections to be held in December, 2021. At the time of publication, the prospect of those elections was still unclear.

CHAPTER 6

Creating the First International Monitor on LGBTI Rights

Asking Too Much or Too Little?

The 2014 negotiations on the issue of LGBTI rights in the United Nations allow us to examine whether negotiators could have done more sooner to advance the creation of a permanent UN mechanism to report on discrimination and violence based on an individual's sexual orientation or gender identity (SOGI). Analyzing whether a negotiator got the best possible deal is always tricky. Hindsight is 20/20. An outsider or Monday morning quarterback can always suggest that the outcome would have been better if the negotiation had been tweaked or different tactics employed. But the cyclical nature of the UN Human Rights Council (HRC) provides a good venue for case studies because the same issues are often raised every year or two. In this way, we can see how outcomes vary from year to year and, with insight on the tactics that were actually employed in the negotiating rooms, one can test certain propositions and examine whether an outcome that was reached later (in this case 2016) might have been achievable earlier (in this case 2014) had different tactics been employed. In this case, we will see how negotiators addressing the issue of LGBTI rights in the UN Human Rights Council in 2014 might have been able to create a UN Special Procedure mechanism two years earlier than they ultimately succeeded in doing in June 2016. This is a case of "leaving money on the table" or not pressing the position of counterparts adequately before making concessions. We will discuss tactics that any negotiator can use to ensure that such an error does not happen to you.

In September 2014, the United Nations Human Rights Council debated how to address the issue of discrimination against LGBTI persons. In the

HRC, the approaches for addressing a thematic topic of concern are relatively limited to public statements, reporting, or holding recurring discussions and meetings. The strongest mechanisms at the disposal of the HRC involve creating institutional mechanisms, known as Special Procedures mandate holders. These unpaid experts carry a UN title, receive funding for travel, and have support of a UN staff person in the Office of the High Commissioner for Human Rights (OHCHR), enabling the mandate holder to research and report on abuses, violations, and trends in the area of human rights they are assigned to follow. Their authority to undertake these investigations and write reports comes from resolutions of the forty-seven-member UN HRC, and creation of such a mandate holder position can be a hotly debated issue. Nevertheless, the use of this position and the bully pulpit of the United Nations can contribute to changes in behavior and international norms. The resolutions that create Special Procedures mandate holders and other decisions of the UN Human Rights Council are also a source of customary international law and persuasive as a form of soft law. So as the HRC considered how to respond to the issue of discrimination against LGBTI persons in 2014, creation of a Special Procedure was one of the key options on the negotiating table.

The issue of violence and discrimination against LGBTI people based on SOGI had surfaced in the HRC in June 2011. At that time, a first, historic resolution was passed by a 23–19 vote with three abstentions (Burkina Faso, Zambia, and China).[1] That resolution, led by South Africa, called for a report on cases of discrimination and violence against people based on SOGI. The report issued by the OHCHR as a result of the 2011 resolution documented a range of abuses, including violent killings of LGBTI people and state-sponsored discrimination.[2]

---

1. See UN Human Rights Council Resolution 17/19, June 17, 2011, "Human Rights, Sexual Orientation And Gender Identity (SOGI)." https://documents-dds-ny.un.org/doc/UNDOC/GEN/G11/148/76/PDF/G1114876.pdf?OpenElement. [Adopted by a recorded vote of 23–19, with three abstentions. The voting was as follows: In favor: Argentina, Belgium, Brazil, Chile, Cuba, Ecuador, France, Guatemala, Hungary, Japan, Mauritius, Mexico, Norway, Poland, Republic of Korea, Slovakia, Spain, Switzerland, Thailand, Ukraine, United Kingdom of Great Britain and Northern Ireland, United States of America, Uruguay. Against: Angola, Bahrain, Bangladesh, Cameroon, Djibouti, Gabon, Ghana, Jordan, Malaysia, Maldives, Mauritania, Nigeria, Pakistan, Qatar, Republic of Moldova, Russian Federation, Saudi Arabia, Senegal, Uganda. Abstaining: Burkina Faso, China, Zambia].

2. UN Issues First Report on Human Rights of Gay and Lesbian People, UN NEWS, December 15, 2011, available at https://news.un.org/en/story/2011/12/398432-un-issues-first-report-human-rights-gay-and-lesbian-people

After the 2011 resolution and report, advocates tried to determine how to present the issue again in the HRC and how to make discrimination against people based on SOGI a more regular and consistent aspect of international nondiscrimination standards. Each time the issue came up, some advocates pressed to create a report that would repeat cyclically or a Special Procedures mechanism that would allow LGBTI rights to remain on the HRC agenda without concern about annual renewal and the political changes that might thwart serious examination of the issue again in later years.[3] Organizers were painfully aware that the vote had been close in 2011 and feared a loss would somehow legitimize discrimination on the basis of LGBTI rights and downgrade the emerging domestic legal norms in many countries protecting people from discrimination and violence based on SOGI. Cognizant of these considerations organizers engaged in a back-and-forth debate about how far to push and how much to ask for to regularize reporting on SOGI-based discrimination. A primary goal was to create something permanent that would report on SOGI-based violence and discrimination, rather than to have to revisit the issue every year or two.

In 2011, South Africa had been a leader of the UN resolution on gay rights in the HRC and in the UN in general. As a strong African voice

---

3. The UN Human Rights Council's Special Procedures include several mechanisms that are routinely renewed and are termed here permanent mechanisms. These Special Procedures mechanisms include:

- Commission of Inquiry: Used to document a serious, ongoing human rights situation and sometimes prepare a record that could be used for an international prosecution or referral to a higher body like the UN Security Council or International Criminal Court.
- UN Special Rapporteurs: Typically created under HRC Agenda Items 3 (thematic issues) or 4 (country situations of concern) to monitor and report on human rights situations within their thematic or country-specific mandate.
- UN Independent Experts: Typically created under HRC Agenda Item 10 (Technical Assistance) to help a country with technical assistance needed to strengthen an aspect of human rights promotion or protection. Often requested by the country concerned. Occasionally, independent experts are created under Items 2 and 3 of the Council agenda for similar purposes, including thematic mandates.
- Intergovernmental Working Groups: Often used to draft documents that might ultimately result in legally binding instruments such as treaties. Working groups meet to provide political support and expert input in the crafting of such documents and to determine whether the political consensus exists to encapsulate the topic under discussion into a legally binding instrument, rather than as persuasive but non-binding "soft law," such as a UN resolution. "Special Procedures of the UN Human Rights Council." 2020. Website of the Office of the UN High Commissioner for Human Rights. https://www.ohchr.org/EN/HRBodies/HRC/Pages/SpecialProcedures.aspx

supporting LGBTI rights, South Africa's voice was important, especially in rebutting claims that gay rights were a "Western invention" being inappropriately foisted on a developing world that was not ready for them. But after the 2011 resolution passed and a series of regional workshops were held to discuss issues of violence and discrimination against LGBTI persons, South Africa controversially took a back seat.[4] South Africa's post-apartheid constitution was one of the first in the world to protect LGBTI rights, but its negotiators in the UN decided that after the 2011 vote, they should no longer play a leadership role on gay rights in the UN, out of deference to the need to maintain support of others in the African group with different views.

As a result, a group of Latin American states (Brazil, Chile, Colombia, and Uruguay) decided to lead as proponents of a new HRC resolution on LGBTI rights in 2014. It was this group that had to make the decisions about strategy and what to try to propose in creating a permanent mechanism. The Brazilian-led "core group" advocated a resolution that continued the focus on discrimination and opposing violence but ultimately fell short of creating a permanent mechanism, instead settling for a mere update to the previous 2011 report (HRC Resolution 27/32).[5] Why, if creating a permanent mechanism was a high priority, did the group settle for creating another one-off report, which the HRC had already done in 2011?

In negotiations on the 2014 resolution, allies of Brazil in the BRICS alignment (Brazil, Russia, India, China, and South Africa) discouraged Brazil from advocacy to create a permanent mechanism. Whittled down by this

---

4. J. Lester Feder. September 8, 2014. "South Africa, Which Once Led on Promoting LGBT Rights Abroad, Could Become a Roadblock." *Buzzfeed News.* https://www.buzzfeed.com/lesterfeder/south-africa-which-once-led-on-promoting-lgbt-rights-abroad?utm_term=.qrLb0n0YZ#.gnmmkwkjB

5. UN Human Rights Council. 2014. "Human Rights, Sexual Orientation and Gender Identity Resolution." HRC Resolution 27/32 (Adopted September 26, 2014). https://documents-dds-ny.un.org/doc/UNDOC/GEN/G14/177/32/PDF/G1417732.pdf?OpenElement HRC Resolution 27/32 was adopted by a recorded vote of 25–14, with seven abstentions. The voting was as follows: In favor: Argentina, Austria, Brazil, Chile, Costa Rica, Cuba, Czech Republic, Estonia, France, Germany, Ireland, Italy, Japan, Mexico, Montenegro, Peru, Philippines, Republic of Korea, Romania, South Africa, the former Yugoslav Republic of Macedonia, United Kingdom of Great Britain and Northern Ireland, United States of America, Venezuela (Bolivarian Republic of), Viet Nam Against: Algeria, Botswana, Côte d'Ivoire, Ethiopia, Gabon, Indonesia, Kenya, Kuwait, Maldives, Morocco, Pakistan, Russian Federation, Saudi Arabia, United Arab Emirates. Abstaining: Burkina Faso, China, Congo, India, Kazakhstan, Namibia, Sierra Leone.

pressure, in the last week of the September 2014 Council session, the core group was positioning to submit a draft resolution that merely proposed an annual report by the OHCHR on violence and discrimination on SOGI. Puzzled by Brazil's retreat from a more permanent mechanism or at least a report, I asked negotiators why they reduced their demand. They said frankly that they had concerns that China and Russia would vote against the bill. These risks were legitimate: certain states viewed LGBTI rights so negatively that they were going to call a vote and vote against a SOGI resolution no matter what content was included. Still my U.S. colleagues and I explained to the Brazilians, the resolution had sufficient support to pass by a comfortable margin even in the face of opposition from China, Russia, and other members of the HRC's so-called "Like Minded Group." The Brazilians were not so sure, citing concerns raised by their BRICS colleagues, especially Russia. In the end, the watered down resolution passed by an absolute majority and a comfortable 25–14 vote with seven abstentions, including four African states and Brazil's BRICS friends China and India. Russia voted no.

So what did Brazil get for watering down the content so it was a one-off report rather than a repeated reporting cycle authored by an appointee with long-term interest in following this aspect of nondiscrimination? Perhaps it got China and India to abstain rather than vote against the resolution. But this was not essential to the outcome or even the margin of victory. China and India abstained but did not support the watered down measure and the resolution would have passed by a majority even with China and India's opposition in the form of a no vote. In addition, China worked with a group of states from the Organization of Islamic Cooperation to support hostile amendments to the resolution that would have completely stripped the language of SOGI from the text. China also supported a hostile "no-action" motion that would have led to the resolution not even being considered.[6]

So if Brazil got nothing from its BRICS allies, why did it give up the chance to create a longer-term mechanism with perpetual reporting on discrimination based on SOGI in 2014? Did it have to make these concessions? Apparently not, because when the SOGI issue came back to the HRC in 2016 with a slightly more hostile group of states serving as members of the Council, the HRC created a permanent mechanism, the Independent Expert on SOGI issues, by a nearly identical margin of

6. "Action on No-Action Motion on SOGI Resolution." 2016. Arc International. http://arc-international.net/global-advocacy/human-rights-council/32nd-session-of-the-human-rights-council/appointing-an-independent-expert-on-sexual-orientation-and-gender-identity-an-analysis-of-process-results-and-implications/annex-ii-description-of-the-vote-on-the-sogi-resolution/action-on-no-action-motion/

23–18 with six abstentions.[7] Again, opposing the Latin pro-SOGI resolution were Brazil's supposed BRICS friends China and Russia, for whom it had conceded the permanent mechanism in 2014, while India and South Africa abstained. None of the BRICS countries for whom Brazil significantly watered down the 2014 resolution ended up giving any concessions or benefits in exchange.

So in this case, Brazil's failure to test the position of its partners and potential adversaries was a negotiating mistake. The vote margin and voting behavior of the parties indicates the negotiator gave up too much without getting anything significant in return. And permanent reporting for a group of individuals who suffer severe violence and discrimination could have received more regularized and repeated scrutiny two years earlier, beginning in 2014 rather than 2016. Instead the creation of the UN Independent Expert on SOGI issues was delayed out of fear, failure to test stated positions, and a failure to deploy tools common to multiparty international negotiations.

As a postscript, it is interesting to note that in July 2019 the SOGI mandate again came to the HRC for renewal. This time, the mandate passed by a clear majority of the Council and HRC Resolution 41/18 was adopted by a 27–12 majority of the HRC, with seven abstentions.[8] Compared with

---

7. UN Human Rights Council. 2016. "Protection Against Violence and Discrimination Based on Sexual Orientation and Gender Identity." HRC Resolution 32/2 (adopted June 30, 2016). https://documents-dds-ny.un.org/doc/UNDOC/GEN/G16/154/15/PDF/G1615415.pdf?OpenElement. The resolution passed by a vote of 23–18 with six abstentions. Results stated in favor: Albania, Belgium, Bolivia, Cuba, Ecuador, El Salvador, France, Georgia, Germany, Latvia, Mexico, Mongolia, Netherlands, Panama, Paraguay, Portugal, Republic of Korea, Slovenia, Switzerland, the former Yugoslav Republic of Macedonia, United Kingdom of Great Britain and Northern Ireland, Venezuela (Bolivarian Republic of), Viet Nam. Against: Algeria, Bangladesh, Burundi, China, Congo, Côte d'Ivoire, Ethiopia, Indonesia, Kenya, Kyrgyzstan, Maldives, Morocco, Nigeria, Qatar, Russian Federation, Saudi Arabia, Togo, United Arab Emirates Abstaining: Botswana, Ghana, India, Namibia, Philippines, South Africa.

8. UN Human Rights Council. 2019. "Mandate of the Independent Expert on Protection Against Violence and Discrimination Based on Sexual Orientation and Gender Identity." HRC Resolution 41/18 (adopted July 12, 2019). https://documents-dds-ny.un.org/doc/UNDOC/GEN/G19/221/62/PDF/G1922162.pdf?OpenElement. The Resolution was adopted by a vote of 27–12 with three abstentions. In favor: Argentina, Australia, Austria, Bahamas, Brazil, Bulgaria, Chile, Croatia, Cuba, Czech Republic, Denmark, Fiji, Iceland, Italy, Japan, Mexico, Nepal, Peru, Philippines, Rwanda, Slovakia, South Africa, Spain, Tunisia and Ukraine. Opposed: Afghanistan, Bahrain, Bangladesh, China, Egypt, Eritrea, Iraq, Nigeria, Pakistan, Qatar, Saudi Arabia, Somalia. Abstentions: India, Angola, Burkina Faso, DRC, Hungary, Senegal and Togo.

2014 and 2016, support for nondiscrimination on SOGI was expanding as states grappled with this issue domestically. Countries in all regions of the globe supported the mandate's renewal, including states from Africa and the Islamic group, and agreed that the UN should evaluate violence and discrimination against persons based on their sexual orientation and gender identity as part of a global assessment of universal standards. This broadening of support helped to overcome an argument of "cultural relativism" voiced by the Organization of Islamic Cooperation (OIC) as a key reason for the ten hostile amendments that the group, plus China, offered. Even there, OIC members Albania and Tunisia refused to agree to the OIC amendments, resulting in the anomalous situation that a group that operates on consensus offered its amendments in the name of "the OIC except Albania and Tunisia."

Moreover, reports authored by the Independent Expert on SOGI have made substantial contributions to the development of international human rights norms. By 2020, concepts of multiple and intersectional discrimination were becoming more common in UN discussions of nondiscrimination as states and institutions considered how multiple factors, such as being a gay women of color or a transgender person, contributed to violence and discrimination based on SOGI. These ideas were popularized in the SOGI Independent Expert's 2018 report to the UN General Assembly looking at multiple and intersecting forms of discrimination in education, health care, housing, employment, and other services.[9] The Independent Expert has also reported to the HRC on issues of violence and stigmatizing discrimination based on SOGI and how the use of "conversion therapy" against LGBTI persons can constitute a form of torture.[10]

Even as positions toward SOGI softened in most regions of the world, the positions of Brazil's friends in the BRICS for whom they made their 2014 concessions remained unchanged or even hardened in opposition to this global trend. China was the only non-Islamic country to support hostile amendments to the resolution and to vote against the 2019 mandate renewal. India, whose Supreme Court decriminalized homosexuality in 2018, abstained in 2019 as it had in 2016.[11] Ironically, even Brazil's delega-

---

9. Report of the Independent Expert on Violence and Discrimination on the Basis of Sexual Orientation and Gender Identity to the UN General Assembly, July 17, 2019, https://undocs.org/A/74/181

10. "Report of the Independent Expert on Protection Against Violence and Discrimination Based on Sexual Orientation and Gender Identity." 2020. So-called conversion therapy, adopted May 1, 2020. https://undocs.org/A/HRC/44/53

11. Devirupa Mitra. July 13, 2019. "Despite SC Ruling, India Abstains Again on Vote on

tion made clear that its leadership on this issue had limits, based in part on the election in Brazil of President Jair Bolsinaro, who removed protections for LGBTI persons from parts of Brazil's government and threatened gay rights activists at home and abroad.[12] All of these developments illustrate how Brazil's willingness to drop the creation of a UN Independent Expert in 2014 was likely a mistake, as Brazil got nothing in return for this concession, and it appears its BRICS allies were never willing to change position or move closer to the pro-LGBTI viewpoint Brazil was articulating.

LGBT Rights at UN." *The Wire.* https://thewire.in/diplomacy/india-abstains-again-on-vote
-expert-lgbt-rights-at-un

12. Morgan Gstalter. January 2, 2019. "Brazil's New President Removes LGBT Concerns
from Human Rights Ministry." *The Hill.* https://thehill.com/policy/international/human-
rights/423594-brazils-new-president-removes-lgbt-concerns-from-human.   Maria   Laura
Canineu. March 18, 2019. "For Brazil at the UN, Rights Values Begin at Home." Human
Rights Watch. https://www.hrw.org/news/2019/03/08/brazil-un-rights-values-begin-home

CHAPTER 7

Surveillance, Free Expression, and the Right to Privacy in the Digital Age

Background: UN Approaches to Internet Freedom or Regulation in the Digital Age

Much as states, individuals, corporations, and societies struggled over how to think about the intersection between human rights and the ubiquity of the Internet, UN agencies, funds, and programs also compete over where and how to address regulation of the Internet. UN technical bodies dealing with telecommunications, spectrum, and intellectual property weighed in with proposals to regulate the Internet coming from within, and sometimes beyond, their areas of technical competency. On the other hand, human rights bodies like the UN Human Rights Council (HRC) argued that the Internet should largely remain unregulated. UNESCO joined in with its own version of a rights-based approach. Nongovernmental and multi-stakeholder organizations like the Internet Governance Forum tried to bridge the gap to offer self-governance proposals created by industry and the tech community in collaboration with states. The environment was ripe for multiparty negotiation, and it largely remains so today with states continuing to disagree about when, how, or whether the UN should have a role in Internet governance or regulation.

In the first UN Human Rights Council resolution to address these questions, HRC resolution 20/8 of July 2012 affirmed that: "The same rights people have offline must also be protected online."[1] This resolution on Inter-

---

1. UN Human Rights Council. July 5, 2012. "The Promotion, Protection and Enjoyment of Human Rights on the Internet." HRC Resolution 20/8. https://undocs.org/A/HRC/RES/20/8

net freedom recognized the global and open nature of the Internet as a driving force in accelerating development and called upon states to promote and facilitate access to the Internet. Two years later, a follow-up resolution reaffirmed the importance for people to enjoy their rights online and noted that security justifications for restricting freedom of expression on the Internet need to meet strict legal justifications. More recently, in 2016, HRC resolution 32/13 called upon states to refrain from Internet shutdowns because of their impact in stifling the exercise of human rights online. The 2016 resolution also urged the United Nations to conduct a study on best practices related to bridging the gender digital divide and advancing access online to persons with disabilities.[2]

In the midst of this discussion about Internet regulation and Internet freedom, the 2013 revelations about widespread U.S. electronic surveillance made public by National Security Agency contractor Edward Snowden made the right to privacy online a new cause célèbre in the human rights community. The Snowden revelations shifted the human rights focus away from countries that used the Internet to identify and detain dissidents and victims of those repressive government policies. Instead the human rights community focused on the U.S. government's influence over aspects of the Internet and the related telecommunications environment. In particular, two partners of the United States—Brazil and Germany—led a resolution in the 2013 United Nations General Assembly on the right to privacy in the digital age,[3] which attacked the United States, albeit indirectly, over its use of mass surveillance and the resulting interference with privacy. The resolution asserted that "unlawful or arbitrary surveillance and/or interception of communications, as well as unlawful or arbitrary collection of personal data, [are] highly intrusive acts, [that] violate the rights to privacy and to freedom of expression and may contradict the tenets of a democratic society."[4] The HRC then picked up the resolution, creating a follow-on mechanism in the form of the Special Rapporteur on the Right to Privacy. This chapter will illustrate key aspects of the Internet freedom negotiations and illustrate lessons going forward, especially those related to the group dynamics occurring as the Internet freedom debate shifted from a focus on free expression to a focus on privacy rights.

---

2. UN Human Rights Council. July 1, 2016. "The Promotion, Protection and Enjoyment of Human Rights on the Internet." HRC Resolution 20/16. https://undocs.org/A/HRC/RES/32/13

3. UN General Assembly. December 18, 2013. "The Right to Privacy in the Digital Age." Resolution 68/137. https://www.un.org/en/ga/search/view_doc.asp?symbol=A/RES/68/167

4. UN General Assembly, December 18, 2013.

The Importance of a Cross-Regional Core Group

The United States' first-ever appointee as ambassador to the HRC was Eileen Donahoe. Having been a professor in Silicon Valley and married to former eBay CEO and PayPal chairman John Donahoe, Ambassador Donahoe was acutely aware of the importance of the Internet and its role as a catalyst for enjoyment of human rights, especially the freedom of expression. She also watched with concern the tools used to constrain free expression online in a range of authoritarian states. Some used old-fashioned techniques of arresting and detaining so-called Internet dissidents for their writings online about democracy. Others used technology itself as a police tool, seeking out dissident views online, blocking key search terms through the "Great Chinese Firewall," and exercising censorship such that even U.S. government websites were sometimes unavailable.

In this context, Donahoe wanted to advance a resolution on Internet freedom in the HRC. But she knew that such an action by the United States would face strong opposition from Russia, China, Egypt, and others who were deploying these online tactics of policing and repression. As a result, she cultivated ambassadors to educate them on the U.S. view of Internet freedom. She arranged to hold an HRC retreat for key ambassadors in Silicon Valley, showing them firsthand the free expression and creativity benefits of an open innovation society. She also created the Internet Freedom Fellows program at U.S. Mission Geneva, an exchange program that brought Internet dissidents, writers, and officials from around the globe to Geneva, to Washington, and to Silicon Valley to learn more about the importance of free expression norms and the culture of innovation and openness that was so important to the Internet's growth and development.

But most important, she created a cross-regional core group of states to lead the campaign for Internet freedom in the HRC. Through personal friendships and professional relationships, she established a core group consisting of Brazil, Nigeria, Tunisia, Turkey, Sweden, and the United States who jointly agreed to lead the Internet freedom resolution. Creating collective leadership, while requiring additional coordination work, can significantly strengthen the prospects for passage of a UN resolution in the following ways:

1. Cross-regional core groups expand the ownership of an issue. This allows the advocates of a resolution to divide the work of lobbying for a resolution, with one or more members of the core group ensuring that those in its own regional group are educated about the resolution and lobby the regional group to support it.

2. In an environment like the UN Human Rights Council where only forty-seven UN states are members and strict two-term limits are imposed, it is important to have at least one member of a core group who is also a member of the Human Rights Council for any given year. For example, in 2016 when the resolution on Internet freedom was renewed, Nigeria was the only one of the core group who was a member. Given the rules of the HRC, it meant Nigeria was also the only state authorized to vote in favor of the resolution and to speak in opposition to hostile amendments at key times.

3. Having a cross-regional group makes it difficult for opponents to brand the issue as purely a case of U.S. hegemony or Western values being imposed on others. In the case of the Internet, it also made it impossible for opponents to brand this as a "U.S. versus Russia" or "U.S. versus China" discussion. By the time I was departing from Geneva in 2016, newer U.S. officials were referring to the Internet freedom resolution as the "Swedish resolution" because of Sweden's role as coordinator of the core group. These officials were so new as to be completely unaware of the past U.S. role in shaping the core group. And the resolution passed by consensus three consecutive times with this group leadership before the Trump administration pulled the United States out of the Human Rights Council.

4. Fourth, an underappreciated benefit of a core group is that it builds capacity among collegial states for future initiatives and negotiations. Some states may be reluctant to lead a resolution by themselves initially but after working together in a core group, it can strengthen their confidence to do so in future.

5. In light of the fact that the Internet regulation discussion was taking place in a range of UN technical agencies, most of whom were headquartered in Geneva, having a core group allowed the lead actors to seek some coherence across the range of UN and multiparty venues where the Internet was being discussed. For example, the Internet freedom core group included Tunisia, host of an important World Summit on the Information Society; Brazil, host of an important 2014 multi-stakeholder meeting, Netmundial; and Sweden, whose foreign minister Carl Bildt was an outspoken advocate of a free and open Internet. Despite differences among the core group members on some Internet governance issues, their shared mission in sponsoring the Internet freedom resolution allowed them to overcome these differences. The bonds forged from working together also helped to

build resiliency against later challenges, such as those that developed when the Internet freedom dispute evolved into one about the right to privacy in the digital age.

The core principle resulting from the Internet freedom resolutions was that "rights people have offline must also be protected online." A relatively simple idea, it has proven durable enough to survive over a decade and has been applied broadly in several human rights domains. Most obviously, the concept is applicable to freedom of expression with the idea that online censorship must follow the same long-standing and internationally recognized rules that would apply in the censorship of a print newspaper, book, or radio or TV broadcast. This has prevented an attempt by some governments to disguise censorship as technical regulation and has shown such efforts for what they are—content-based restrictions that almost always violate internationally agreed rights.

But the principle that rights apply the same online as offline extends beyond freedom of expression. For groups that form online and have members, for example, the principles of freedom of association should apply equally online and offline. On issues of discrimination, hate speech, and racism, discriminatory acts should be equally punished online as they are offline. And the balance between free expression and other rights should be respected equally online as offline. But when it came to the right of privacy, recognized as a qualified right under international law, the U.S. position became a bit of a thorn in the side. The United States found its cherished principle that rights apply online the same as they do offline in conflict with Edward Snowden's 2013 revelations of mass surveillance programs in the United States, which raised to the fore important new issues of the right to privacy in the digital age.

Privacy in the Digital Age

The resolution on the right to privacy in the digital age was a unique experience where the United States, the United Kingdom, and their allies Canada, Australia, and New Zealand were at a relative disadvantage in the distribution and allocation of power in the United Nations on an important human rights issue. As leaders of the resolution on privacy and the digital age, Germany and Brazil formed a powerful bloc and the focus of their criticism was behavior by the United States and the United Kingdom in the realm of surveillance, which Brazil and Germany considered to violate international norms. Press reports of the United States overhearing conversations of Brazilian president Dilma Roussef and German chancellor Angela Merkel[5] made the German and Brazilian leadership especially strong—those delegations knew that they could reach back to their respective capitals and, when necessary, get the attention of their very highest policymakers to assist in lobbying for positions favorable to the German and Brazilian draft. Moreover, the issue split these Anglophone countries from the European and Latin American regional groups—the UN's regional groups most likely to advocate for human rights protections.

Even without the handful of largely German-speaking states who joined them, the Brazilians and Germans constituted a formidable core group. Many of the lessons of Ambassador Donahoe's work to create a strong core group on the Internet freedom resolution were employed by the Brazilians (fellow Internet freedom core group members) in advocacy for the resolution on privacy in the digital age. Brazil's strengths came in many forms—its leadership role in Latin America, in the developing world bloc known as the G-77, and in the BRICS (a coalition of Brazil, Russia, India, China, and South Africa that often resisted the power of the United States and Western Europe). Moreover, Brazil added to its core group Mexico, the other strongest country in Latin America and the one state that could have possibly sided with the United States and produced some division within Latin America. Brazil coupled this strength with Germany, the EU's strongest voice. Germany was embedded at the center of the Western European grouping and held the HRC presidency at the time. The Western Europe group is comprised of the EU and a collection of non-EU Western states called JUSCANZ.[6] Along with Brazil, Germany, and Mexico, the other core group members for the resolution were Norway, and the German-speaking states of Switzerland and Liechtenstein. By including these states in the core group, the United States and United Kingdom would face challenges in the EU, in WEOG, and even in JUSCANZ, so that they could not count

---

5. See, e.g., Alison Smale. Oct. 23, 2013. "Anger Growing Among Allies on U.S. Spying." *New York Times*; "Stung By the NSA's Reach, Brazil and Germany Prepare for Closer Ties." August 13, 2015. *Deutsche Welle*.

6. JUSCANZ is an acronym from the original members of this group (Japan, the United States, Canada, Australia, and New Zealand) but has now become known as the UN body to which all non-EU members of the UN's WEOG group belong, and in addition to which Japan and the ROK are members. JUSCANZ is occasionally spelled JUSCANNZ in recognition of the core membership in the group of Switzerland and Norway, the largest Western European countries who are not members of the EU (up to the point of Brexit at least). The group is an ad hoc body whose membership can change depending on the issue. It is not a policy coordination body, unlike the European Union.

on support even among their most natural core allies if they attempted to defuse or limit the scope of the right to privacy resolution. Thus, from the very start, the right to privacy issue had a strong core group, and without even discussing the substance of their idea, the resolution's sponsors had sufficient power to guarantee passage of almost any text addressing the topic.

Even so, and perhaps because of this apparent overwhelming advantage, the group made mistakes in negotiation practice that weakened their hand. First, perhaps because of the strength of their core group, they did not seek true cross-regional support. No African or Asian state was brought into the group as a supporter, nor did they have support in the UN's 5th regional group, Eastern Europe. Second, and perhaps more importantly, they committed a major error in how they handled their draft text. The group kept their text secret, refusing to discuss or share it with other states until almost the opening of negotiations. This meant that the many states in Asia and Africa were unaware of the resolution's content. Even if they supported the principles of the resolution, they were ignorant of its language and could not be brought on board as early supporters.

Control of the draft of a resolution is seen as a key source of power in negotiations.[7] As drafters of the resolution, a core group has this key source of power and can set the agenda for the negotiation by controlling what language goes into the draft. By "controlling the pen," the core group can add or reject suggestions made by other delegations, leaving other parties in a take-it-or-leave-it posture if their proposals were not accepted. When producing its text, the core group relied significantly on the draft resolution on privacy in the digital age, which had already been passed by the UN General Assembly's Third Committee, resolution 68/167. The General Assembly text had passed by consensus after language was agreed to that reflected some concerns of other states. But Brazil and Germany tried to overplay their hand in the Human Rights Council. They reasserted only the language that they liked from the General Assembly resolution while deleting all the balancing text. When the text was unveiled so late—literally table dropped at the time of the first informal negotiation—American negotiators pointed out this "cherry picking" of only parts of the UNGA resolution text. The U.S. approach won sympathy from several Asian and African states who also had been kept out of the drafting until the first open negotiation and viewed as unfair the late tabling of a draft resolution that chose selectively from the UNGA resolution.

Moreover, the Germans and Brazilians focused some of their rhetoric on

---

7. Salacuse, *The Global Negotiator*, p. 40.

the governing principle of the Internet freedom resolution—that the enjoyment of human rights should be the same online as offline. Using this perspective, they argued for the concept of protecting privacy in the digital age and sought to hoist the Americans on their own petard. At first glance, the analogy was a strong one: if people enjoyed a right to privacy in their correspondence and homes, it seemed that governmental opening of their emails would clearly be an online infringement.

Ironically, the Germans and Brazilians tried to take the HRC resolution further than they had in the General Assembly and further than the resolution on Internet freedom had gone before. They wanted to address complicated issues on surveillance. For example, they wanted to declare that collection of metadata (the web of who communicates with whom via email, text messaging, Facebook friending, and other digital communication) violated the right to privacy. However, this argument faced a problem in the analogy with the offline world. In almost every state in the United Nations, postal services began as a government function. That meant that the government had always been aware of the addresses of those who were receiving mail and even those who were writing to others. How else could that most ubiquitous of government employees—the mail carrier—deliver the mail? Similarly, in many states, telecommunications ministries controlled telephone connections. This again raised problems with the core argument of the Brazilians and Germans: the idea that government collection of metadata in the form of who was communicating with whom gave the government a new way of infringing privacy in the online world that it did not have in the offline world.

Finally, the very groupings that made the Brazilians appear so powerful as a proponent of the resolution also worked to their detriment. Brazil was insistent that the resolution focus only on infringements of privacy online that could be seen as a result of surveillance by the United States and United Kingdom. It made this choice because it did not want to create opposition from its powerful allies in the BRICS grouping, including Russia and China, who use surveillance to jail Internet dissidents and to close organizations for the content of their work, especially those who advocate domestic reforms or democratization. Thus throughout the negotiations there was intense silence about the actual damage caused by any violations of the right to privacy in the digital age other than those created by the United States' and United Kingdom's electronic surveillance programs.

In the end, these weaknesses in approach caused the privacy in the digital age core group to compromise. They removed key language on the digital age from aspects of the resolution, added back in deleted paragraphs from the UN General Assembly resolution that had balanced the concepts they emphasized, and allowed the concepts to be broadened so that they focused on all aspects of the right to privacy, not just those related to surveillance. The United States and the United Kingdom joined consensus on the measure, which is today used to address all aspects of privacy rights online, to include issues related to sexual health and LGBTI rights, as well as questions of surveillance and online policing of Internet dissidents and nongovernmental organizations. The passage of a more balanced, rights respecting resolution on privacy in the digital age resulted in a healing of the divisions between advocates for the two different HRC resolutions seeking an open Internet. Today, most members of the Internet freedom and privacy in the digital age core groups work together to advocate for an open, rights respecting Internet in the HRC and in other technical agencies where the pressure for regulation of the Internet remains oppressive.

CHAPTER 8

Sudan

Giving Respect and Salvaging Compromise from the Worst Alternatives to a Negotiated Agreement

Sudan's human rights violations under the regime of Omar al-Bashir presented one of the most serious human rights situations in the world. Especially in the run-up to al-Bashir's indictment by the International Criminal Court in 2009 on charges of war crimes and crimes against humanity,[1] the international community struggled to adequately address this barbarity. Sudan had been criticized by the UN Human Rights Council (HRC) under its Item 4 for the most serious situations of human rights concern from 2006–2009. The ongoing systematic attack of the al-Bashir regime against rebels in South Kordofan and Blue Nile, and the government-supported attack against the people of Darfur, produced a human rights situation that governments outside Africa and on the continent could no longer ignore. The African Union also used strong language condemning Sudan's human rights abuses against its own people. Before 2009, a series of HRC resolutions condemned Sudan and appointed Dr. Sima Samar, a medical doctor from Afghanistan, as the special rapporteur to highlight human rights problems in Sudan. Then in 2009, Sudan's resolution was moved from Item 4 to Item 10, which dealt with technical assistance to countries for their human rights efforts. Dr. Samar was replaced by a series of independent experts who had shorter terms of focus on Sudan and less-detailed knowledge, resulting in progressively less and less detailed criticism of the country's human rights situation. International NGOs and some European member states of the

---

1. The Prosecutor v. Omar Hassan Ahmad Al-Bashir, 2019, ICC 02/02–01/09, available on the website of the International Criminal Court at https://www.icc-cpi.int/darfur/albashir

UN began to accuse the HRC of treating Sudan too softly, but at the same time none of them were able to negotiate a more satisfactory description of the Sudanese regime's abuses into UN language.

In the HRC, the African group traditionally defended its own members and would usually line up its thirteen (out of forty-seven) votes in the HRC unanimously to support any African state being criticized. African diplomats felt pressure to maintain solidarity with Sudan to protect it from excessive international pressure on its human rights record, even though many states, particularly in western and southern Africa, expressed serious concern about the Sudanese regime's mistreatment of its own people. The pressure for united resistance to criticism of an African state by the international community was not just based on ideological approaches or theoretical solidarity. It was also a very practical concern for African delegations who knew their human rights situations could also change due to political changes on the continent and, indeed, in their own domestic politics. A feeling of "there but for the grace of god go I" motivated African states to resist efforts by those outside the African continent, largely Europeans and North Americans, to impose resolutions of the international community onto African human rights situations. Rather the African group preferred to police its own situations and approaches to human rights problems on the continent, ideally through African institutions. Close cooperation among African diplomats also led them to see their counterparts as human beings. This also held true for diplomats from Sudan, many of whom were longtime professional diplomats and lawyers whose technical work earned the respect of colleagues, even if those colleagues disagreed with the human rights abuses of the al-Bashir regime that the Sudanese professionals were defending.

This was the situation when I arrived in Geneva at the end of 2013. While Sudan had relied on the pressure of the African group to get out from under the scrutiny of Item 4, it could not escape a human rights situation that was horrific and increasingly attracting negative public attention. Systematic human rights violations were continuing in Darfur. Media publicized the flogging of a Muslim woman who converted to Christianity and was charged with apostasy. As if in scenes from *The Hunger Games* films, planes of the Sudanese air force were caught on film bombing civilian hospitals in the Nuba mountains. And just as the HRC session in September 2013 was ending with the adoption of an Item 10 resolution on Sudan's human rights situation, the government opened fire on peaceful protesters at Khartoum University and elsewhere in the capital city, many protesting vast increases in prices of fuel and other commodities. No objective observer could see this as an improving situation. Incredibly, in response to this situation, Sudan overreached. The approach backfired.

Damaging Package Deals by Taking Too Hard of a Line

For Sudan, its most important redline at the UN HRC had been to avoid criticism under the "condemnatory" Item 4 of the HRC's agenda. Having its human rights addressed under Item 4 left Sudanese officials with the feeling of being "unfairly" labeled as among the world's worst violators of human rights and with no reason to cooperate with the Council. But since 2009, Sudan and the United States had agreed to treat Sudan's situation under Item 10, so long as Sudan agreed that the HRC resolution would include accurate factual language critical of its human rights record.[2] In this environment, it was surprising that in 2014 Sudan pushed so hard to escape the Council's consideration altogether, rather than to accept the deal it had achieved to have its situation addressed as one needing technical assistance. Perhaps because of its negotiators' relative inexperience with multilateral negotiations or perhaps because of a sense or relatively unequal bargaining power, Sudan repeatedly made the mistake of taking too hard of a line with the United States.

In 2014, just as the human rights situation was reaching a nadir and as the process of negotiating its resolution for the September HRC session was beginning, Sudan went on the offensive. It circulated a diplomatic note in Washington, New York, Geneva, and many African capitals proclaiming the advances it had made in human rights and "national dialogue" and insisting that the time had come for Sudan to "graduate" and be removed from the UN Human Rights Council's agenda altogether. In discussion with Sudanese negotiators later, they said that this was merely an opening gambit on their part. But their counterpart in these negotiations was an American lawyer used to the zero-sum environment of financial settlement in legal cases. Instead of letting Sudan shift the playing field with its talk of having no resolution, the U.S. ambassador announced—without consultation with African delegations about his chance of success—that the United States would be introducing the Sudan resolution that year under Item 4. In so doing, he explained that Sudan's record since the previous Council session,

---

2. Focusing on the factual basis for criticism was what Fisher and Ury would term an "objective criteria" for resolving differences during the negotiation. Fisher and Ury, *Getting to Yes*, chapter 5.

including the government's decision to fire on peaceful demonstrators just as the 2013 Item 10 resolution was being finalized, made it impossible to consider that the situation had improved or remained the same. To reflect the reality of the worsening situation, the resolution would be introduced under Item 4, and if Sudan or the Africans did not like it, they were welcome to introduce their own resolution, he said.

Initially, Sudan did just that, posturing as if it would introduce its own separate resolution under Item 10 on technical assistance. But as soon as it did so, Sudan's overreaching gambit of trying to claim that it had "graduated" and needed no resolution was lost. For the United States, it was facing the best of all possible worlds. Either it would end up negotiating an Item 10 resolution with Sudan, as it had in the previous years, or it might prevail on its proposal to shift the situation back to Item 4. Because some delegations at the HRC valued consensus over consistency in their voting pattern, it was possible that on a close vote, both the Item 10 resolution sponsored by Sudan and the Item 4 resolution sponsored by the United States would succeed. This was true, even though the U.S. gambit of tabling an Item 4 resolution was uncertain. It had no sure vote count of success under Item 4 and many swing voters in Asia and Latin America expressed concern about the move back to Item 4 only a few years after the Council had unanimously agreed to shift from Item 4 to Item 10. But, for the settlement-minded U.S. ambassador, the only way to deal with Sudan's claim that there would be no resolution was to up the ante and press back that the resolution's condemnatory nature would be increased to Item 4, despite past compromises under Item 10.

Sudan's BATNA and How to Adjust It

The above example illustrates classic negotiation theory and posturing while trying to change the other side's BATNA. Sudan initially tried to restructure the playing field of alternatives through its public statements. It viewed, or at least tried to frame, the range of possible options as:

1) No resolution on its human rights
2) Ending a mandate for an independent expert looking at its human rights
3) Continuing with the status quo Item 10 mandate

In this case, Sudan tried to shift the spectrum of options so that its bottom-line acceptable outcome (continuation of the status quo) became the worst of three choices on a spectrum in which all other choices would represent for Sudan strong successes. Sudan also tried to portray a series of options in which the middle one—which psychology indicates is the one most often chosen[3]—was the goal it sought to achieve in the negotiations.

The Americans quickly saw they needed to change Sudan's view of the possible options, as well as changing the spectrum of alternatives. As a result, by announcing the United States' intention to raise the situation of Sudan under Item 4, the United States introduced a new spectrum of possible alternatives, changing the BATNA for both parties (and introducing for Sudan a new WATNA—Worst Alternative to a Negotiated Agreement). The new options were:

1) A resolution condemning Sudan under Item 4 with a mandate holder
2) A strengthened mandate holder under Item 10
3) Continuation of the current mandate under Item 10

Again this spectrum established a range of options where all three choices presented "wins" for the U.S. delegation, with the middle choice representing the U.S. view of the most desirable likely option. Note that in both Sudan's spectrum of choices and the U.S. spectrum, there was one option in common—continuing with the status quo item 10 for the mandate. Had Sudan seized on that choice early, rather than pushing for more, it might have walked away with that result and be seen by all parties as a win-win outcome.

Sudanese Overreaching and Return to Interest-Based Negotiation in Search of Win-Win Options

In fact, however, the Americans' gambit worked and seemed to force a reevaluation by Sudan. After the dueling threat of no resolution or an Item 4 resolution was announced and bandied about publicly, I worked behind the scenes with Sudanese experts to come up with a resolution under Item 10 that accurately reflected the factual situation on the ground and that both Khartoum and Washington could live with. The Sudanese negotiators and I reached this point by following a pattern of exchange—taking note of some positive element of Sudan's claimed human rights improvement in exchange

---

3. Nicholas Christenfeld. 1995. "Choices from Identical Options." *SAGE Journals*. http://journals.sagepub.com/doi/abs/10.1111/j.1467-9280.1995.tb00304.x; "People Prefer the Middle Option." April 30, 2012. *British Psychological Society's Research Digest*.

for every "negative" mention of a fact that constituted the Sudanese government's violation of human rights. Then a visiting Sudanese minister arrived in Geneva in order to claim credit for having negotiated the deal, which was reaching its final contours and keeping Sudan under the Item 10 on "technical assistance." The minister raised new objections to language that experts had already agreed upon. The minister used the negotiating ploy that "until everything is agreed, nothing is agreed." This undermined both Sudan's bottom line of staying off Item 4 and ignored the fact that the United States had already agreed to take note of positive developments in Sudan. The first time he tried this tactic, I walked out of the room, noting that there was no point in all our previous negotiations if he was going to come in and revisit every issue, so he did not need the benefit of my experience on what had happened up to his arrival. When he persisted, the result was reversion to a previous draft text that gave Sudan less positive credit for its human rights improvements. At the end of the day, Sudan was stuck with a harsher Item 10 resolution than it could have negotiated at the start of the session, had it merely settled for continuing the status quo.

Treating Your Adversaries with Respect and as Human Beings

As we discussed above, respect for one's negotiating adversary is a tool that a negotiator can give without cost to one's national position and whose value is often underestimated. In negotiations with Sudan, the relationship of the two countries, in which the United States had for years justifiably imposed sanctions on the Khartoum regime, made respect a particularly powerful tool.

In the negotiations over Sudan's HRC resolution in 2014–2016, Sudan elected to negotiate its human rights resolution directly with the United States, rather than through the African group. While the African group ultimately sponsored the text that was agreed bilaterally, the dynamic made it clear that the Sudanese delegation was seeking the respect and equality that could be inferred from negotiating directly with the United States.

This meant that treating Sudanese diplomats with respect was a key bargaining tool that I could offer and one that significantly improved our negotiating dynamics. At the beginning of our negotiating interactions, the Sudanese often would start negotiation sessions on a weekend afternoon and drag them on through the evening, knowing that the Americans would grow impatient and want to be home on the weekends. In response to these approaches, I was polite but firm, refusing to engage in the weekend negotiating sessions. But instead of doing so rudely, I issued a corresponding invitation for the following workday, often to pick up negotiations over lunch or coffee. The process of invitations gradually grew with an exchange of Sudanese dates or chocolate being a key measure of how the atmospherics would carry forward in a given negotiating session.

The Sudanese also believed, mistakenly, that working well with me as a person meant a change in the U.S. position toward their country. This was illustrated once through a discussion about Sudan's press strategy. Sudan believed that its controlled press indicated a government view and it issued a press item in 2014 that criticized American diplomats in New York for being too tough on Khartoum. Why are you not more like the U.S. delegation in Geneva, the article asked? I explained to my Sudanese counterparts that, while I appreciated the sentiment that they were trying to convey, nothing could have been worse for Geneva diplomats than an impression that the Sudanese government liked them or was softer on them than American diplomats based in New York. They also learned a lesson in the power of the media shortly thereafter. In an early meeting on Sudan in 2015, I showed other potential Western partners a video of a Sudanese air force plane strafing a civilian hospital run by Doctors without Borders in the Nuba Mountains, killing dozens. The media impression was a powerful one and Sudan had no response to the footage, claiming only that the plane at issue was not the government's, even though no rebel or private force had a plane capable of producing that type or airstrike or damage of that magnitude. This did not change our friendly personal interactions, but it drove home the point that, no matter any positive personal interactions, all of us were advocates for the position of our governments. The United States could not accept the kind of wanton killing and disregard for international human rights and humanitarian law depicted in the video.

Finding a Solution through Compromise on Words

Nonetheless, positive interactions, goodwill, and mutual respect that I established with Sudan's delegation from the 2014 negotiations carried over into the substantive interactions on the 2015 resolution. Sudanese counterparts had some redlines that they were instructed to object to as offensive to the government and its sovereignty: "monitoring" of their human rights situation, blaming violations only on the government rather than the rebels whom they were fighting in areas like South Kordofan and Blue Nile, claims of "excessive force" or disproportionate response. And in a reminder that all governments have their own interagency power dynamics, they seemed truly scared of specific mentions that would criticize Sudan's powerful National Intelligence and Security Services (NISS).

To disarm the conversation and lower tensions about these topics that were beyond the authority and redlines of my foreign ministry counterparts, I used a tactic that works best when negotiating about words. I emphasized that the United States was most concerned that the resolution accurately reflected the facts of the human rights situation in Sudan, and that we had some flexibility about the words used to reflect them. So, for example, we came to an understanding early on that the United States would insist on a certain number of references to human rights facts that were extremely challenging for Sudan and offensive to its ideas of sovereignty. But rather than repeatedly insisting on words that offended them (especially during a negotiation in the Sudanese embassy no doubt bugged by the aforementioned officials of the NISS), we agreed to be flexible on the language. In effect, we knew that we were talking about violations by Sudan and its security officials, but we agreed to call them something else. Originally using the Shakespearean phrase "a rose by any other name will smell as sweet," I would say that the United States would insist on a "flower" in this or that paragraph, which my counterpart knew was code for a mention of government or security agency responsibility for a human rights violation. I delighted when she picked up the tool and turned it to her advantage, insisting that we no longer talk about adding "flowers" to the text, but instead that we add mentions of a "stinky fish" to represent the language or names Sudan found objectionable. We followed this approach and ultimately found compromise on a significant mention of "stinky fish"—such as the bombing of civilians, the shooting of unarmed protesters, national security laws that violated international norms, and the monitoring that the international community so strongly insisted upon and that Sudan so fervently rejected.[4]

This negotiation illustrates the importance of seeking win-win compromise on language and how to "avoid the nasty words, but get the content addressed" as outlined in chapter 3's list of negotiating tactics. Agreement ultimately became possible by working around offensive words and concepts while remaining true to the underlying substance. As a result, the Human

---

4. The ensuing resolution, HRC Resolution 30/22, referred specifically to each of these types of human rights violations in paras. 10–16 and 22–23, and included a mandate for the independent expert to "assess, verify, and report" on the human rights situation in Sudan. See UN Human Rights Council. 2015. "Technical Assistance and Capacity-Building to Improve Human Rights in the Sudan." HRC Resolution 30/22 (adopted October 2, 2015). https://documents-dds-ny.un.org/doc/UNDOC/GEN/G15/233/12/PDF/G1523312.pdf?OpenElement

Rights Council ultimately passed a 2014 resolution that clearly stated the international community's condemnation of aerial bombardment of civilians, of the shooting of protesters, and of the ongoing abuses in Darfur and the "Two Areas" of Blue Nile and South Kordofan States. The resolution also strengthened the mandate of an independent expert to monitor and report on these situations.

Ratifying the Bilateral Agreement across the Broader Membership

Finally, this case study illustrates the potential challenge in getting capitals and a broad, membership-based group like the UN to ratify an agreement reached bilaterally. First, the ratification by capitals differed for Sudan and for the United States. On the U.S. side, we remained in close touch with our capital throughout the negotiations. Redlines usually were well established ahead of time and American negotiators knew where they had flexibility and where they did not. Occasionally an ambassador or a negotiator would seek to renegotiate a redline or explain why it was not going to work. But close consultation throughout the negotiation process allowed the United States to have a common position and to avoid the problem of moving the goalposts. In the U.S. Department of State, officials handling Africa were especially interested in working with the HRC to accomplish U.S. policy goals. As a result, special envoys like Ambassador Donald Booth (Sudan and South Sudan) and Tom Perriello (for the Great Lakes region) frequently visited Geneva to both inform and lobby member states about U.S. positions. It was still possible that some domestic pressure from politicians or NGOs would result in an effort to change the U.S. bottom line. But at least in the U.S. government, it was well understood that such a late change would be nearly impossible to pull off.

On Sudan's side, the ratification process was used as a chance to get "one more bite at the apple." In each year that I worked with Sudanese officials to negotiate a resolution, Sudanese officials would come to Geneva from Khartoum late in the negotiation process and seek to change a few key terms that had already been agreed. In the case illustrated above, a minister arrived and engaged in brinksmanship which nearly scuttled a deal. The minister later came back. But after observing this insistence on renegotiation by an official arriving from the capital late in the process over three successive years, I realized that this was not only a tactic but was a required performance for the Sudanese. The minister could not sell the final deal to his own government for ratification until he had personally tried to get a better deal, even if that meant undoing work that had already been agreed upon.

In addition to ratifying a deal with capitals, each side had to ratify its position with other HRC member states. For Sudan, this meant working with the African group, which typically took the position that it would support the "state concerned" on any HRC resolution. Historically in the UN, the African group has taken bloc positions on country-specific resolutions, usually in defense of an African member state. This meant that all thirteen of the group's votes would follow the position of the bloc. But when no common position could be reached, as happened on some egregious cases of human rights abuse, such as in Sudan and Eritrea, there would be no common African group position. This meant each African voting member of the HRC could vote according to its own national position or conscience. What was unique about Sudan's decision to negotiate bilaterally with the United States is that Sudan gave up its support network in the African group in order to have more control over the tradeoffs made in the resolution in its name. Sudan also recognized that its interests in cooperation with the United States diverged from the African group's interests somewhat, but that it would not lose the group's support because of the group's tendency in multilateral human rights negotiations to defer to the country concerned. Just as with the visiting Sudanese minister, the African group sometimes used its "ratification" as a chance to try to get another bite at the apple and change terms of the already reached bilateral agreement. This was especially true for Sudan's powerful neighbor Egypt. But the United States rarely accepted last-minute changes requested by the African group. When we did accept a late change, it was accompanied by a countervailing tit-for-tat change to improve the text in a direction that Washington requested.

U.S. ratification with its own European partners was sometimes more difficult. Diplomats in Brussels, London, and Oslo double-checked and second-guessed every edit and compromise on the Sudan text to ensure that too much was not being given over to those they saw as the "Butchers of Khartoum." There was no guarantee that European colleagues would support the outcome reached in bilateral negotiations. As a result, the United States had to maintain parallel consultations, especially with UK, Norwegian, and EU negotiators, throughout the period of bilateral negotiations with Sudan. In general, European negotiators would reach the same conclusion as their American counterparts about what was advisable as content of the resolution, or at least on what was attainable. At the end of the day, colleagues realized that they could not get the votes for a more stringent criticism of Sudan, but this did not stop some delegations from voicing on the floor of the HRC their displeasure about certain contents in the bilaterally negotiated agreements about Sudan, or for that matter other resolutions.[5]

Conclusion

From a multiparty negotiations perspective, negotiations with Sudan illustrate the importance of having a system for bringing all of the various interests together at the end of a negotiation so it can be ratified. Vesting the power of negotiations in a single party on either side of an international negotiation can work if the key participants are included, but the possibility that parties in broader penumbras of the interest group will try to spoil the deal is always present in multiparty negotiations, especially in international fora. The risks of error are higher if there is a disparity of power and experience between the parties, and Sudan's attempt at overreaching in 2014 is one example of the way in which a negotiation can get waylaid on its path to success. Nonetheless, negotiations with Sudan at the UN Human Rights Council illustrate that good diplomats can usually find compromise if they work in an environment of respect and good faith, even when the domestic political environments and the value-based perspectives on a topic like human rights are as different as they were between Sudan and the United States. Interestingly, some of the Sudanese diplomats involved in these discussions joined the side of protesters who ultimately overthrew Omar al-Bashir's dictatorship in April 2019, and they are now working to help Sudan in its challenging transition to becoming a country that better respects human rights and the rule of law.

---

5. See, e.g., UN Human Rights Council Webcast Archives. 2015. Video. Geneva: October 2, 2015, under Item 10, Sudan, including statements by the European Union and the United Kingdom.

CHAPTER 9

Waking the Sleeping Dragon

Overplaying the Hand on Human Rights
Negotiations with China

American negotiators also fared poorly in negotiations with China that pre-ceded a resolution on China's human rights at the March 2004 session of the UN Commission on Human Rights in Geneva. China's human rights situation was a contentious topic in Sino-American relations and in the international community dating back to the June 4, 1989, killing of student protestors at and around Tiananmen Square. Hundreds, if not thousands, of peaceful protesters were killed as the Chinese government sent military forces to suppress the protests and arrest some ten thousand of its own citi-zens.[1] For the decade after Tiananmen, China's human rights policy became an issue of debate in the international community and in several Western countries, including the United States. Tiananmen also symbolized the Chi-nese Communist Party's harsh opposition to political dissent, enforced by the intelligence, security, and judicial arms of the government. Criticism of China's opposition to dissent and the way this opposition was enforced was a central element of international, and some domestic, criticism of China's human rights policies. American critics of China's human rights policies focused on annual congressional debates about whether the United States should grant China Most Favored Nation trading status. Internationally, the United States and others voiced concerns about China's human rights

---

1. John Kamm. June 3, 2009. "Remarks to the Commonwealth Club of San Fran-cisco, 'How Tiananmen Changed China.'" The Dui Hua Foundation. http://duihua.org/wp/?page_id=2520

through resolutions in the UN Commission on Human Rights (CHR) in Geneva. These resolutions were raised in several years, from 1999 until the Commission was replaced in 2006 by the UN Human Rights Council.

In the years just before and while I was in China, the United States began trying a different approach.[2] U.S. diplomats worked with Chinese officials to see if China would make actual, concrete improvements in its human rights policies and implementation, perhaps in lieu of the U.S. raising a resolution critical of China's human rights at the UN in Geneva. This effort at cooperation, rather than confrontation, as the Chinese called it served both parties' interests. For China, it avoided the public humiliation of a sanctioning resolution in the United Nations. "Saving face" is so important to China that the government, prodded by those who valued the U.S.-China relationship and by those who sought a more balanced legal and security environment in China, was prepared to make concrete concessions rather than face public censure in the United Nations. China even went so far as to permit a $12 million rule of law assistance program to operate in the country, which I helped administer.[3] Funds went to U.S. academic and nongovernmental institutions in the United States who then provided training on topics such as reform of criminal law and administrative detention, the adversary system in criminal procedure, women's rights, and environmental litigation. In the United States, this cooperative approach allowed a focus on concrete results

---

2. See, e.g., Lorne Craner. January 29, 2004. "Remarks by U.S. Assistant Secretary for Democracy and Human Rights Lorne Craner, 'A Comprehensive Human Rights Strategy for China,' Delivered at the Carnegie Endowment for International Peace." https://2001-2009. state.gov/g/drl/rls/rm/28693.htm

3. Craner, "A Comprehensive Human Rights Strategy for China." ("Through a congressional appropriation, the State Department is catalyzing long-term efforts to lay the foundation for the rule of law, greater public participation and a robust civil society. We are supporting programs to foster the development of the legal and democratic institutions that will hopefully serve as a means to check human rights abuses in China. The programs we support address some of our most serious human rights concerns, including the right to due process of law, the harassment and detention of criminal defense lawyers, and lack of judicial independence. We are supporting efforts to help non-governmental organizations become effective advocates for their communities and the disenfranchised, such as workers suffering under sweatshop-like conditions and those living with HIV/AIDS. The State Department is also backing programs to give citizens a greater voice in governance by improving public participation through elections and public hearings. The judicial and legal reform projects we support aim to establish the rule of law in China. I am proud to say that in the last three years, the amount of funding available for rule of law programs in China has grown more than fivefold, from $2 million to over $12 million. In fact, the U.S. government funds more projects to promote democracy, human rights and the rule of law in China than any other foreign government or international aid agency in the world.")

in the improvement of human rights rather than a mere "naming and sham-ing" through reports, UN resolutions, and public statements. For human rights victims in China, as well as for Chinese officials brave enough to advocate reforms, it allowed an environment where China could admit its need for external help to improve aspects of its domestic criminal, legal, and security systems. The program of legal assistance was a way to test whether, as one U.S. participant put it, China's system had grown strong enough to tolerate dissent.

Sometimes this cooperative approach worked. But in other years the negotiations broke down and the United States pressed forward with rais-ing the resolution on the situation of human rights in China in the United Nations Commission on Human Rights. This chapter tells one story of United States' overreaching in these human rights negotiations in 2004, resulting in the loss of a compromise, leaving one human rights champion languishing in prison, and damaging prospects for future cooperation on human rights and the rule of law.

By 2004, a pattern of positive momentum had been established in nego-tiations to avoid the resolution critical of China at the UN Commission on Human Rights. In 2002 and 2003, for example, China released political prisoners, abolished forms of detention such as reeducation through labor, and agreed to permit scrutiny of its domestic conditions by international monitors like the United Nations Special Rapporteur on Torture. Several Tibetan political prisoners were released as part of these negotiations, as were others, like China Democracy Party cofounder Xu Wenli.[4] As a result, negotiators for both sides approached the 2004 negotiations optimistic that a deal could be found. As had happened in previous years, China began slowly, offering in January and February to release political prisoners ahead of the March UN CHR session. Preliminary negotiations led to incremen-tal progress and the tentative outlines of an agreement. As a first gesture of goodwill, China Democracy Party cofounder Wang Youcai was released on medical parole to the United States on March 4, 2004.

In the course of negotiations, the United States repeatedly requested that a second political prisoner be released, Uighur businesswoman Rebiya Kadeer, who had been detained while preparing to meet a visiting U.S. con-gressional delegation. China was reluctant. Ms. Kadeer had been a Chinese official who ran afoul of the powerful provincial head of the Xinjiang Uighur Autonomous Region, Wang Lequan. For the central government to release

---

4. Mickey Spiegel. December 6, 2003. "China's Game with Political Prisoners, Op/Ed." *International Herald Tribune.*

Ms. Kadeer, it felt it would lose domestic political capital with the powerful governor and would take a risk that her release might lead to further activism in Xinjiang by the restive Uighur minority. Nonetheless, efforts were made to enable Kadeer's release and Beijing awaited final word from Washington to seal the deal.

With time running short before the conclusion of the UN Commission on Human Rights, a young Deputy Assistant Secretary of State for East Asia and Pacific Affairs was sent to China to work with U.S. ambassador Clark "Sandy" Randt to finalize a deal. The Deputy Assistant Secretary was not experienced in these negotiations. He wanted to demonstrate to his constituents in human rights groups and among the defense establishment in Washington that he could hold a tough line with the Chinese. He recommended, and his mentor Deputy Secretary of State Richard Armitage ultimately accepted, that China had not done enough on human rights that year and the deal should be scrapped.[5] Chinese officials were told this in late March 2004. Viewing this as the United States "shifting the goalposts," they were angry. One of the forms of retaliation Beijing instituted was to ban a young human rights officer from the U.S. embassy from coming to the Chinese foreign ministry to discuss human rights for the period of a year. That banned officer was me.

Analysis: Why Did Negotiators Pass up a Win-Win Agreement? What Can Be Learned from This?

To some extent, U.S. negotiators in the China human rights case erred in rejecting what previously had been a win-win process of negotiation in which concrete improvements in China's human rights and releases of political prisoners were made by China in exchange for a U.S. agreement not to publicly embarrass China through a resolution critical of the country in the United Nations. By passing up a deal that would have released another prisoner in exchange for foregoing a symbolic resolution, U.S. negotiators may have missed a chance to get concrete improvements. They may also have played to emotion or domestic pressure. Another more rational reason for rejecting the win-win deal was a feeling that China had not lived up to promises made in the previous year. Assistant Secretary of State for Human

---

5. See, e.g., Randall Schriver. 2009. "Testimony Before House Foreign Affairs Committee, Subcommittee on Oversight, June 16, 2009." http://project2049.net/documents/uigher_testimony_of_randall_schriver.pdf

Rights Lorne Craner indicated publicly a few months before the deal broke down that the United States was concerned about China's "backsliding" on commitments made the previous year.[6]

But was anything achieved by going ahead with the China resolution on human rights in the UN instead of striking an agreement? Arguably not. At the United Nations, the United States did advance a resolution on China's human rights. As in past years, the resolution failed in spectacular fashion. In the end, China blocked the resolution raised by the United States from even being considered, using a procedural maneuver called a no-action motion so that the March 2004 session of the UN Commission on Human Rights did not even vote on the resolution.[7] Advocates of the decision to press ahead with the UN resolution argued that just filing the resolution, even if it was not considered, "kept up the pressure" on China and brought some solace to Chinese human rights activists that the international community stood with them in their struggle to improve human rights. The release of a few political prisoners was insignificant, they argued, because tens of other dissidents would be detained, even if a few were released as the "revolving door" of China's prison system continued to spin. But the United States did not really seem to value this symbolic criticism.

And by ignoring a potential deal, real harm came to individuals as a result. For one, Kadeer had to spend another year in jail until her release on March 17, 2005.[8] Chinese officials released Kadeer to my custody and

---

6. Craner, "A Comprehensive Human Rights Strategy for China." ("During the December 2002 Human Rights Dialogue, we were pleased when China made several commitments, and we viewed it as incremental but important progress. Since then, I have traveled to China twice to discuss the status of these commitments and our human rights concerns. For example, China agreed to host visits by the UN Special Rapporteurs on Torture and Religious Freedom, as well as the UN Working Group on Arbitrary Detention. We believe that these kinds of interactions would help to integrate China into the international human rights regime, enabling medium-term improvements in due process, extra-judicial sentencing, religious freedom, and the practice of torture. It was on this basis that we decided to forego offering a resolution on China at last year's UN Commission on Human Rights in Geneva. . . . As a result of our concern about backsliding across a range of key human rights issues, the United States is seriously considering sponsoring a resolution on the human rights situation in China at the commission this spring, a decision which will be made at the highest levels of our Government. If China expects to be a fully-accepted member of the international community, China must live up to international human rights norms, and they can begin by fulfilling the pledges they made more than a year ago.")

7. "Commission on Human Rights Adopts Resolutions." UN Press Release HR/CN/931 (April 23, 1999); Elizabeth Olson. April 24, 1999. "China Escapes Censure in Vote by UN Human Rights Agency." *New York Times*.

8. "Rebiya Kadeer's Release Part of China's Hostage Diplomacy." March 18, 2005. Radio

I flew her to the United States, to a future of both freedom and exile. On the flight, we discussed the difficult choices that would face her: whether to speak out about her situation or whether to remain silent in the hopes that China would improve treatment of Uighurs and release other political prisoners in the future.

In addition, what China saw as the United States "shifting the goalposts" caused it to rethink its strategy of compromise. Beijing decreased its willingness to (1) release political prisoners and (2) take U.S. threats of action on Chinese human rights in multilateral venues seriously. Kadeer's ultimate release in March 2005 was a turning point in China's view of the costs and benefits of releasing political prisoners. Prior to Kadeer's release, China saw cooperation on global issues such as counterterrorism and even human rights as strengthening its place as a responsible stakeholder in the UN system. Those Chinese dissidents who were released as a result of international compromise and flown to exile in the United States were essentially quiet. After an initial media splash, the dozens of Tibetans and handful of Han Chinese democracy activists who were released from prison into exile in the United States in the five years after the September 11, 2001, attacks essentially faded from public and media attention. Not so with Kadeer, who founded

---

Free Asia. Some reports highlighted that Kadeer's release took place days ahead of Secretary of State Condoleezza Rice's visit to China, but it was also days ahead of the opening of the 2005 session of the UN Commission. See Elise Labott. 2005. "U.S. Drops China Rights Censure— Mar 17, 2005." CNN.com. http://edition.cnn.com/2005/WORLD/asiapcf/03/17/china. humanrights. Citing "important and significant steps" by China to improve its human rights record, the U.S. Department of State has said it will not introduce a resolution condemning Beijing this year at the UN Human Rights Commission. Deputy department spokesman Adam Ereli said on Thursday that while "persistent systemic problems" remain, the Chinese government has taken action to increase religious freedoms and allow more leniency for political prisoners. Those steps include allowing political prisoners the same rights to sentence reductions and parole as other prisoners, Ereli said. He also pointed to Beijing's agreement to visits by the UN Special Rapporteurs on Torture and Religious Intolerance and the UN High Commissioner for Human Rights. The Chinese government has also agreed to host the U.S. Committee on Religious Freedom. China has also begun to allow family churches to operate in their homes without registering with the government, Ereli said. "Taken together, these are important steps that get at some of the structural issues concerning human rights in China as well as noteworthy steps in the reduction of the number of prisoners," he said. He cited the release of Rebiya Kadeer, a Uighur businesswoman who was detained in August 1999 and sentenced to eight years in prison on espionage charges when she sent newspaper clips to her husband in the United States. The State Department has been pushing China for Kadeer's release. She was released Thursday on medical parole. A senior State Department official added that out of fifty-eight high-profile cases of political prisoners that the United States was following, twenty have been released early, thirty-three have received reduced sentences and five are being considered for early release or reduced sentences this year.

a movement based on her experience in Xinjiang that joined with disparate Uighur actors to be known as the Uighur American Association. Associates of Kadeer's within these groups called for improved treatment of Uighurs in China, while others made more extreme or direct calls for independence of "East Turkestan," as they called the Xinjiang region. Kadeer's vocal advocacy for Uighur rights exacerbated China's fear that a released prisoner would be used to strike at China's core interests and even to foment terrorism in Xinjiang. To China, it didn't really matter if Kadeer advocated for using peaceful means or for violence in the pursuit of independence. Leaders of China's Communist Party and security systems saw Kadeer's platform in the United States as promoting the "three evils" of terrorism, "splittism," and religious extremism, all of which it saw emanating from Xinjiang.[9] This made China much more cautious about future prisoner releases because Kadeer for the first time made the cost of such a release much higher.

Second, China began to see U.S. threats of UN action as a paper tiger. It saw what happened when a resolution was raised: the resolution never passed and sometimes was not even heard on its merits because of China's raising of a no-action motion. This failure of UN CHR action helped China realize that the dangers of a UN resolution about its human rights situation were limited. Of course, China would prefer not to have the negative publicity and reminders of human rights problems dating back to Tiananmen paraded in front of the world, regardless of the resolution's ultimate success or failure. But a series of Chinese successes in defeating the resolution culminating in 2004 left it less concerned about the damage to its reputation that might have resulted.

The 2004 negotiations marked the last time that the United States effectively raised the threat and tabled a UN resolution on the situation of China's human rights. In 2005, as noted, the United States struck a deal allowing for Kadeer' s release, along with several commitments for "systemic" improvements in human rights. These improvements included

---

9. One of the demands raised by the United States in negotiations was to put an end to "strike hard" campaigns in China, resulting in large-scale arrests, including of Uighurs. These strike hard campaigns were a more lenient precursor to the mass incarceration of Uighurs in reeducation and labor camps that began in 2017. Ironically, one of the main systemic reforms that U.S. negotiators saw advanced in 2003 was a decision to abolish custody and repatriation, one form of reeducation through labor. See "Strike Hard Campaigns in Xinjiang," December 28, 2013, *China Daily*, available at http://www.chinadaily.com.cn/china/2013-12/28/content_17202294.htm. See also Sheena Chestnut Greitens, Myunghee Lee, and Emir Yazici. Winter 2019/2020. "Counterterrorism and Preventive Repression: China's Changing Strategy in Xinjiang." *International Security* 44 (3). https://www.mitpressjournals.org/doi/pdf/10.1162/isec_a_00368

Beijing permitting monitoring visits by the UN Special Rapporteur against Torture and the U.S. Commission on International Religious Freedom, as well as a public statement about China not discriminating against Christian "house" churches. And in 2006, the United States did not even demand concessions of China in exchange when it decided not to raise an anti-China motion at the commission's successor, the new UN Human Rights Council. The U.S. administration decided that the new UN Human Rights Council did not yet have the credibility required for the United States to actively engage and use the forum for criticism of others on the world stage. The 2006 decision particularly puzzled and delighted Chinese officials, who had previously offered huge concessions on human rights to avoid a UN resolution, and who now saw the United States refusing to table the resolution because U.S. officials believed that the UN's preeminent body for addressing human rights did not have sufficient credibility. The 2006 end of this cycle of negotiations was in many ways a final lost opportunity to extract concessions from China on human rights, and essentially ended a process that had been a win-win negotiation. To this day, the process has not fully resumed.

This stalemate situation over China's human rights continued for years. In fact, not until I joined the U.S. delegation at the UN Human Rights Council did joint action critical of China's human rights again take place in Geneva. In 2016, a dozen countries issued a joint statement critical of Chinese human rights abuses, including extraterritorial actions such as kidnapping of booksellers from Hong Kong and forcing them to face charges in the mainland.[10] At the same HRC session, Canada and other UN member states hosted the Dalai Lama to speak at an event on Nobel Peace laureates and human rights, which again seriously angered the Chinese delegation. China was so angered by the prospect of the Dalai Lama appearing at the United Nations that it called UN Secretary General Ban Ki-Moon and threatened financial and political retaliation if the UN allowed the event with the Dalai Lama to be held on the UN grounds. UN officials ultimately relented and the panel discussion with Nobel laureates (including the Dalai Lama, 2011 Yemeni Nobel Laureate Tawakkal Karman, and a representative of Iranian laureate Shirin Ebadi) was moved

---

10. UN Human Rights Council Joint Statement. 2016. "March 10, 2016, Item 2 Joint Statement on Human Rights Situation in China." https://geneva.usmission.gov/2016/03/10/item-2-joint-statement-human-rights-situation-in-china/

to the next-door Graduate Institute of Geneva.[11] Thus, even though China claimed to no longer be concerned about criticism of its human rights record at the United Nations, it stopped using tactics of negotiation or cooperation to find win-win solutions at the HRC.

Ironically, in 2018, the idea of win-win cooperation also took on a new twist at the UN Human Rights Council. China offered a resolution of its own at the March 2018 37th UN Human Rights Council session focused on the value of win-win cooperation in human rights. Perhaps as an attempt to preempt any negative action on Chinese human rights or show that China has "arrived" as a power whose human rights could not be criticized, China proposed and the HRC ultimately passed this resolution, which drew on the widespread but somewhat controversial phrase from Xi Jinping's publications. Opponents argued that the draft resolution was flawed in that it undermined the importance of a state's responsibility to protect citizens from human rights violations. They also claimed that the resolution ignored the situation of human rights victims and emphasized cooperation between and among states rather than the responsibilities of states to cooperate with the UN Human Rights Council's special procedures mechanisms or with independent judicial bodies and human rights arbiters or ombudsman. Opponents also noted the irony that a resolution focused on the principle of win-win cooperation was so divisive as to be impossible to pass by consensus.

Also in 2018, the mass detention of Uighurs was raised in China's appearance before the Committee for the Elimination of Racial Discrimination (CERD) and in China's November review under the HRC's Universal Periodic Review mechanism. But these relatively limited criticisms came in the context of processes to which all UN member states are subject. In July 2019, twenty-two states offered a joint statement at the UN Human Rights Council condemning the surveillance and detention policies in Xinjiang, while thirty-seven states offered praise for China's policies in Xinjiang.[12]

---

11. See "U.S. Mission Geneva, March 11, 2016 Side Event of the UN Human Rights Council." 2016. Facebook. https://www.facebook.com/usmissiongeneva/photos/his-holiness-the-dalai-lama-participates-in-a-side-event-of-the-un-human-rights-/10153728017638876/

12. The twenty-two states criticizing China's policies in Xinjiang were largely from the Western European and Others Group (WEOG) and the European Union. Some thirty-seven states signed a joint statement supportive of Chinese policies. Compare Patrick Goodenough. 2019. "China Thanks 36 Countries, Half of Them Islamic States, for Praising Its Uighur Policies." CNS News, July 15, 2019. https://www.cnsnews.com/news/article/patrick-goodenough/china-thanks-37-countries-including-islamic-states-praising-its. "UN: Unprec-

To date, no negotiations have resumed to find a possible win-win path forward on human rights between the United States and China. And in an environment of increasing hostility over trade, intellectual property, mass detention of Uighurs in Xinjiang, and strategic military confrontation, it appears that the opportunity to resume the win-win cooperation of improving China's rule of law adherence at the same time as it reformed its international human rights reputation has now past.

edented Joint Call for China to End Xinjiang Abuses, 22 Countries Decry Mass Detention, Seek Monitoring." 2019. Human Rights Watch. https://www.hrw.org/news/2019/07/10/un-unprecedented-joint-call-china-end-xinjiang-abuses. This process of dueling pro and anti-China joint statements has since become a regular, annual activity with the number of states endorsing China's statement regularly larger than those signing the anti-China statement.

PART II

Multiparty International Negotiations and Structural Factors

CHAPTER 10

Participants, Observers, and Guarantors

Is Anyone Truly Neutral?

Multiparty international negotiations carry with them their own dynamics not only for the parties most closely involved with the issue but also for other actors who choose to use multiparty international negotiations to enhance their own positions. Typically, those actors for whom the issue is most central remain at the heart of the negotiations and others are brought in or insert themselves as observers, guarantors, mediators, or even to put pressure on one or the other side to make a deal. The role that a party plays in a multiparty negotiation has a significant influence on the type of negotiating tactic and approach that will work best. The latter part of this book will analyze how to use the specific roles that different parties seek to have in a multiparty international negotiation to get more back for your state or client. In so doing, we will also look at the specific characteristics and roles of multiparty negotiations, both inside and outside a formal multilateral (e.g., UN-type) setting.

In this chapter, we define the types of roles that different actors may play during a multiparty international negotiation. Subsequent chapters then expand on specific characteristics of multiparty negotiations to look at their unique aspects and how a negotiator can take advantage of some of those aspects to maximize results for the state or client he or she is serving.

Multiparty negotiations can find a negotiator (or the state that the negotiator represents) in several different roles. We focus on the roles of direct participant, indirect participant, observer, and guarantor. **Direct participants** are those whose interests are so central that the negotiation and an agreement cannot be reached without addressing these concerns. **Indirect participants** may also have interests affected by a negotiation, but their interests are not as central to the negotiation as those of direct participants. The interests of indirect participants could be resolved in a parallel forum and need not be resolved at the same time and in the same forum as the issues of the direct participants. **Observers** are just that, parties outside the negotiation who are observing, rather than trying to achieve a specific goal for themselves in the negotiation. Some observers are also mediators, providing good offices,[1] but not all play that role. In multilateral negotiations, such as in the United Nations, it is more common that a member state, or even a part of the United Nations itself, plays the role of mediator. Fourth, we will look at a particularly important role for some negotiation participants in multiparty talks, the role of the guarantor. **Guarantors** are defined as parties whose participation in the negotiation arises because of the real or perceived influence that the guarantor can bring over one of the direct participants. A guarantor state is one whose power allows it to enforce or help enforce a deal, convincing, cajoling, or otherwise persuading one or more direct participants into taking a certain action.[2] Occasionally, guarantors also use their powers to undo or block a deal, which can convert them into **spoilers**.

The role a state plays in a negotiation can shift over time. This shift in role can result in changes in the environment, in deception about a party's true interests, in variation of its level of commitment to its initial goals, and in changes to the party's prioritization of its initial and subsequent goals. Negotiation participants—including states and even the United States—are often confused about the role they are playing at any given time. The lack of clarity about one's role in a negotiation is often a symptom of a lack of unified policy direction by the state or a reflection of competing interests. It manifests itself most often in dispute over the instructions a state is providing to its negotiators. Especially when considering the negotiation instruc-

---

1. See, e.g., Theresa Whitfield. February 2010. "External Actors in Mediation." Centre for Humanitarian Dialogue Practice Series. Geneva. https://www.hdcentre.org/wp-content/uploads/2016/08/35Externalactorsinmediation-MPS-February-2010.pdf. (Role of states as mediators and importance of getting all external actors to a conflict generally united in support of the mediation).

2. In their study of the use of power-sharing arrangements at the end of civil wars, Hartzell and Hoddie define guarantors as "[t]hird parties . . . called upon to guarantee that groups will be protected, terms will be fulfilled, and promises will be kept." Caroline Hartzell and Matthew Hoddie. April 2003. "Institutionalizing Peace: Power Sharing and Post-Civil War Conflict Management." *American Journal of Political Science* 47 (2): 318–32. Citing Barbara Walter. 1997. "The Critical Barrier to Civil War Settlement." *International Organization* 51 (3) 335, 340. Hartzell and Hoddie also hypothesize that a guarantor can protect security interests of former warring parties, convincing them to rely on democratic institutions which the actor might otherwise find distrustful.

tions and guidance that a capital provides to its negotiators, determining the role a state will and should play in a multiparty negotiation can result in a negotiation within the negotiation.

In modern international conflicts, conceptual boundaries that previously separated negotiation participants from mediators and guarantors are merging and shifting. Today, for example, a country like Saudi Arabia or the United Arab Emirates may offer itself as a mediator over conflict in Libya or Yemen even though it has clear political interests in the success of certain participants and in the outcomes. The number of truly disinterested mediators is shrinking. Even the United Nations, who should be the ideal disinterested mediator, finds itself biased by its institutional goals. In Libya, for example, the UN was so invested in the success of the December 2015 Libyan Political Agreement it brokered that it lost sight that its UN-backed government lacked public support and failed to provide any form of basic services to the Libyan people. So, the government had to be replaced in February 2021.

Thus our current chapter seeks to clarify the roles of parties, based largely on their proximity to the issues under negotiation, so that students and analysts of negotiations can separate the position of biased would-be mediators from their roles as participants, indirect participants, or guarantors in a negotiation. Once you identify the role each party is playing, you can place your client in a position that maximizes his or her leverage.[3] For example, chapter 12 talks about how to use proxies to advance your interests in a multiparty negotiation in the United Nations—something Glendon and Crump might characterize as "cooperative relations between parties on the same side."[4]

The following chart offers illustrations of the different types of actors based on four multiparty negotiations that are key case studies of this book: the

---

3. One of the more thoughtful articles on multiparty negotiation dynamics, "Towards a Paradigm of Multi-Party Negotiation," by Glendon and Crump, identifies five types of relationships in a multiparty negotiation: 1) primary party relations; 2) cooperative relations between parties on the same side; 3) noncooperative relations inside a single party not behaving in a unitary way; 4) third-party relations; and 5) relations that provide support to a single party. These relationships cover some of the functions of direct participants, indirect participants, observers, and guarantors but not all, nor do they consider the importance of establishing roles so one can influence the type of relationships one has with other participants. A. Ian Glendon and Larry Crump. 2003. "Towards a Paradigm of Multiparty Negotiation." *International Negotiation* 8 (2): 197–234. doi:10.1163/157180603322576112. While it is clearly valuable to classify other parties in a negotiation as friend or foe, as Glendon and Crump do, our focus rests with how to use different roles in a negotiation process to maximize leverage for yourself and your client.

4. Glendon and Crump, "Towards a Paradigm of Multiparty Negotiation."

Table 1. Negotiation Roles in Four Multiparty Case Studies

Based on party's proximity of interests and centrality to resolve conflict

Role	Oslo Accords	DPRK 6PT 2003–9	DPRK 2017–20	Libya after Qaddhafi
Direct Participant	Israel, Palestinian Authority	DPRK, USA, China, ROK	DPRK, USA	Libyans (GNA, Haftar/LNA, Other Libyan Stakeholders)
Indirect Participant	Palestinian's Arab supporters, USA	Japan, Russia	China, ROK	Egypt, UAE, Qatar, Turkey
Observer	USA	All 6PT states		UN, P3+Italy, EU, Libya's Neighbors
Host or Mediator	Prior Mediator: Norway	Host: China	Mediator: ROK Hosts: Vietnam, Singapore	UN, France, UAE, Italy (minimal success)
Guarantor	USA for both sides	USA for ROK, China for DPRK	China, ROK	Egypt/UAE for Haftar/LNA; USA/UK for GNA

1997–1999 talks between Israel and the Palestinians over implementation of the Oslo Accords; the Six-Party Talks on the North Korea nuclear issue from 2006–2010; the subsequent Trump-Kim negotiations over North Korea's nuclear program during the 2017–2020 period; and the talks attempting to reach a unified government in Libya from 2015 through 2020. We will briefly consider each of the types of actors across these four case studies, along with some additional examples, to help understand key characteristics of each of the roles that actors can and should play in these types of negotiations.

Israel-Palestinian Negotiations and Implementation of the Oslo Accords

In the Israel-Palestinian negotiations I observed to implement the Oslo Accords, the roles were fairly straightforward. The Oslo negotiations over troop and territory exchanges and political representation had been completed in 1993 and 1995,[5] with Norway playing a key role as mediator and

5. Oslo I, known as the Declaration of Principles, was a result of secret Israeli and Pal-

convener. When I arrived on the scene as a junior diplomat at the U.S. embassy in Tel Aviv in 1997, the discussions underway focused on implementation, in particular implementation of certain economic agreements documented as annexes to the Israeli-Palestinian Interim Agreement.[6] Several working groups had been established to implement different provisions of the accords. I participated in support of the United States as an observer in two of these groups—those seeking to establish, respectively, an airport and a seaport in the Gaza Strip. In the Oslo negotiations, one of the principles resulting in a deal was an exchange of economic opportunity for guarantees of security.

As direct participants, the Israeli negotiators aimed to ensure control of security in both the airport and the seaport. For the Palestinians, their objective was primarily to achieve a connection for direct links to the outside world for purposes of trade and transportation. In this negotiation, the Palestinians' indirect supporters included other Arab states, particularly in the Gulf region, who were potential trade partners or travel destinations. But these parties were not very influential in the implementation phase and were not present in the formal negotiations. They did, however, wield some influence over the negotiations, but not always a constructive influence. For example, the Palestinians' Arab state allies did not use their influence to press for a win-win deal in the Oslo implementation talks. But some of them did use their roles as indirect participants in the negotiations to play the spoiler. For example, some Arab state allies discouraged the Palestinian Authority negotiators from striking a deal that might benefit the Palestinian economy because such a deal might also leave the Israelis looking reasonable in the eyes of the international community.[7] These outside actors preferred

---

estinian negotiations in 1992–1993 in the Norwegian capital, while Oslo II, known as the Israeli-Palestinian Interim Agreement, was announced in 1995 and focused on Israeli withdrawals from Palestinian territories and the process of Palestinian Authority government formation. See "Oslo Accords Fast Facts." September 3, 2013. CNN. https://edition.cnn.com/2013/09/03/world/meast/oslo-accords-fast-facts/index.html

6. See, e.g., Israeli Ministry of Foreign Affairs. February 10, 1999. "The Israeli-Palestinian Interim Agreement on the West Bank and the Gaza Strip." https://mfa.gov.il/mfa/foreign-policy/peace/guide/pages/the%20israeli-palestinian%20interim%20agreement%20-%20annex%20iii.aspx. These agreements were later elaborated in the Sharm El Sheikh Memorandum of 1999.

7. In other contexts I have observed, Saudi and Egyptian representatives also blocked Palestinian-Israeli compromise. For example, in late March 2014, when the HRC President was selecting a candidate for Special Rapporteur for the Palestinian Territories, Palestinian officials agreed to the appointment of Indonesia's Makarim Wibisono, but Saudi and Egyp-

to encourage the Palestinians to hold out for extreme positions, and given their indirect role in the outcomes, they really suffered no losses if a deal on implementation could not be reached. This is a classic example of how an indirect participant can play a role that is destructive, to the point of becoming a spoiler.

The United States was, however, present at each round of negotiations. Given the United States' formal role as an observer, both parties often postured and pleaded in efforts to draw the country into the negotiations more directly, either as a mediator or even as a guarantor of behavior of one or the other side to press for an agreement on terms more favorable to them. In her memoirs, Condoleezza Rice expresses surprise over this phenomenon where Israelis and Palestinians would offer lengthy explanations or grandstand for the sole benefit of the American observer:

> Negotiating with the Palestinians and the Israelis was no easier. Every encounter seemed to produce either a history lesson or a lecture about some UN resolution. One of my aides, seeing my frustration, noted that Israelis are among the most legalistic people on Earth; after all, the Torah is mostly about keeping the law, he said. I asked how this explained the Palestinians' behavior. "They are cousins," he answered.[8]

In one negotiation where I was an observer, the Palestinian captain leading the seaport negotiations dramatically "abandoned ship" and threatened to walk out as the lead Palestinian negotiator. This was as much for my benefit as a U.S. observer as for any real impact it might have, and it was aimed at winning sympathy to his side about the perceived unfairness of the situation and excessive Israeli leverage. But I found that if I walked away from the negotiations, perhaps not returning after a coffee break for more than an hour, the parties would talk constructively in my absence and could often make progress.

My supervisor during the Oslo implementation period, Jeffrey Feltman, would ultimately go on to serve as Under Secretary General for Political Affairs at the United Nations. When I was working for him, Jeff served as observer in the Israeli-Palestinian talks aimed at construction of an air-

---

tian diplomats blocked the choice and pressured Palestinians to do the same. Tovah Lazaroff. March 29, 2014. "UNHRC Delays Appointing New Special Rapporteur to Replace Falk." *Jerusalem Post.* Wibisono was ultimately appointed only after a delay in the process and Palestinian officials speaking more strongly in favor of their own position.

8. Rice, *No Higher Honor*, chapter 14, Kindle location 3794 of 12657.

port and of allowing for Israel-Palestinian trade to expand across the then-passable Gaza border. Sadly, these efforts were ultimately for naught. Following terrorist attacks in which a Palestinian suicide bomber passed from Gaza through a joint trade industrial park to enter Israel and kill several people at a crowded Jerusalem market, the effort at joint trade was ended. Even the runway at the Gaza Airport was bulldozed, and today Gaza remains even more isolated as Hamas' political takeover has furthered the political and economic blockade of the strip. This sad outcome shows that observers may have goals in a negotiation, such as to make progress on joint trade, but it is often easier for spoilers to block progress than for any party to advance negotiations, or in this case, their implementation.

Six-Party Talks on the North Korean Nuclear Issue

In the Six-Party Talks on North Korean denuclearization, complexities between roles and the shifting of roles between parties is also easily illustrated. Determining which parties are direct participants and which are indirect participants often depends, as do most things, on your perspective. In this case, North Korea was no doubt the direct subject at the center of the negotiation and without whom no negotiation could otherwise continue. No matter your perspective, North Korea would have to be defined as a direct participant. The North Koreans were the sole party able to truly implement any agreement on denuclearization and its denuclearization was the primary goal of the talks.

Even though all six of the parties participated in each round of talks, it would not be accurate to consider all of them direct participants. There was a significant difference in the extent of involvement and influence among the DPRK, ROK, China, Russia, Japan, and the United States. For example, Russia sometimes participated in the talks only through its local ambassador in Beijing.

Historically, the United States was the other main participant in denuclearization talks with North Korea from the time of the Clinton administration's bilateral talks with the DPRK. The tradeoffs that North Korea wanted in order to consider denuclearization included a web of security and economic guarantees that brought five additional parties to the table: the United States, China, South Korea, Japan, and Russia. From North Korea's perspective, the direct participants were itself and the United States. The DPRK had engaged in a series of bilateral talks with the United States about its denuclearization during the Clinton administration, and one of its primary goals was to attain the degree of international respect (and in its eyes legitimacy) that could be inferred from seeing the North Koreans as direct negotiation partners of the United States.[9] Moreover, many of the bilateral talks that were most influential to moving the Six-Party Talks forward were between the DPRK and the United States.

Because these two parties' participation was indispensable to the talks, I would define them as the direct participants. Indeed, in periods where either the United States or the DPRK refused to come to the negotiating table during the six rounds of the Six-Party Talks, no talks took place.

But many of the security guarantees North Korea was seeking have antecedents dating back to the Korean War. During that war, North Korea (today's DPRK) and South Korea (today's ROK) were clearly direct participants, and the United States and China quickly joined into the war on each of the opposing sides. While the four parties, all signatories of the Korean War Armistice (to this day, there still is no peace treaty), would be considered direct participants in the negotiations over the end of the Korean War, should all four also be considered direct participants in the subsequent denuclearization talks?

Other Definitions of Direct Participants?

The North Korean view that the armistice defined the key participants also is a useful framework for evaluating the extent of other parties' interests and their proximity to the primary goal of the negotiation: the denuclearization of the Korean Peninsula. I would classify South Korea as an indirect participant in the talks although it could be argued that South Korea was a direct participant for some purposes. At one point, South Korea had been a direct participant in denuclearization talks, when North and South Korea had reached the 1991 Joint Declaration on Denuclearization of the Korean Peninsula. But as time went on, it was possible for U.S.-DPRK talks to

---

9. The United States and North Korea previously had direct negotiations on the nuclear issue. The United States in 1994 entered into the agreed framework, which sought to end the DPRK's nuclear programs in exchange for heavy fuel and construction of two light water reactors in North Korea. Clinton administration Secretary of State Madeleine Albright explained that a primary motivation for DPRK ruler Kim Jong Il to participate in denuclearization talks was his desire to be seen as having the legitimacy and stature to sit across the table from the United States in the 1990s. "Interview: Madeleine Albright." March 27, 2003. *Frontline*. PBS. org. http://www.pbs.org/wgbh/pages/frontline/shows/kim/interviews/albright.html

proceed without the ROK's participation and Seoul was often briefed before and after consultations between the North Koreans and the United States. As a result of these changing circumstances, I would classify South Korea under this framework as an interested indirect participant.

In the case of South Korea, deciding whether it is a direct or indirect participant is not merely an academic exercise. Much of the political debate today in the ROK about the U.S.-ROK alliance and even which domestic political party a Korean citizen supports focuses on the degree to which South Korea directly participates in determining the future of the Korean Peninsula. Critics of the ROK government who participated in the Six-Party Talks said that the ROK position was too passive, a critique also aired today by those who object to Seoul paying a greater percentage of the costs of U.S. Forces Korea stationed on the peninsula. Moreover, North Korea frequently criticizes Seoul as being an indirect player, incapable of making its own security decisions without permission from the United States.

China, too, could be argued to be a direct participant given its role in the Korean War Armistice, but during the period when I was observing these talks Beijing primarily served as a guarantor of North Korean behavior. China also used its role as host of the Six-Party Talks for its own purposes, to strengthen its bilateral relationships with the United States, South Korea, and Japan and to enhance its international reputation as a responsible actor in the international community. In part because of the importance it gave to its role as host of the Six-Party Talks, China refused to veto a series of UN resolutions sanctioning North Korea over its nuclear and missile tests. The extent to which China used its convening power as "host" of the Six-Party Talks and the impact of such convening power on Beijing's international reputation will get further detailed attention in chapter 11. From my perspective, while China may have wanted to appear as a mediator in the Six-Party Talks, its interests in the discussion were too direct for it to have the level of impartiality required of a mediator. As an indirect participant and host, China retained influence on the outcome, gained international prominence, and scored points with its American and South Korean coparticipants for making efforts to contain the North Koreans. In this way, China could be seen as a guarantor of the North Koreans' behavior. But because China had sufficient interests of its own separate from the main goal of denuclearization, I would consider Beijing an indirect and interested participant that sometimes acted as a guarantor.

The final two participants in the Six-Party Talks—Japan and Russia—joined the discussions in part for parity. Having three on a "side" (U.S.-ROK-Japan and DPRK-China-Russia) provided balance at some points of the negotiations. Group dynamics were important: Russia could ensure that China was not "selling out" the DPRK for China's own interests in improving relations with the West, for example, and helped to soothe DPRK paranoia in that regard. Russia brought deep expertise in denuclearization in the UN system but rarely participated directly in the talks. As chair of a working group on regional issues, Russia seemed content to observe and ensure that its interests were not being disregarded, as well as to be included in any regional structures that might emerge from a Korean peace agreement. In some Six-Party rounds, Moscow was represented solely by its local ambassador in Beijing. But it contributed, as a P5 member and a wealthy energy exporter, to the economic assistance for fuel oil compensation for the DPRK's denuclearization. It was also a positive player in communicating international standards of nonproliferation to Pyongyang. Russia was clearly an indirect participant in these aspects of the talks, but it could also be considered a guarantor, given its primary purpose to influence the North Koreans to further denuclearize.

Finally, Japan's role was the most complicated in the Six-Party Talks. Japan cannot be considered a direct participant because it was not essential for achieving the denuclearization of the DPRK. The DPRK sometimes underscored this indirect role for Japan in a pique by refusing to hold bilateral talks with the Japanese delegation. Japan had significant interests in the negotiation and made significant financial contributions to the compensation that was designed to elicit North Korean denuclearization. But Japan's interests in the talks extended beyond the nuclear field.

Like the ROK, Japan was a significant target of North Korean hostility. DPRK missile launches often headed to the Sea of Japan, demonstrating an ability to reach and threaten Japan. This conventional threat was just as real as any nuclear threat might be in the future. Japanese citizens had also been victimized by a DPRK spate of abductions in the late 1970s and early 1980s. A campaign to find out about the abductees' whereabouts and return them safely to Japan if they were still alive was a strong domestic political topic on the right wing in Japan. This issue sometimes gave Japan aspects of a spoiler, willing to sacrifice progress on the DPRK nuclear issue unless sufficient progress was made on this important, but parochial and largely bilateral, issue of abductions.

Again, among the ROK-Japan-U.S. trio, group dynamics played a significant role. For Japan, when the DPRK froze it out of bilateral talks, its U.S. and ROK partners could help by raising the abductions issue in the course of their bilateral meetings with the DPRK. Group meetings before and after U.S.-DPRK or U.S.-ROK bilaterals also helped the other parties to be sure that negotiations and their positions were synchronized. Japan, in particular, feared that the others might "sell out" its interests in the abductions issue to strike a deal or make progress on denuclearization without it. Moreover, for political reasons, the U.S. administration did not want to be seen as "rewarding" the DPRK with direct talks and therefore wanted to frame the discussions as multilateral ones, including U.S. allies in Seoul and Tokyo. While bilateral talks often took place during the rounds of the Six-Party Talks, it was an important limit on North Korea's ability to gain international respect and legitimacy from the United States that they were not always rewarded with such bilateral meetings. Finally, group dynamics and trust issues within the United States internal political structure were also important factors for having the U.S.-ROK-Japan trio operate as a group. Within the U.S. administration during the Bush years, there was deep skepticism that Ambassador Hill and the State Department negotiators might be too soft on the DPRK in their efforts to strike a deal. Those more conservative voices in the Pentagon and the Office of the Vice President relied in part on the presence of Japan to serve as a check on progress proceeding too quickly and to make sure that interests in comprehensive verifiable and irreversible denuclearization were protected. This is just one example of the competing interests that can be at stake between and among the parties and why Japan was not a disinterested observer, but either an indirect participant or at times a spoiler in the talks.

Finally, it is worth noting that the United Nations had no role in the Six-Party Talks, and no party was a true mediator. In early 1992, North Korea entered into a comprehensive safeguards agreement with the United Nations under the Non-Proliferation Treaty allowing the IAEA to conduct inspections of nuclear sites. On occasion, the topic of return by the IAEA inspectors to the Yongbyon nuclear facility was discussed in the Six-Party Talks and even requested by the United States. But the days of those direct, or even UN mediated talks, were over by 2003 when the Six-Party Talks began. Unlike the Libyan example, the United Nations was not, in any way, a participant in talks on DPRK denuclearization. This essentially remains true for North Korea even at present.

CHAPTER II

Host or Matchmaker?

*Using Convening Power as a Vehicle for
Mediation, Influencing Counterparts, and
Controlling Outcomes*

Chapter 10's analysis of whether participants in a multiparty negotiation are direct participants, indirect participants, observers, or guarantors is important for analyzing the options to influence a negotiation as a mediator or other broker. An important part of a negotiator's toolkit can involve restructuring the relationships between direct participants, indirect participants, and mediators, especially if you see that your state or client is being moved to the periphery of a multiparty negotiation. Even when a party is not directly involved, it can use the offer to host negotiations and related convening power to influence a negotiation's outcome and become a more central player than its direct interests might otherwise suggest.

The power to bring parties in dispute around the negotiating table is a strong source of power in any negotiation. A judge or mediator who brings economic disputants together for settlement talks or for negotiations to resolve a financial dispute clearly wields power and authority, derived largely from his independence. This potential source of "soft power" is available to countries regardless of size, interests, and extent of involvement in a given dispute or conflict. In fact, it is often better that a mediator not be a superpower, influential neighbor, or other interested party. The United Nations is often looked to as the convening power of choice. But anti-UN sentiment and failure of the UN to play this role has led to an expansion of state efforts to serve as conveners and mediators, including strong contributions to global peace from Norway, Switzerland, and others. International guidelines for mediators indicate the importance of mediators maintaining neutrality in efforts to convene disputing parties, be this in the economic or political realm.[1]

Multiparty international political negotiations offer an opportunity for participants in a negotiation to use convening power not only to mediate but also to advance their goals in the negotiation. One of the reasons we have focused on the different roles a party can have in a multiparty negotiation is to avoid confusion between a truly neutral mediator and the kinds of guarantors, direct, and indirect parties who might seek to advance their own interests through the use of convening power. Conducting this analysis and determining how neutral your host is in a meeting can be another key tool in a negotiator's toolkit. At the same time, properly using convening power can offer the host a range of advantages, depending on the goals of the party offering to host a meeting. These include:

- Setting the agenda for the participants;
- Creating an opportunity for third-party mediation;
- Earning goodwill and reciprocal gratitude from direct participants;
- Allowing observation and surveillance of the talks and planning sessions;
- Controlling allies and proxies while boxing out competitors; and
- Influencing outcome documents by controlling the pen.

By and large, these advantages can accrue to any party hosting a negotiation session, be they a member state, an international organization, or a private company or client.

In this chapter we will look in detail at the North Korea and Libyan examples to analyze how some parties used convening power to their advantage and how others failed to do so. On North Korea, we will look briefly at the differences between how Beijing exercised convening power during the 2003–2009 Six-Party Talks, and how the ROK has tried to exercise a brokering role in the 2018–2020 nuclear summitry between President Trump and Chairman Kim over North Korea's nuclear program. On Libya, we will look at how the United Nations alternately won and lost the confidence of key negotiating parties in its bid to serve as the convening power, opening the door to a confusing mix of hosts and conveners, each of whom

---

1. See, e.g., "A Guide to Mediation: Enabling Peace Processes in Violent Conflict." 2008. Centre for Humanitarian Dialogue. http://www.hdcentre.org/wp-content/uploads/2016/08/83Guidedelamediation-February-2008.pdf

sought to influence participants, control proxies, or advance its own role. The chapter will conclude with a few observations on the role of online and distance technologies as they relate to convening power, especially during the COVID-19 pandemic when travel and face-to-face meetings have been made more difficult by public health control measures.

Hosting Six-Party Talks on North Korea: A Pillar of Chinese Foreign Policy

China originally gained significant international and bilateral prestige and credibility as the convener of the Six-Party Talks on the North Korean nuclear issue beginning in 2003. At this time, there was a significant debate about whether China, as a rising power, would seek to change the existing international order or would be a "responsible stakeholder" within the existing structures.[2] One of the primary ways that China demonstrated to the world that it could be a responsible stakeholder was through its convening power, exercised as the host of the Six-Party Talks.

China moved to host the talks in 2003 as it became clear that the administration of President George W. Bush was taking a tougher position on North Korea's development of nuclear weapons. Talks had been ongoing about North Korea's nuclear program for years in various formats: the four-party talks; bilateral and trilateral talks including the United States, ROK, and DPRK about the Korean Peninsula Energy Development Organization (KEDO) and its mission to provide light-water reactors to the DPRK; and even bilateral U.S.-DPRK talks about constraining the DPRK's missile program at the end of the Clinton administration. After the September 11 attacks, tension about the DPRK's developing nuclear and missile programs became more pronounced, especially with President Bush labeling the DPRK as part of an axis of evil in his 2002 State of the Union address. At about this time, Beijing began efforts to improve its international reputation and maximize its influence on North Korea with many of the other Northeast Asian powers and the United States. A primary tool in China's toolbox to advance this effort was for Beijing to serve as host and convener of what came to be known as the Six-Party Talks.

First, as convener, Beijing could help to determine who were the rel-

2. Robert Zoellick. September 21, 2005. "Whither China: From Membership to Responsibility? Remarks of the U.S. Deputy Secretary of State to National Committee on U.S.-China Relations, New York City." https://2001-2009.state.gov/s/d/former/zoellick/rem/53682.htm

evant parties to discuss the issue and how and when should they sit down to meet. The Six-Party format produced a relative balance between a "communist" bloc of China, Russia, and the DPRK that often looked to ensure North Korea was being treated fairly and an "allied" block of the United States, Japan, and South Korea that looked to move forward on denuclearization and to contain the DPRK security threat. But far more than this macro-level control over the negotiations, Beijing's convening power also let it exercise micro-level control. It could determine the schedule of bilateral meetings that filled the majority of the time during which Six-Party negotiations were convened. This could allow China, for example, to consolidate a position between itself and the DPRK first, before floating that position with members of the allied bloc. Sometimes it helped China to marginalize or minimize the influence of a rival like Japan. China often denied or delayed opportunities for Japan and DPRK bilateral meetings because of a perception that Japan was pushing too hard on the issue of abducted Japanese citizens for political purposes and as a distraction from the focus on the DPRK's denuclearization.

Second, as host, China had access to the schedules and locations of the participants in all delegations dealing with the North Korean nuclear issue. By holding the DPRK nuclear talks in Bejing, it quite literally made it easier for China to overhear, and thereby know, what each of the delegations was saying and thinking about the DPRK situation. This was true not only for the plenary negotiations but also for more private interactions like bilateral meetings and planning sessions, where delegations may speak in a more unguarded fashion about their bottom lines, interests, and BATNAs. In countries that use electronic surveillance, one should not underestimate the comfort that a government or its security services can derive from listening in and discovering or confirming views about other parties' positions.

Third, China used its convening power to advance its own interests concerning the DPRK. This meant balancing its neighborly and traditional support for the DPRK as a socialist brethren country with China's national interests in regional stability and global interests in nonproliferation of nuclear weapons. In 2003, when the Six-Party Talks began, China was focused on its economic reforms and export-led growth. China wanted stability above all in its international affairs so that it could focus on export-led growth, and the DPRK's unpredictable steps toward gaining nuclear weapons disrupted China's goal of having a stable regional environment.

Fourth, China's work on the DPRK talks helped to improve its relations with the international community generally, and specifically with other Asian countries. As we discussed above, during this time period China's economic and trade relations with Asia were expanding exponentially.[3] China's export growth saw it selling significant volumes across Asia and, in some cases, importing raw materials and other natural resources to fuel this manufacturing boom. With South Korea and Japan, the trade relationship was even more complex.[4] South Korea and Japan were investors in China's manufacturing-led, export economy. While these Asian allies were skeptical of China's communist and control-oriented political system, they were also attracted to its huge market, resources, and low-cost labor. China used the Six-Party Talks to show the ROK and Japan that it had a pragmatic, development focused side to its international political philosophy. China did not let ideological affinity for North Korea overcome practical economic benefits of an improving relationship with traditional rivals in Seoul and Tokyo. This led to a booming trade relationship, even though some aspects of politics remained tense, especially when enmities with Japan resurfaced over official government visits to the Yasukuni Shrine, which memorialized Japan's World War II-era leaders.

But most important, the convening power China exercised in the Six-Party Talks was part of China's grand strategy to use the North Korean nuclear issue to improve its relations with the United States. China positioned itself as a partner to the United States in dealing with the threat the DPRK posed to the international security order. China organized bilateral meetings during the Six-Party Talks so that the first bilateral was almost always between China and the United States. China's Six-Party Talks' envoy Wu Dawei would hear the U.S. position toward North Korea and then

---

3. See OECD. March 20–21, 2011. "China's Emergence as a Market Economy: Achievements and Challenges." OECD Contribution to the China Development Forum, Beijing. http://www.oecd.org/governance/public-finance/47408845.pdf

4. In 2005, the ROK aimed for a future trade volume with China of $100 million. Young-rok Cheong. 2009. "Presentation by Seoul National University Professor Cheong Young-Rok." KEIA Conference on Dynamic Forces on the Korean Peninsula. http://keia.org/sites/default/files/publications/09.Cheong.pdf. By 2012, China-ROK trade had grown to $215 billion per year and trade-reliant South Korea's economy was heavily dependent on China as a partner. Shannon Tiezi. June 2, 2015. "It's Official: China, South Korea Sign Free Trade Agreement." *The Diplomat.* doi: https://thediplomat.com/2015/06/its-official-china-south-korea-sign-free-trade-agreement/ Japan-China trade was a higher volume and also increasing rapidly. Official statistics show that in 2006 Japan-China trade had crossed the $200 billion threshold. Japanese Ministry of Foreign Affairs. 2006. "Japan-China Relations, Basic Data." https://www.mofa.go.jp/region/asia-paci/china/data.html. As early as 2003, the Bank of Japan recognized this trend was having a significant influence on bilateral relations. See Hitoshi Sasaki and Yuko Koga. August 2003. "Trade Between Japan and China: Dramatic Expansion and Structural Changes." https://www.boj.or.jp/en/research/wps_rev/ec/data/rkt03e03.pdf

shape that message in delivering it to the DPRK delegation. China often tried to play matchmaker, drawing the United States and DPRK closer by the way it organized the meeting and relayed messages.

In an environment where China could have been seen as a strategic competitor, China aimed to convince the United States that it could be counted on as a "responsible stakeholder" in the international community.[5] Mediating between North Korea and the other members of the Six-Party Talks was one way China showed the United States that it could be a responsible partner, not only a rising competitor. When China's own international behavior threatened international nonproliferation norms—for example when Chinese firms sold technology to Iran and other sanctioned governments in violation of sanctions—China often returned to its role as a host of the Six-Party Talks to convince the United States of its overall positive, or benign, intentions.

For all the success China found from its hosting of the Six-Party Talks on the DPRK nuclear issue, ten years later many in China criticize this approach as a failure. North Korea retains and has expanded its nuclear arsenal. It appears to have used the time granted it during the Six-Party Talks era to refine a covert uranium enrichment program.

Since 2018, China's leadership on the North Korean issue has taken something of a back seat to the ROK, which effectively replaced China as mediator and matchmaker between North Korea and the United States. ROK President Moon Jae-In from 2018–2019 became the most important host and mediator pressing for peace on the Korean Peninsula. Motivated by a desire to improve relations between North and South, Moon led a complex effort to draw North Korea to attend the Pyeongchang Winter Olympics and participate in a series of summits with himself and with U.S. President Donald Trump, a phenomenon we will examine in more detail in chapter 14. For present purposes, it is sufficient to note that the role of a convener is not necessarily a permanent one, and maintaining convening power can require significant expenditure of effort, resources, and time. Expectations of other parties also can burden the party who is a convener and the convener might find itself being influenced as much by the participants as it is doing the influencing. As the shift between China and the ROK in hosting North Korean peace efforts reveals, agreement about who is host and who is participant is a two-way street. North Korea used shifting allegiances and even willingness to be hosted for discussions on Korean Peninsula peace and security as an intentional part of its strategy. As will be discussed in more detail

---

5. Zoellick, *Whither China Remarks.*

in chapter 13, Kim Jong Un was largely successful in playing China and the ROK off one another in his effort to see which of them could best deliver the most important negotiating partner for the DPRK: the United States.

Outsiders in the Libyan Civil War: Letting Proxies Battle or Conveners Seeking a Solution?

The multiplicity of outside actors who sought to host and influence parties and negotiations aimed at encouraging Libya to form a unified government after the ouster of Qaddhafi was a veritable musical chairs. From the 2015 Libyan Political Agreement, through four years of implementation, up to the summer 2019 siege of Tripoli and the military stalemate between eastern and western Libyan authorities, Libya has been a playground for outside actors to use Libyan parties to advance their own interests. The parties involved range from Libya's neighbors (Egypt, Tunisia, and Algeria) to leading Middle East powers fighting a proxy war over their views of political Islam (Turkey and Qatar versus Saudi Arabia and the United Arab Emirates), to European powers and the United States, who largely used the UN Mission and UN-backed Government of National Accord to advance their own economic and political interests. I will use the frameworks and the different roles for multiparty international political negotiations outlined in chapter 10 to analyze how the different actors used the Libyan situation to advance their own interests and consider which approaches were most successful. Whether outside actors were motivated by self-interest or thought they were advocating what was best for Libya, the victims of more than five years of infighting, posturing, and manipulation are largely the Libyan people, who continue to face a country torn by political divisions and who must live with constant insecurity, shortages, and suppressed opportunities because of the proxy war being fought in their names.

Efforts to Forge a Unified Libya: Getting Enough Parties in Line to Deliver a Capable Government

In Libya's effort to form a unity government and implement provisions of the 2015 Libyan Political Agreement, negotiations among international parties reflected their roles and links to different parties within the country. For some, like the UAE, Egypt, Qatar, and Turkey, the Libyan conflict was a venue in which to fight a proxy war concerning issues of ideology and

Islam that were much broader than Libya's political issues, and many aspects of their conflict took place outside of Libya's borders. For others, typically those in Western countries who supported the UN-backed Government of National Accord (GNA) led by Fayez Sarraj, their interests were more indirect, placing them less as guarantors of any particular party's behavior but as significant potential guarantors and donors in support of an overall agreement. Unfortunately for ordinary Libyans, the indirect nature of their interests also meant that the United States, France, Italy, and others were unlikely to shed too much blood or treasure to resolve the Libyan conflict for the parties, or to force the other feuding international actors to "get in line" behind a single solution. This—coupled with the weakness of Libyan institutions and the deep political divisions within the country—led to a significant governance vacuum and a failure to establish a single unified government in Libya to replace the transitional governing provisions of the 2015 Libyan Political Agreement.

Given the complicated mixture of domestic and external factors and interests involved in the Libyan negotiations, identifying the roles of direct and indirect participants among the domestic and international actors in post-Qaddhafi Libya merits some background discussion. The direct participants were those in Libya's dueling governments—the Western and UN-backed Government of National Accord (headed by PM Fayez Sarraj), the Eastern House of Representatives and its nominally aligned military leader Khalifa Haftar backed by Egypt and the UAE, and the Qatar and Turkey-backed Government of National Salvation, most prominently led by defunct General National Congress (GNC) leader Khalifa Ghweil and Libya's Mufti Gheriyani. Most of the international parties were indirect participants and even guarantors because of their roles in arming or financially and politically supporting some of the direct participants. Among these, many international players attempted to pass themselves off as conveners, and even neutral mediators, for helping the Libyans achieve a new political direction or settlement to replace the LPA.

Key Domestic Libyan Actors

For a negotiator to maneuver in this environment, it is important to understand better each of the main domestic actors and to appreciate their perspectives and their interests, especially as those interests relate to counterterrorism and political Islam. The Islamist-aligned National Salvation Government briefly controlled Libya's government after elections in 2012 and again in

2014. This government was supported by a range of Islamist political parties and militias, some of whom got their financial support from Qatar and Turkey. The largest such party was the Muslim Brotherhood-aligned Justice and Construction Party (JCP). During Qaddafi's time in Libya, the Muslim Brotherhood was the most organized opposition to the dictator. After Qaddafi's fall, the Muslim Brotherhood in Libya had significant grassroots experience and organizing power, which led it to be a strong political and electoral force. In 2012, the Muslim Brotherhood-aligned JCP fared well in Libya's first elections and worked to pass a law in 2013 that banned former Qaddafi-era officials from participating in the government. Qatar's government and significant wealthy individuals in Turkey provided financial backing to many of the political forces aligned with this Government of National Congress. Most of these Islamist forces ended up aligned behind NSG Prime Minister Khalifa Ghweil, who had some control of Tripoli in 2014–2015, a period when Islamist militias grew in power and influence. Ghweil was evicted from Tripoli in summer 2017 by forces loyal to the Government of National Accord and he has periodically mounted efforts to come back and retake parts of the capital ever since.

Until March 2021, the United Nations-recognized government was the Government of National Accord (GNA), led by a nine-member Presidency Council. The GNA was created as a result of UN-led negotiations in Libya and Morocco, which resulted in the December 2015 Libyan Political Agreement (LPA). The LPA authorized the creation of the Presidency Council, led by Prime Minister Fayez Sarraj, which seated itself in Tripoli in April 2016 and has exercised executive power for the nation since that time. The GNA has, in fits and starts, assumed control of the mechanisms of government and tried to subdue the militias governing Tripoli, ultimately ousting Ghweil and establishing a cease-fire in March 2017. The GNA has been a main partner of the United States in counterterrorism, authorizing the air strikes and equipping the Misratan ground forces who combined to push Daesh out of Sirte, a city located between Tripoli and Benghazi and the hometown of former dictator Mohamed Qaddafi.

Finally, Libyan National Army General Khalifa Haftar's eastern forces were aligned with a parallel government structure established as a result of elections of a House of Representatives (HOR), which was recognized internationally during the period 2014–2015. The eastern government was created by a vote of the House of Representatives in Tobruk, near the Egypt-Libya border in September 2014. Led by so-called Prime Minister Abdullah al-Thinni, this eastern government set up executive ministries in the eastern city of al Beyda and received financial support from Russia, which allowed it to print currency and issue a budget. Egypt and the UAE provided political and other support to the al-Thinni government and provided military support to Khalifa Haftar and his Libyan National Army. The al-Thinni government and the HOR were reluctant to cede authority to the new executive in Tripoli, repeatedly blocking formation of a true national government as anticipated by the LPA, failing to produce a quorum to approve GNA decisions, and otherwise acting as a spoiler. Throughout much of the post-Qaddafi period, General Haftar's LNA controlled parts of Libya, instituting a system of military mayors and governors when they have taken territory. Following an April 2019 telephone call with President Trump,[6] Haftar's forces marched on Libya's capital Tripoli, the last remaining stronghold of the GNA. After initial successes, Islamist-aligned militia forces from the city of Misrata—many of whom had aided the United States in its efforts to cleanse Daesh from Libya—rallied to the GNA's defense and a military stalemate held in 2020 with Haftar's forces essentially encircling Tripoli but unable to enter the city.

International Players and Their Roles

The analytical points I wish to draw from the Libya negotiation have as much to do with the framing of a negotiation environment among the various parties as with the actual content of the negotiations themselves. In part, this is because the competing domestic and international parties spent so much time fighting a proxy war in Libya over their differing quests for power that it is hard to have an interest-based analysis of the conflict. True, for the UAE, Egypt, Turkey, and Qatar, part of the proxy war within Libya was a battle over ideological views of the Muslim Brotherhood and the role of political Islam. But even that was a largely binary discussion with limited opportunity for compromise or creating value. The international community, particularly the UN, had some role in and responsibility for this failure to bring the parties into an effective negotiating environment. Constantly fighting Libyan parties hardly needed an excuse to squabble, but international actors who encouraged dispute among their proxies made the problem even worse. As a result, the rest of this chapter will look at the positions and interests of each of the main international players in Libya and see how their competing efforts to serve as guarantors of a certain outcome undermined, rather than

---

6. Ryan Browne. April 19, 2019. "Trump Praises Libyan General as His Troops March on US Backed Government in Tripoli." CNN.com. https://edition.cnn.com/2019/04/19/politics/us-libya-praise-haftar/index.html

facilitated, successful negotiations among Libya's power brokers. It remains unclear whether the Government of National Unity (formed in 2021 as this book went to press) will suffer the same fate.

Egypt and UAE's Interests

Egypt is the outside party that has expressed the most significant interests in Libya. A neighboring country that relies on stability in Libya to prevent terrorists from crossing the border, Egypt also has strong economic interests in Libya given that tens of thousands of Egyptians were guest workers in eastern Libya during the Qaddhafi era. Egypt unhesitatingly backed HOR speaker Agila Saleh Issa and LNA general Haftar in their governance efforts and their counterterrorism operations. In some cases, Egypt may have provided direct air support to Haftar's forces as well as consistent intelligence about the location of alleged terrorist groups. Like Haftar, Egypt in the post-Morsi era took a dim view of political Islam and considered many actors from a Muslim Brotherhood background in Libya as supporters of terrorism or terrorist fighters themselves. In that way, Haftar and Issa were not just Egyptian proxies in Libya but they shared a view of the policy solutions for Libya's troubles that made them natural allies.

The UAE had a similarly dim view of political Islam and offered strong military and financial support to Haftar to help him achieve his counter-terrorism objective. The UAE provided air support to Haftar's operations and funded many of his weapons purchases, if it did not provide the weapons to him directly. Both Egypt and the UAE shared Haftar's ideological opposition to the Muslim Brotherhood and his view that all Brotherhood-associated forces were terrorists or supporters of terrorists, including some representatives of the UN-backed Presidency Council governing Libya. In June 2017, the eastern government in Libya joined the UAE, Saudi Arabia, and others in severing relations with Qatar. In this way, the eastern government was a true proxy for some of the UAE's most significant domestic and international objectives and it used the eastern government and Haftar's forces as a vehicle for carrying out a kinetic battle against the Qatar-backed forces of political Islam in Libya, in addition to supporting them politically.

Because Egypt and the UAE exhibited so much influence over Haftar, they could be seen as guarantors of Haftar's behavior. As one example of this influence, the two governments pushed Haftar to join direct talks with Sarraj, which finally took place for the first time on May 2–3, 2017, in Abu Dhabi and again on July 25, 2017, in Paris.

Turkey's and Qatar's Interests

Qatar and Turkey allied themselves with post-Qaddhafi political forces in Libya who came from a Muslim Brotherhood background and had an activist view of the role of political Islam in Libya's political future. This was especially true for a Salafist political party called Watan that was launched by former Libyan Islamic Fighting Group member turned millionaire investor Abdelhakim Belhadj.[7] Along with his allies, Belhadj, who today owns the Libyan Wings airline, a major television station, and numerous others business, is a primary Turkish funder of Libyan political parties from this ideological perspective. Belhadj also is the financial supporter for certain Tripoli militias, to whom the Turks and Qataris also provided money for weapons. Together they empower these militia allies on the ground, including not only some of Tripoli's strongest militias but also some of the Islamist-backed militia fighters in Benghazi and Misrata. On the economic front, some analysts have also claimed that Turkey and Qatar wielded significant influence over the governor of Libya's central bank and that the central bank often gave favorable lines of credit to businessmen and militia supporters affiliated with Qatar and Turkey's brand of political Islam. In this way, the Libyan actors affiliated with Qatar and Turkey act in more of a proxy relationship. This should also mean that Qatar and Turkey could be important external guarantors of the behavior of key Libyan actors under a new Libyan Political Agreement.

Western Actors

In the West, the United States, the United Kingdom, France, and Italy have offered indirect support to the UN-backed GNA but each outside power again has its own interests. For the European parties, especially Italy, stopping the flow of migration from sub-Saharan Africa through Libya to Europe was of paramount concern. A government at least sufficiently functional to accomplish this goal was an important outcome of political reconciliation talks for Europe and especially Italy. France has interests in counterterrorism across Libya's Southern borders, which led it to cooperate in certain military aspects with General Haftar. France also appears to have attempted to take

---

7. Cameron Glenn. August 8, 2017. "Libya's Islamists: Who They Are and What They Want." Wilson Center. https://www.wilsoncenter.org/article/libyas-islamists-who-they-are-and-what-they-want

a leadership role as convener based on the involvement of French President Macron in the July 25, 2017, Paris meeting. Italy too had direct economic interests, not least in oil and gas, as well as in support of certain members of the GNA Presidency Council who provided lucrative business opportunities to Italian firms.

While the United States and United Kingdom were in a somewhat more neutral position with fewer direct economic interests, neither government was willing to exert the necessary commitment to play a role as a convener or mediator. The two countries are therefore classified as interested observers, with the United States having played a role in the country in 2016 by bombing terrorist locations and supporting GNA troops to remove al-Qaeda from the city of Sirte, its last major stronghold in the country. But neither the United States nor the United Kingdom took on a greater role to exert pressure on the GNA for a particular outcome, although they probably had sufficient leverage to do so if necessary or desired. Legacies of the past, including the murder of former U.S. ambassador J. Christopher Stevens in Benghazi on September 11, 2012, played a role in limiting U.S. involvement.[8]

Other International Actors

Libya's neighbors—notably Sudan, Algeria, and Tunisia—had various, often competing interests in supporting certain players within Libya. Algeria had a strong interest in containing the terrorist threat to it that came from its one thousand-mile desert border with Libya across which terrorists, smugglers, and other forces could easily pass, sometimes influencing political interests among Libya's competing groups.[9] Tunisia also had an interest, largely based on its status as Libya's neighbor. Tunis wanted to avoid the dangerous return of thousands of poor, young Tunisians who served as hired terrorist fighters in Libya. At the same time, it wanted

---

8. My primary experience working with Ambassador Stevens was during 2010–2012, in my role supporting the task force led by Ambassador Bill Taylor, which sought to mobilize financial resources for countries emerging from the Arab Spring. Libyans I worked with in 2016–2017 continued to remember Ambassador Stevens fondly and saw his interest in their country and his death as symbolic of the hopes and challenges of better U.S.-Libyan relations.

9. See Yacine Bouhane. August 28, 2014. "Op/Ed: Algeria's Role in Solving the Libya Crisis." https://www.washingtoninstitute.org/policy-analysis/view/algerias-role-in-solving-the-libya-crisis; "Interests of Neighboring States in Libya's Civil War." *The Maghreb and Orient Courier*, 2015 final edition.

Libya to attain sufficient stability that the many thousand Libyans who took refuge in Tunisia after the ouster of Qaddhafi could return home. Regional groups like the African Union, Arab League, and European Union offered their help as conveners or coordinating bodies but without the requisite influence or heft to drive any kind of negotiations process. This left primarily the United Nations as a potential neutral mediator. Unfortunately, both Martin Kobler—the SRSG until 2017—and Ghassan Salame—who took on the task in summer 2017—were too weak to pull the competing international or domestic players together in an effective negotiating process. After Salame fell ill, acting SRSG Williams convened Libyan military parties in Geneva, resulting in the selection of an interim prime minister in March 2021.

Efforts to Convene a Push toward Unity Government

A proliferation of actors and conveners who have used Libya as a playground to push forward their own supporters, and along with them their own interests in this oil-rich but essentially ungoverned swath of North Africa. Neither the Libyans themselves nor other potential convening powers knew what process would continue from day to day and when or where talks would occur, and under the leadership of which country.

From 2016 to 2018, the U.S. and European actors at least nominally followed the lead of the UN Special Representative, but even among those parties, Italy and France frequently scheduled competing meetings. In 2017, Italy brought legislative leaders to Rome to try to work out a power sharing agreement, while France brought the contenders for executive power to Paris (along with the recently announced new Special Representative Ghassan Salame, who was teaching in Paris).[10] France's efforts to convene a meeting were aimed at boosting the role and stature of Salame as the UN Secretary General's Special Representative, as well as ensuring that French troops deployed in countries near Libya's southern border received cooperation from the authorities in Tripoli. At the same time, Italy's efforts aimed at ensuring the continued flow of pure Libyan crude oil across the Mediterranean. Italy was also motivated, along with the rest of the European Union, to stem the flow of African migrants who continued to arrive unwelcome

---

10. Frederica Saini Fasanotti and Ben Fishman. October 31, 2018. "How France and Italy's Rivalry Is Hurting Libya." *Foreign Affairs*.

on Italian shores and to stop the human tragedy of the hundreds who died attempting the voyage.

Rather than a unified approach toward Libya's future, international players competed over which of them would be seen as the international statesman that could "solve" the Libya problem. The P3 sometimes worked in concert with Italy to discuss Libyan affairs.[11] In other cases, the P3+Italy expanded its reach to try to include "regional actors," but again it was not consistent in setting a lineup for these negotiations. At one point, the United States, United Kingdom, Egypt, and UAE convened several discussions. At other times, the P3 added Libya's North African neighbors (Algeria, Tunisia, and Egypt) to the mix. Despite a brief period of high-level activity in 2017–2018, the United Nations did little to bring order to the chaos of meetings, mediators, and conveners.

Throughout early 2017, Italy, Russia, and even the United States tried to convene a meeting between Haftar and Sarraj. In January, Russia brought its aircraft carrier into the Mediterranean as a show of support and offered Haftar a visit on board,[12] as President Putin tried to expand his influence in Libya and serve as a thorn in the U.S. side in the region.[13] Italy convened leaders of two moderately influential legislative bodies, the HOR and State Council, in April 2017 in Rome, in part because it could not get Sarraj and Haftar to attend in person.[14] Some of these efforts may have been motivated by a desire to help Libya but they were also motivated by a desire to increase their own roles as convener of Libya's internal political discussions. On the U.S. side, the history of Ambassador Stevens' death in Benghazi left the United States reluctant to get too involved in brokering a deal among Libyans.[15] As a result, no outsider pushed effectively for the political compromise

---

11. "Libyan Officials Meet in London in Hopes of Economic Stabilization." October 31, 2016. *Libya Gazette*. https://www.arraedlg.com/libyan-officials-meet-in-london-in-hopes-of -economic-stabilization

12. "East Libya Strongman Visits Russian Aircraft Carrier in Mediterranean: RIA." January 11, 2017. Reuters. https://www.reuters.com/article/us-libya-russia-haftar/east-libya-stron gman-visits-russian-aircraft-carrier-in-mediterranean-ria-idUSKBN14V1T2

13. Lincoln Pigman and Kyle Orton. September 14, 2017. "Inside Putin's Libyan Power Play." *Foreign Policy*.

14. Alessandro Pagano Dritto. April 23, 2017. "Libya's HOR's Ageela Saleh and State Council's Abdul Rahman Sewehli Met in Rome, Italy, for the First Time." *Between Libya And Italy*. https://betweenlibyaanditaly.wordpress.com/2017/04/23/6950/

15. On April 20, 2017, President Trump told a press conference that the United States would not be heavily involved in solving the Libyan crisis. Glenn Thursh. April 20, 2017. "No U.S. Military Role in Libya, Trump Says, Rejecting Italy's Pleas." *New York Times*. https:// www.nytimes.com/2017/04/20/us/politics/trump-italy-prime-minister-paolo-gentiloni.html

necessary to produce an agreement between Sarraj and Haftar. But the many interested participants and spoilers spent significant political capital trying to enhance the position of their own proxies and their own supporters inside Libya.

Convening Power as a Way to Empower Proxies

Among those competing for influence, Egypt and the UAE seemed the most successful in convening the parties, in part because of their closer contacts to Haftar, who was most often the recalcitrant party or the one least willing to join in an international political negotiation. Neither Egypt nor the UAE could be considered neutral power brokers or mediators because both were intimately involved in offering political and military support to Haftar and the LNA in the effort to eradicate terrorism in Libya. Yet precisely because of their roles as guarantors—influential parties in the negotiation with an ability to put pressure on one or multiple direct participants—Egypt tried and the UAE ultimately succeeded in carrying off this power broker's meeting, but it took almost three years to do so. In the lengthy period of time that the parties tried and failed to initiate political compromise among the Libyans, General Haftar's confidence grew, and by 2019 he attempted to unify the country by force with a military march on Tripoli.

Throughout much of 2016, Egypt had been playing the role of spoiler in efforts to bring together the Libyan political leaders. A strong backer of LNA General Khalifa Haftar, it preferred to see Haftar's LNA forces make advances on the ground and in their attacks on terrorist and Islamist groups, regardless of the impact on Libya's future as a democracy or a unified state. Egypt's approach was consistent with its own domestic anti-Islamist campaign as well as its political and security interest in having Haftar secure eastern Libya as a buffer zone against insecurity and potentially a place where Egyptian guest workers could return for work and income. Following the formula that the convening party could earn a greater role in influencing the political process inside Libya, Egypt in 2017 tried to convene a power broker's meeting and tried specifically to get Sarraj and Haftar to meet and discuss Libya's future across the east-west divide in the country. On February 13–14, 2017, Sarraj, Haftar, and Speaker of the Libyan HOR Agila Salah Issa all traveled to Cairo and met with Egyptian officials, headed by the Egyptian Armed Forces chief of staff General Mahmoud Hegazy. While all three parties were present in Cairo at the same time, Haftar refused to meet Sarraj in person. This embarrassed and angered the Egyptians, who had prepared a "Cairo Communique" that summarized commonly agreed proposals for minor amendment to the Libyan Political Agreement. Cairo issued the communique after what it called "indirect" talks among the leaders, but it was clearly unhappy that its effort to convene a Libyan power brokers meeting and to gain prestige on the international stage had been rebuffed.

When, in early May 2017, Prime Minister Sarraj and General Haftar met face-to-face in Abu Dhabi, rather than in Egypt, the Egyptians were furious. Their efforts to brand themselves as the leading international force capable of resolving the Libyan political stalemate were damaged. But the Emiratis succeeded in bringing Haftar to the table for a two-hour meeting aimed at coming up with amendments to the LPA that would give Haftar and the army a sufficient role to bring him back into the political fold, rather than remaining at odds, and in conflict, with Sarraj and his Misratan military allies. Why did the UAE succeed where so many others had failed?

On one hand, the UAE succeeded and Egypt was able to host proximity talks because of the military influence they wielded over General Haftar. Prime Minister Sarraj was never the problem. Reports out of the Cairo proximity talks indicated that Sarraj was willing to meet Haftar, but it was the general who declined a meeting in Cairo. With Haftar not meeting Sarraj in Egypt, it provided greater prominence to Egypt's ally and proxy in Libya, HOR Speaker Agila Issa Saleh. When the UAE successfully convened the parties a few weeks later, it was no surprise that the HOR speaker was not included.

The UAE succeeded in convening actual talks largely because its influence with Haftar was more direct than Cairo's influence, but also because the UAE did not have to overcome Libya's historical suspicions of a neighboring power that has often interfered in Libya's affairs. On the question of its military influence, the UAE provided Haftar a huge proportion of his military and economic support, dating back to 2014.[16] This backing included air support in the form of bombing raids against alleged terrorists.[17] This gave the UAE the leverage to convene a meeting where others failed. In this case,

---

16. "UAE Provided Military Aid for Haftar, Says Libyan Politician." April 27, 2017. *Middle East Eye*. https://www.middleeasteye.net/news/uae-provided-military-aid-haftar-says-libyan-politician

17. Jared Malsin. May 9, 2017. "U.S.-Made Airplanes Deployed in Libya's Civil War, in Defiance of U.N." *Time*. http://time.com/4746914/libya-civil-war-airplanes-haftar-uae/

the meeting was not really a means of enhancing the convener's power but of demonstrating it to other parties, including other indirect parties like the West and Cairo, who hoped to similarly place themselves in the convener's role. As the conflict continued, the UAE continued to successfully manage its proxies in eastern Libya, including Haftar, in part through convening negotiations. For example, in November 2019, the UAE brought Haftar to Abu Dhabi to consolidate his position vis-à-vis the civilian forces of the government in eastern Libya.

Other parties were less successful in stemming the outbreak of conflict. Italy tried again to convene a peace process in November 2018 but was quickly rebuffed. Italy's prime minister hosted an international conference in Palermo aimed at setting a new path to peace. Sarraj, Haftar, Egypt, Tunisia, Qatar, and Turkey attended, but the Turkish delegation pulled out when Haftar demanded Turkey be excluded from a discussion among the key parties. After a year of steady gains on the ground by Haftar forces throughout 2019, in January 2020 Turkey overtly entered the Libyan conflict by sending ground troops and increasing armament to back the GNA. Among the weapons sent by Turkey were armed drones, used—Turkey claimed—to counter the increasing deployment by the United Arab Emirates of air bombardment using manned aircraft as well as unmanned drone attacks. At least one alleged UAE-backed bombing by Haftar's LNA killed an old man and three children at an equestrian school outside of Tripoli in October 2019. In stopping the escalation of violence, the UN and Europeans expressed public statements of opposition and condolence. But leadership in terms of convening power was nowhere to be seen.

Conveners So Focused on Own Interests, Libya's People Are Victims

In the framing of these negotiations, where are the interests of the Libyan people? Why did none of the international actors working on Libya—including the United Nations—pay significant attention to the needs of the Libyan people, including basics such as physical security, economic development, or governance? Libyans were known to say they wanted the revolution to give them liberty, but after the revolution all they wanted was security, electricity, and liquidity. Focused on a supposed role as a mediator of political compromise, the United Nations did little to address these problems. The United States and United Kingdom convened an economic dialogue among officials of the Central Bank of Libya, the Ministry of Finance, and the National Oil Company, among others, to try to ensure that funds that went to the central government flowed to municipalities and regions and that development programs got underway. But even these efforts failed to provide the most basic solutions to Libya's economic problems, such as its huge black market exchange rate or the fact that, even though most Libyans had a monthly salary deposited into their bank accounts by the state, very few of them could actually go to the bank and withdraw their money because of massive liquidity shortages. And Libyan leaders did not encourage too much outside involvement or transparency, in part because of the massive opportunities for corruption that a government post provided.

Behind all these problems lay the fact that the UN-installed government provided little leadership for its cabinet agencies and ministries. The GNA suffered from a lack of institutional management, which resulted in it providing little actual governance. As I observed while serving for the United States in its Libya External Office based in Tunis, Libyan citizens got little from the national government amidst the squabbling and interests of these multiple factions. Security seemed anecdotally better in areas under the control of the LNA, including in Benghazi. By most accounts, 2018 saw Haftar's Libya National Army extend and cement administrative control in many parts of Libya's south and east, bringing governance and administrative improvements, which were still hard to find in the parts of Libya under the de facto administration of Sarraj and the GNA. But none of the international players competing for influence in Libya spent significant time focused on the needs of the Libyan people, at significant cost to the Libyan economy and Libyan lives. This is probably why the political stalemate in the country extended from 2015 until the formation of the March 2021 interim government.

Technology as a Tool, and Obstacle, to Convening Powers in the Age of COVID

The outbreak of the coronavirus in early 2020 effectively put a hold on efforts to host in-person peace negotiations, be they concerning North Korea, the Middle East, or other international problems. This situation in part led UN Secretary General Guterres to call for a global cease-fire in response to COVID, stating that our common global fight should be against the coronavirus pandemic and not with each other.[18] The global call was heeded for

---

18. See, e.g., United Nations. April 3, 2020. "UN Secretary General Reiterates Call for Global Ceasefires." https://www.un.org/press/en/2020/sgsm20032.doc.htm; United Nations.

a few months before conflict parties essentially returned to business as usual in many parts of the world, regardless of the extent of coronavirus outbreak.

Given pressure to move some forms of negotiation to online platforms and spaces, it is useful to reflect how those platforms affect convening power in negotiations, and how most of the tools available in the offline world remain accessible to good negotiators using online platforms.

First of all, organizers seeking to convene peace negotiations using technology can have the same advantages in controlling the agenda, drafting outcome documents, and managing an online platform as they can in hosting an in-person meeting. An organizer is expected to create the agenda and oversee the outcome of a meeting, even when the discussion takes place online. Online negotiations usually require more focus than those that take place offline and may also require more patience. In-person negotiations often feature some period of emotional outbreak, or letting off steam, such as the outbursts between Palestinian and Israeli seaport negotiators described in chapter 10. Online platforms are usually less conducive to such shows of emotion and therefore sometimes require more detailed preparation. But once an online negotiation begins, parties are typically able to focus on the negotiation and hold back on peripheral or emotional issues.

Second, the ability to have informal interactions is limited online in comparison with in-person negotiations. In-person negotiations allow significant opportunities for a host to use breaks, coffee, meals, and social outings before and after the negotiation session as a tool to break the ice and create good atmosphere among the negotiating parties. A convener can and should use atmospherics to help bring parties closer. In the offline world, China spent significant time hosting banquets, providing coffee, and using the marginal meetings and breaks to allow participants to break the ice and establish relationships in the Six-Party Talks. In my experience, Chinese diplomats are particularly skilled at using these social opportunities and sightseeing tours to advance their negotiation objective, while Western participants sometimes see these activities as peripheral and press to more quickly "get to the point." A skilled negotiator should see these opportunities for informal interaction as a key chance to gain information about other parties' positions, styles, and BATNA. Moreover, the skilled use of breaks is also a way for a convener or host to control the emotional dynamics of a meeting and keep the discussion headed in the direction that he or she wants, or conversely, to allow emotional outbursts to derail a discussion that is not consis-

July 1, 2020. "Security Council Backs Long-Delayed Call to Support SG Call for Humanitarian Ceasefires." https://news.un.org/en/story/2020/07/1067552

tent with the host's interests. Creating opportunities for informal discussion and breaks is harder in the online space, but not impossible, as activities like virtual happy hours have made clear.

Security is an obvious difference between online and offline meetings. Online meetings are more easily monitored using electronic surveillance and the well-publicized stories of security lapses on various online platforms make this problem even more serious. Since offline meetings can also be subject to surveillance, parties often proceed and assume some security risk, having little other choice when an in-person meeting is not possible.

Finally, online meetings have some advantages. For delegates who are introverted or reluctant to speak, the "Chat" function on many online platforms can allow ideas to come out without the pressure of speaking publicly. Similarly, for delegates who require instruction, the ability to multitask and communicate with their political leaders during an online negotiation but out of sight of the other participants can sometimes increase the robust participation of such delegations.

In sum, technology is unlikely to allow online negotiation to replace in-person negotiation any time soon. But in general the same tactics that one would use as a participant—or a convener—of an in-person meeting can also be deployed in an online session.

CHAPTER 12

Combatting Genocide with a Little Help from My Friends

Empowering Partners

In multiparty negotiations, one tactic that often produces great results in an international setting involves working with and through other parties. Especially in a United Nations or other formal multilateral setting, working in coordination with others allows opportunities for tactical maneuvering and deployment of soft power. The idea of a core group leading an issue, as opposed to a single sponsor or party, can cut away political and regional rivalries. Group dynamics are always an issue in the UN. The support of a cross-regional core group in advocating for a position can significantly strengthen the effort and can also press other member states to decide their positions in a negotiation based on the merits, rather than purely a regional approach to the negotiation. Leading a UN negotiation with the support of a cross-regional core group (typically one member from each of the UN's five regional groups) can also provide benefit by allowing a member of each regional group to advocate for a position from within.

This chapter will focus on two case studies in which the United States empowered partners in the effort to combat mass atrocities. First, we will discuss the violence against civilians in South Sudan that took place beginning in December 2013 and that culminated in action at the UN Human Rights Council (HRC) in the summers of 2015 and 2016. Second, we will look at the HRC action on Burundi in late 2015 and how cooperation by a cross-regional group of partners, including particularly brave African and Latin American partners, allowed the council to hold its first-ever special session aimed at preventing an atrocity before it occurred.

South Sudan

In December 2013, a civil war broke out between supporters of South Sudan's president Salva Kiir and the country's former first vice president, Riek Machar. The war quickly took on an ethnic tone with supporters of the Dinka-dominated government targeting Nuer ethnic groups aligned with Machar and vice versa. By mid-2014, international observers were warning of the risk of an all-out ethnic conflict. More than two million South Sudanese were internally displaced with another 1.5 million remain refugees outside the country.[1] More than one hundred thousand took refuge in UN compounds in South Sudan and government soldiers and officials attempted to enter those compounds to pursue civilians. As of March 2016, one UN official estimated that fifty thousand people had been killed in the conflict.[2] Untold numbers of targeted killings and cases of sexual violence have occurred. As the June 2015 session of the UN Human Rights Council approached, it was clear that the human rights consequences of the political violence were staggering. UNICEF reported in June 2015 that as many as 129 children were killed in a three-week period the previous month. "Survivors report that boys have been castrated and left to bleed to death. . . . Girls as young as 8 have been gang raped and murdered. . . . Children have been tied together before their attackers slit their throats. . . . Others have been thrown into burning buildings."[3]

Beginning shortly after the conflict erupted in March 2013, a cross-regional group of diplomats had been watching the conflict in mounting horror and pledged to do something about it. In 2014, the African Group in the HRC stymied efforts to create an independent investigation into South Sudan, noting that the African Union's first-ever Commission of Inquiry (COI) was underway, headed by former Nigerian president Obasanjo. President Obasanjo came to a special panel of the UN Human Rights Council in September 2014 and placed the blame for the violence squarely on the country's political leaders. He warned that the conflict had taken on an ethnic dimension and that there was a risk of genocide. Despite Obasanjo's

1. United Nations. 2017. "Report of the Commission on Human Rights in South Sudan." UN Document A/HRC/34/63, March 6, 2017. https://ap.ohchr.org/documents/dpage_e.aspx?si=A/HRC/34/63

2. Fleur Launspach. March 3, 2016. "ÚN: Tens of Thousands Killed in South Sudan War." *Al Jazeera*.

3. UNICEF Executive Director Anthony Lake. June 17, 2015. "Unspeakable Violence Against Children in South Sudan—UNICEF Chief." https://www.unicef.org/media/media_82319.html

strong remarks calling for accountability, the AU COI's report was blocked from public release and regional and international action to do something to stop the killings or establish accountability appeared stymied. The HRC refocused attention on the need for independent action from outside the region. A broad support group was formed of representatives from the European Union and its member states, plus Norway, Switzerland, Mexico, Paraguay, North Macedonia, Montenegro, Albania, Japan, South Korea, Australia, and New Zealand, hosted by the United States. The group heard reports about the situation in South Sudan from experts from the Office of the High Commissioner for Human Rights and special envoys working on the issues, including U.S. ambassadors Donald Booth and Susan Page. The group worked to determine how it might create an additional monitoring body to document the widespread human rights abuses that had occurred and call for accountability. Rather than sit back and watch a few states with strong interests in East Africa decide the response for the entire United Nations, the group became empowered. Ultimately, a core group of four member states—Albania, Paraguay, the United Kingdom, and the United States—was selected to take the matter forward into the HRC, while the remaining states continued to network with civil society, advocate with other delegations, and remain updated on developments in the region as part of an extended core group.

The presence of Albania and Paraguay in this core group was particularly important. In 2015, both countries' permanent representatives served as vice presidents of the HRC. While the crisis in South Sudan was far from their territories and not a preoccupation of their peoples, their presence in the core group signified that these governments were putting their credibility, and the credibility of their roles as vice presidents of the HRC, behind the push to establish a special procedures mechanism in South Sudan. Albania's and Paraguay's national histories also gave them credibility: they had experienced human rights issues and conflict in their own countries. Finally, their presence made it difficult to label the core group as an imperialist or anti-Africa effort. The South Sudan government had already attempted that—blaming the U.S.-U.K.-Norway troika of donor states for providing inadequate support to postindependence South Sudan after it became independent in 2011. Finally, Albania could reach into the UN's Organization of Islamic Conference and the HRC's Eastern Europe Group, while Paraguay could help communicate with and deliver support from colleagues in the important swing Group of Latin American and Caribbean States (GRULAC).

Negotiations of a resolution at the UN Human Rights Council, and indeed most any UN body, take place through "informal consultations." In these discussions, experts from the member state delegations typically read through the proposed text in a meeting chaired by the core sponsor, or in this case, the core group. Because the extended core group had participants who were extremely well-informed about the situation in South Sudan and the history of delays to allow the AU COI report to address the topic, they were well-prepared to respond to arguments for yet another delay in favor of actions by the regional body. Briefed about the facts, ambassadors from states like Portugal took the floor to condemn the killings documented in the UNICEF report. Even those from outside the extended core group, states as diverse as Botswana and the Maldives, expressed serious concern about the loss of life and the lack of a credible regional response taking place in South Sudan, echoing the call that the credibility of the UN and its Human Rights Council would be damaged if an atrocity of this magnitude could occur without a response. The European Union, as well as a group of female ambassadors from a range of states, expressed concern about the extent of sexual violence documented in recent reports by the Secretary General's Special Representative for Violence Against Women. A similar type of specialization of argument emerged from the core group. Albania's permanent representative and expert, both of whom were female, emphasized the horrific allegations of sexual violence. Paraguayan expert Jorge Brizuela, who chaired the informal sessions, focused his advocacy on South Sudan's humanitarian situation.

Amid facts so damning, the debate about the text of the language was relatively simple. Like the case study of the negotiation on Sudan discussed previously, South Sudan's position centered on avoiding creation of a monitoring mechanism. Initially the core group tabled a draft resolution under the council's agenda Item 4 proposing the creation of the HRC's strongest type of monitoring mechanism, a Commission of Inquiry. South Sudan said it could not accept the creation of a mandate of any kind, whereas the core group held firm that the situation in South Sudan was so serious that it should be addressed by an investigative commission under Item 4. The core group emphasized that human rights violations on the scale of those in South Sudan could not be addressed credibly as a matter of "technical assistance" under the council's agenda Item 10. With an apparent impasse reached, it became necessary to convene large negotiation sessions between the African Group ambassadors, chaired by South Africa, on one side, and the four states of the core group on the other. Initially, the African ambassadors tried to uphold African unity in support of South Sudan. But the South Sudan position was unreasonable. At one point, South Sudan charge d'affaires John Cheikh Awol argued that it was the United Nations' fault that

South Sudanese soldiers and government officials attacked a UN protection of civilians site where thousands of South Sudanese had fled from the violence, because the UN had "violated its status of forces agreement" with the government. At this point, even African ambassadors became enraged, with the Algerian ambassador and previous African Group chair telling the South Sudanese "you don't get to talk anymore." The South Africans and Algerians worked with the core group to have the resolution text document the facts of South Sudan's atrocities, but still urged, on behalf of South Sudan, that the parties find a compromise and perhaps shift the resolution to rarely used Item 2. African and core group officials at that point gave South Sudan a choice: either it could accept a Commission of Inquiry-like investigation and the core group would shift the resolution to Item 2, or South Sudan could file a competing resolution that opted to make the investigatory mechanism something less than a Commission of Inquiry and face the vote of the entire Human Rights Council on the competing alternatives. African Group leaders wanted merely to avoid the specter of an Item 4 resolution. But to their (and most other negotiators') surprise, South Sudan failed to file a competing resolution by the deadline. Then faced with a choice about whether it wanted the investigative mechanism to be created by the council to be a single person or a three-person panel, the South Sudanese chose a three-person panel, essentially conceding to the creation of a Commission of Inquiry in everything but name. African states were also satisfied that the council's credibility had been upheld and only a few outliers, led by Egypt, objected because they did not like the idea of an additional Item 4 resolution being advanced about an African state.

On March 23, 2016, HRC resolution 31/20 passed without a vote. The resolution created a three-member Commission on Human Rights in South Sudan "(a) To monitor and report on the situation of human rights in South Sudan and make recommendations for its improvement; (b) To assess past reports on the situation of human rights since December 2013 in order to establish a factual basis for transitional justice and reconciliation; (c) To provide guidance on transitional justice, accountability, reconciliation and healing. . . ."[4] African states Ghana and Senegal even joined as cosponsors. On June 14, the HRC president appointed Yasmin Sooka, Kenneth R. Scott, and Godfrey M. Musila to serve as the three members of the commission,

---

4. UN Human Rights Council. March 23, 2016. "The Situation of Human Rights in South Sudan." HRC Resolution 31/20 (Adopted March 23, 2016). UN General Assembly. https://documents-dds-ny.un.org/doc/UNDOC/GEN/G16/086/91/PDF/G1608691.pdf?OpenElement

with Ms. Sooka as its chair. The commission made two trips to South Sudan and continued to document the horrific abuses and violations on both sides, leading to an additional special session of the HRC in late 2016 to publicize the situation and their response. It continues its important work to this day.

Among the lessons that can be drawn from the South Sudan example are the benefits of establishing a broad, cross-regional core group and empowering as many states as possible to support your position. Unlike a two-party negotiation, when decisions are made by multiple parties, compromise tends to dilute the results because multiple interests are at stake. But in the South Sudan case, the early empowerment and buy-in of many states led to a stronger and more durable result. This was especially important because in 2016 when the resolution was adopted, neither the United States nor the United Kingdom was a member of the Human Rights Council. As a result, Paraguay and Albania had to be prepared to defend the resolution on the floor of the council and against any procedural challenges. And while the horrific violence in South Sudan continues, it is at least being documented professionally, setting the stage for possible future transitional justice measures as a result of the HRC's strong resolution 31/20.

Burundi

The issue of atrocity prevention was particularly important to me in my diplomatic career. From 2010 to 2012, I worked for the Undersecretary of State for Human Rights and Democracy who was tasked by Secretary of State Hillary Clinton to represent the State Department in the planning to create an Atrocities Prevention Board. The brainchild of Samantha Power, the National Security Council senior director, the Atrocities Prevention Board (APB) aimed to harness a whole-of-government approach to identify and intervene to prevent situations of potential mass atrocities before they could occur. I was assigned to chair a State Department task force charged with looking at the results of President Obama's Presidential Study Directive-10 on Atrocity Prevention. Atrocity prevention theory argues that most conflicts follow a cycle of acceleration and exacerbation that transforms clashes or violent incidents into continued clashes and then cycles of recrimination that turn into mass atrocity. Similarly, the theory posits that actors in the international community who understand and can identify this cycle could, with appropriate political will, intervene to prevent the outbreak of violence from escalating into an atrocity—even if they cannot prevent the outbreak of the conflict itself.

With a team of more than thirty-five experts from across the State Department and USAID, and in cooperation with the intelligence community and other colleagues, our APB task force prepared materials explaining the APB's goal and theories for the public launch of the board by President Obama at the U.S. Holocaust Memorial Museum on April 23, 2012. The task force I chaired prepared the launch and continued to analyze steps to implement the board's mission: we discerned lists of warning signs for mass atrocity, catalogued tools to deploy as interventions to prevent atrocity from occurring and escalating, and documented public and private ways of communicating these interventions for use in training U.S. diplomats, NGO aid workers, and officials in other governments. Public statements and attention highlighting the possibility that an atrocity could be underway was deemed by the task force as one of the most important tools for deterring those who might undertake or order an atrocity, and convincing them to change course.

The Human Rights Council had an opportunity to deploy some of the lessons learned by the Atrocities Prevention Board in the 2015 case of Burundi. Burundi was on everyone's "Watch List" for atrocity prevention ever since President Nkurunziza insisted in April that he was going to stay in office for an unconstitutional third term and a coup attempt to force him out of office was suppressed. In late 2015, government officials in Burundi began making public statements and motivating forces that appeared to be a return to the environment that allowed the mass genocide of thousands of Hutus and Tutsis in Rwanda and Burundi in the 1990s. Comments like we have to "finish the work" and "take those people out" coming from the mouths of Burundi's leaders, including its president of the senate, hearkened back to other inciting statements, like those from Nazi Germany, Srebrenica, and even Libya's Qaddafi who threatened to "hunt down" those involved in the revolution against him "like rats."

Up to that time, no single country had taken a lead in the HRC on the issue of atrocity prevention. Armenia was a leader in an annual resolution on prevention of genocide, along with a group of states including Rwanda and Hungary. But this was a politically charged resolution, which often became a political football between the Turks and Armenians. Hungary too had led discussions of atrocity prevention, including several at which I spoke, but the rise of Viktor Orban had led Hungary to be seen as a somewhat questionable leading state on human rights issues. Rwanda was clearly biased and potentially implicated in the violence in its neighboring state. Australia, the Netherlands, and Rwanda had formed a cross-regional group called the Friends of the Responsibility to Protect. But those states were not prepared to take country-specific action, afraid of tarnishing the general brand of the R2P Friends group. Traditionally, the European Union had been the most active entity within the council on Burundi. The EU, led by Belgium, sponsored previous joint statements on Burundi and had worked on the situation when an independent expert was appointed to help improve the country's judicial system nearly a decade previously. But none of those parties appeared ready to take any action against Burundi prior to the end of 2015, a date both real (because of the amount of violence in Burundi and the president's extra-constitutional stay in power) and symbolic (because in 2016 Burundi would take a seat on the HRC as a member and this was the last chance to emphasize the violations being committed and seek to encourage the UN General Assembly to replace Burundi, or to convince the delegation to resign its seat out of embarrassment).

The week of December 7 two important events independently took place that resulted in the HRC determining to hold a special session to focus on Burundi. First, the United States decided it would lead a call for a special session so long as the session took place before the end of 2015, given that the United States was rotating off the council and would not be a voting member in 2016. In a working-level briefing on Burundi (much like the extended core group meetings on South Sudan discussed above), Ghanaian deputy permanent representative Ebenezer Appreku announced that his delegation was prepared to sign onto a call for a special session. This decision was important, in fact momentous, for two reasons. First, no African state had ever before signed onto a call for a special session to be held on another African state. In the meeting, attended by many swing states in Eastern and Western Europe, Appreku delivered passionate remarks on why it was inappropriate for African governments to stand by silently without acting in the face of the Burundi government's action against its own civilians. Second, many European Union member states had announced that they were not prepared to take action on Burundi prior to the end of the year unless African states joined the call. Under the rules of the Human Rights Council, sixteen of the council's forty-seven member states must sign a call for a special session. Ghana's announcement broke the logjam, but on the morning of December 11, I still had received the signatures of only fourteen member states calling for a special session. Given the upcoming Christmas and New Year holidays, Washington had decided that if we did not succeed in holding the special session before December 18, we would have to wait until the following year. That would make the situation challenging because membership on the Human Rights Council would change in 2016. In addition to the United States rotating off the council, African states had elected Burundi to rotate onto the council. As a member of the council in 2017, Burundi could exercise its voting power as one of only forty-seven members to trade influence and try to prevent a special session from happening.

With the clock ticking, my ambassador had arranged to host that day at lunch several ambassadors from the HRC member states and key observers in the Group of Latin American and Caribbean States. During the lunch, we outlined the case for action on Burundi, explained the thinking of Ghana in its willingness to support the call, and urged the Latin American delegations to take action. As dessert was being served, none had agreed to sign onto the statement, and I made the candid point that we were desperate. We were two signatures short of the sixteen needed for a special session. The Republic of Korea, usually a reliable vote, wanted to avoid signing the call because its ambassador had just been named to serve as the council's president for 2016. At this point, Ambassador Martelli of El Salvador stepped forward. His country had seen the horrors of human rights abuses in its own history, he said. If ownership from Latin America was needed to bring this special session about, he would sign. Colombia's ambassador was also willing to sign, but as a nonmember would not influence the needed count. Argentina, which had just completed an election establishing a new government, agreed to call for instructions as soon as business opened in Buenos Aires. Mexico agreed to do the same. As the lunch finished, I received a text message from the Korean expert: if we still lacked one signature at close of business, Seoul would sign on. This meant the sixteen signatures required for holding the special session were assured. And as the business day opened in the Western Hemisphere, both Mexico's government and the new Argentine foreign minister, UN veteran Suzanne Malcorra, authorized their governments to sign, bringing the total number of member states demanding a special session on Burundi to eighteen. The letter was filed with the HRC secretariat at close of business December 11, 2015.

This demand for a special session could not have been more timely. On the weekend of December 12, the actions of Burundi officials turned from rhetoric to violence. Nearly ninety people were killed in that one weekend alone in a series of coordinated, ethnically charged attacks.[5] Many were young boys who had been shot execution style, with their hands tied behind their backs. Government-affiliated militias were implicated as responsible, according to eyewitnesses.

On December 17, the twenty-fourth special session of the HRC was held focusing on the human rights situation in Burundi. The country's lead-

---

5. Jessica Elgot. December 12, 2015. "Burundi: 87 Killed in Worst Violence Since April Coup Attempt." *The Guardian.*

ing opposition human rights figure, Pierre Claver Mbonipa, received special permission from the Belgian government to travel to Geneva and participate in the session, even though he was still in the process of claiming political asylum. Mbonipa testified about how his son and son-in-law had both been killed by pro-regime forces as a result of the protests against Nkurunziza's unconstitutional third term, and he addressed delegates with his neck heavily bandaged because he had been shot in the face weeks earlier in an assassination attempt. Nonetheless, his vivid description of the politically charged nature of the violence and the sacrifices of Burundi's civilian population in the face of mounting risks of atrocity were highly persuasive. The council unanimously passed a resolution on preventing the deterioration of the human rights situation in Burundi. This was the council's first-ever resolution on atrocity prevention and it ordered that a mission of existing independent experts urgently be dispatched to draw attention to the violence in the country and to try to stop the deteriorating rights situation.

Had the end of year gambit not worked, it is possible that the HRC would have held a special session the following year, but it was unlikely to have been as effective or to have passed a resolution by as strong a vote margin as that passed in the 2015 session, for two reasons. First, Burundi's rotation onto the council almost guaranteed some "No" votes against any resolution, including Burundi's own. Finally, midway through 2016 Ghana's Appreku died of a heart attack and his impassioned voice for Africans taking responsibility for African affairs was lost forever. Appreku's bravery on behalf of Ghana helped to empower others to be willing to direct criticism toward an impending atrocity. He was joined in his bravery by the Salvadoran ambassador, who made the call that action was necessary, even when his other colleagues from Latin America were unwilling to sign their names to the task.[6] Such examples show that the actions of individuals can make a significant difference to the outcome of negotiations, even when taken by representatives of small and medium-sized states in large multilateral venues like the United Nations.

---

6. Interestingly, Martelli's decision to sign the call for a special session was the first in a series of leadership actions he took on behalf of his tiny Salvadoran delegation. As a result, later in 2016, he was elected president of the Human Rights Council, representing all GRULAC states.

CHAPTER 13

North Korea Back Again

A Victory for Trumpian Negotiation or a Defeat for Everyone?

The table was set, literally. Chefs prepared a luncheon of foie gras, snow fish, and candied ginseng to serve on the table of ceramic plates, crystal glass, and the finest silver inside the Metropole Hotel, where Kim Jong Un and Donald Trump were to celebrate their success at the Hanoi Summit.[1] According to a schedule for February 28, 2019, already distributed to journalists and the public, the luncheon was to be followed by the signing ceremony for a U.S.-DPRK agreement that would be a significant step in North Korea's denuclearization and that would bring the world closer to ending one of the last vestiges of the Cold War.

So what went wrong? When White House spokeswoman Sarah Sanders told the press corps in Hanoi that the luncheon was canceled, confusion and pandemonium ensued. A spokesperson for South Korean president Moon Jae In, whose tireless mediation efforts had brought the two participants to this second summit and who hoped that the meeting would give him the green light for continued efforts at improving economic ties between Seoul and Pyongyang, candidly told the world that the ROK government had no idea what was going on either. Later President Trump explained in a press

---

1. Siobhain O'Grady. February 28, 2019. "A Shared Dinner, a Canceled Lunch: What Trump and Kim Did—and Didn't—Eat in Vietnam." *New York Times*; Ju-min Park and James Pearson. February 28, 2019. "Inside the Dying Moments of the Trump-Kim Summit at a Hanoi Hotel." *Reuters*.

conference that the DPRK's denuclearization offer and demand for sanctions relief was just not good enough and "sometimes you have to walk."[2]

Walking away is a tried and true tactic in negotiations over money and one that Trump had used dozens, perhaps hundreds, of times before in real estate and other deals. He had also used it previously with Kim Jong Un, announcing in May 2018 that their planned Singapore Summit had to be postponed because of inadequate progress in preparations.[3] In the case of postponing the Singapore Summit, Trump was walking away because North Korea had stalled his lead nuclear negotiators, insulted his vice president and national security adviser, and was holding out to negotiate any denuclearization concessions with him personally. Trump's gambit worked that first time, as North Korea increased its willingness to negotiate in preparation for the Singapore Summit, and the Singapore meeting was rescheduled for June. As he had done before, the president found that by walking away, his negotiation counterpart improved its offer and he got more of what he wanted. The lesson he took: brinksmanship allowed him to proceed as a victorious dealmaker, rather than a failed aspirant.

As anyone knows who has shopped in a market in the non-Western world with no fixed prices, walking away can be a successful tactic to determine the other side's bottom line in a price negotiation. If a potential buyer walks away from a carpet or souvenir vendor, merchants from Tianjin to Tunis will chase the buyer down and say "okay, okay." This usually indicates their agreement to take the last price offered and close the deal. Similarly, the person walking away can feel they held their bottom line and got a fair deal by refusing to pay too much. Hence the president's statement that "sometimes you have to walk" reflected a tried and true negotiating tactic.

In a more formal sense, walking away sharpens a negotiating counterpart's sense of their BATNA (Best Alternative to a Negotiated Agreement). When your negotiating counterpart demonstrates they are prepared to walk away, one literally sees a deal slipping away and has to assess whether any deal is better than the alternatives. That is a real world example of deploying the BATNA theory. The negotiator facing a walkout must immediately assess whether the alternative to a negotiated agreement really is better than striking a deal, even an imperfect one. How much would they lose by the loss of an agreement? Was there a risk that the loss of the

2. Julian Borger. March 1, 2019. "Vietnam Summit: North Korea and US Offer Differing Reasons for Failure of Talks." *The Guardian*. https://www.theguardian.com/world/2019/feb/28/vietnam-summittrump-and-kim-play-down-hopes-of-quick-results-nuclear-talks

3. Mark Landler. May 24, 2018. "Trump Pulls Out of North Korea Summit Meeting with Kim Jong Un." *New York Times*.

process meant that no agreement would ever be forthcoming? Or should the party who threated or actually walked away try to go back? Put in our marketplace example, the customer might have to ask: is it really worth leaving this country without that souvenir in an argument over $10? Similarly, the shopkeeper must ask herself: if I am making a profit, even a small one, should I take the deal now before this customer does not make the purchase or buys it from someone else?

In a marketplace and even a real estate deal, the possibility of an alternative negotiating partner affects one's BATNA. A potential purchaser can simply try another vendor to see if the same item can be purchased for a better price. Similarly, the shop keeper can wait for another customer hoping to make more profit from the sale of the same item. But in international negotiations over political issues, alternative suppliers are not always an option. With respect to denuclearization negotiations, only the DPRK can strike a deal with Washington to give up its nuclear devices. Guarantors and indirect parties like China, Russia, and South Korea can offer their good offices as mediators but they cannot offer up the nuclear devices. Similarly, the DPRK appears cognizant that it cannot get a peace agreement or the security guarantees it is seeking from anyone besides the United States. In this, as in many multiparty political negotiations, alternate suppliers do not exist. So the BATNA calculation a party makes when it decides it is "time to walk" is increasingly important.

At the end of this chapter, we will consider whether the 2020 elections functioned as a kind of alternative supplier for the United States in its negotiations with the DPRK, or with other parties such as Iran. Did the DPRK have any incentive to strike a deal with the Trump administration before the elections given the risk a different president would be elected? Before the 2016 U.S. election, candidates from both parties had taken strong positions that partisan differences stop at the nation's edge, allowing some certainty that the United States would have continuity in foreign policy regardless of election outcomes. But the Trump administration's reversal of many Obama foreign affairs actions made it increasingly likely that this reliability in U.S. foreign policy is under threat. Other countries may begin to treat U.S. elections like alternate suppliers as they assess their BATNA in negotiations with the United States. Just like President Trump failed to uphold the Iran nuclear deal, the Paris climate change deal, and many trade commitments of previous administrations, so the North Koreans must have asked themselves whether it was worth signing a deal with President Trump in the run-up to elections when a subsequent U.S. president might not honor the deal. In considering alternatives to a negotiated agreement, a wise DPRK negotiator must take into account waiting for a future U.S. administration as among those alternatives.

Beside the Snow Fish: What Was Left on the Table When the United States Walked Out?

President Trump's decision to walk away from the Hanoi luncheon table in February 2019 was an effort to get the North Koreans to change and improve the offer that was on the negotiating table in a complicated exchange over denuclearization, sanctions relief, and future steps to improve relations, including ending the Korean War and opening the door for North Korea's reentry into the community of nations. According to participants and second-hand accounts of the Hanoi meeting, North Korea had offered to close a key nuclear production site at its Yongbyon nuclear complex. This was the same complex I visited many times and where, in 2008, our negotiations resulted in the demolition of the nuclear reactor's cooling tower as a visible symbol of the DPRK's commitment to denuclearization.

But Yongbyon is just one of many sites where fissile material for North Korea's nuclear program is produced. With North Korea demanding removal of all of the UN Security Council resolution sanctions that targeted its domestic economy, the United States felt it needed more on denuclear-ization. The UNSC resolutions North Korea wanted to have rescinded— totaling five in all—were the key part of a U.S. maximum pressure campaign of sanctions during the Trump administration. The resolutions implemented sanctions measures in response to North Korea's aggressive steps in 2017 to test a thermonuclear device and a long-range missile that could theoreti-cally become an ICBM-like delivery vehicle for a nuclear device capable of striking the United States. According to press and participants, the United States responded to this demand for major sanctions with a "bigger deal" and asked for all nuclear facilities in the DPRK to be shut down in exchange for such widespread sanctions relief.

North Korea had a history of concealing its nuclear production facilities, as we discussed in chapter 4. In October 2002, U.S. Assistant Secretary of State James Kelly confronted North Koreans over evidence that it had highly enriched uranium facilities where nuclear materials were being produced that could go into a bomb.[4] Kelly's accusations and North Korea's evasion

---

4. David Sanger. October 17, 2002. "North Korea Says It Has a Program on Nuclear Arms." *New York Times*.

and denials began a spiral of confrontation and escalation that was only eased when the Six-Party Talks began as a new structure of regular negotiations to promote North Korean denuclearization. In 2008, the Six-Party Talks collapsed because of failure to agree on a verification protocol that would be broad enough for international monitors to inspect and follow-up to ensure that all North Korean nuclear programs—plutonium, tritium, and uranium enrichment—would be shut down. In the February 2019 Hanoi Summit, the United States evidently raised similar evidence about nuclear sites outside of Yongbyon and production of nuclear fuel beyond the Yongbyon plutonium reactor. How, the Americans reasoned, could they agree to remove all sanctions on North Korea if the DPRK was continuing its nuclear and missile production at sites outside of Yongbyon? In effect, the money that would be pumped into the DPRK economy by sanctions relief could potentially be funding these covert efforts by North Korea to increase its threatening nuclear and missile stockpile, according to U.S. thinking.

So both the luncheon table and the negotiation table were set, but the parties did not eat and instead returned home largely empty handed. When President Trump and his advisers decided that "sometimes you have to walk," and Hanoi was one of those times, the package that was left on the table included an offer to close North Korea's most significant nuclear production and research complex and to keep in place a missile and nuclear testing moratorium in exchange for major relief from UN sanctions for the DPRK economy. Trump walked away with a smile and a handshake with Kim Jong Un and the promise that future talks would follow. But in hindsight did the president of the United States—the commander in chief and leader of the free world—make the right call for protecting the American people?

President Trump's behavior at the Hanoi Summit was all about adjusting the North Korean BATNA. By walking away, he was saying that the deal he had on the table with Kim Jong Un was not good enough. In negotiation theory language, President Trump was trying to make it clear to North Korea that it might have to accept its Best Alternative because it might not get a Negotiated Agreement. But in so doing, he may have miscalculated not only the North Korean response but his own Worst Alternative to a Negotiated Agreement or WATNA. It appears that, before walking away, President Trump did not accurately consider that some steps the DPRK might take—such as a resumption of nuclear and missile testing—might actually be worse for U.S. national security than a mediocre negotiated agreement. After the summit, Kim Jong Un pressed ahead quickly to take precisely those steps, and remind the Americans to reconsider their BATNA as well, lest they end up with the Worst Alternative to a Negotiated Agreement—a nuclear armed North Korea unrestrained by a diplomatic process with a perfected ICBM truly capable of being launched and hitting a U.S. city on the American mainland.

Could Trump Have Been Both Right and Wrong at the Same Time?

According to many aspects of negotiation theory and much of the analysis in this book, President Trump was right to walk away in Hanoi. First, he was sending North Korea the clear message that its proposal was not reasonable. The U.S. negotiators in Hanoi apparently felt that any steps the United States took to remove the hard-won international sanctions from its maximum pressure campaign would never be put in place again. Under this line of reasoning, UN Security Council veto-wielding defenders of the DPRK, Russia and China, would not agree to restore any such sanctions because of the DPRK's diplomatic charm offensive waged since the beginning of 2018. In effect, giving up those sanctions, the United States believed, was an "irreversible" diminution of its maximum pressure. This step was not worth the dismantlement of one North Korean facility—that of the Yongbyon compound. Moreover, the sanctions being rolled back were so significant that they were more than just half of the UN sanctions resolutions. They constituted all of the sanctions passed to punish the DPRK for its ICBM test. By walking, the United States was making it clear to the North that the deal was too lopsided.

Second, the president was making clear that, in future, more preparatory work needed to be done at working levels before the leaders got personally involved in trying to strike a deal. Prior to the Hanoi Summit, North Korean negotiators repeatedly ignored and rejected attempts by Secretary of State Pompeo and Special Representative Steve Biegun to explore the details of a U.S.-DPRK deal such as might be addressed by the leaders in a summit. This was probably the foremost reason that the Hanoi Summit was breaking down—unlike typical summits in the past, North Korean refusal to engage in preparatory negotiations with Biegun and others meant the summit content was not adequately prepared. The DPRK felt it could ignore preparations for the Hanoi Summit with American negotiators because it succeeded in the past in going "over their heads" and having their leader speak directly to President Trump. In the Singapore Summit preparations, the DPRK's preference for engaging Trump directly seems to have been rewarded: the outcome document from the Singapore Summit seemed largely one-sided and in favor of the DPRK. In the June 12, 2018, Singapore Communique, the DPRK agreed to "work toward" the complete denuclearization of the

Korean Peninsula, while the United States and DPRK jointly agreed to build new relations, work toward lasting peace on the Korean Peninsula, and to resume Korean War remains recovery repatriation.[5] When it was revealed after the summit that President Trump had also agreed to freeze U.S.-ROK military exercises on the Korean Peninsula, commentators widely agreed that the Singapore outcomes were a major win for North Korea.

If the North Koreans hoped that in Hanoi they could again get a better deal from the president, Trump's decision to walk away showed them that they were wrong. For the future, it probably was also the right decision because it empowered his real negotiators—Special Representative Steve Biegun, Secretary of State Mike Pompeo, and their successors in the Biden administration —to be able to negotiate details of denuclearization and "corresponding measures" with their DPRK counterparts. By walking away, Trump may have hoped that this would make it more possible for experts to quickly follow-up on the agreed but ill-defined goal from Singapore: the complete denuclearization of the Korean Peninsula. Experts might also be able to synchronize steps that might lead to a win-win outcome of complete denuclearization, complete sanctions relief, and security guarantees like an end to the Korean War that would open the way for the DPRK to reenter the international community.

Third, the president appears to have tried a range of negotiating tactics with Kim Jong Un before he decided to walk away. President Trump certainly gave the DPRK face and respect by agreeing to meet with Kim Jong Un. In the Singapore Summit of 2018, the DPRK finally was seen on the world stage as an equal to the United States. In the months following Singapore, President Trump continued to give Kim Jong Un respect and tried to personalize the friendly relations by talking about exchanging "love letters" with the DPRK leader. Trump also tried to avoid negative statements about Kim Jong Un, going so far as to state that he didn't believe the DPRK leader knew of the abusive treatment of American student Otto Wambier. This marked a complete reversal of the frequent barbs and Twitter jabs the president had leveled at North Korea during his first year in office, such as calling the North Korean leader "Rocket Man" and suggesting that Trump's nuclear button was bigger than Kim's.

In addition to its tactical influence on North Korea's perception of nego-

---

5. The White House. June 12, 2018. "Singapore Summit Communique." https://www. whitehouse.gov/briefings-statements/joint-statement-president-donald-j-trump-united-states-america-chairman-kim-jong-un-democratic-peoples-republic-korea-singapore-summit/

tiations, President Trump's decision to meet the North Korean leader face-to-face also made the world safer. Trump's businessman's confidence and style of negotiating was a key element in allowing the June 12 Singapore Summit to take place. His CEO's mindset made Trump want to be the first American in the room with Kim Jong Un, and he believed he was the person to strike a deal and talk the DPRK out of further enhancing its nuclear and missile programs. Trump's predecessors, going back to George H. W. Bush, Bill Clinton, George W. Bush, and Barack Obama, refused to meet with North Korean leaders because they did not want to reward one of the most brutal and dictatorial regimes on the planet with a chance to meet the leader of the free world. Where such summits were explored, for example late in the Bill Clinton administration, they fell apart in the preparation stage because the North Koreans would not commit to prerequisites demanded at lower levels, such as Secretary of State Madeleine Albright's October 2000 visit to Pyongyang to meet Kim Jong Il, Kim Jong Un's father.[6] As a result, all previous efforts to allow for presidential summits between the United States and North Korea failed.[7] Trump's willingness to meet Kim Jong Un and his belief that he could judge Kim's good will and guide the leader on a path to denuclearization where Kim would "be running his country, his country would be very rich, his country would be very industrious"[8] opened the possibility of Northeast Asia turning into a region of peace and prosperity.

A final reason that peace on the Korean Peninsula seemed to be drawing near in the second half of 2018 was because Koreans—rather than the American president—were taking huge steps to advance peace on the Korean Peninsula and denuclearization in North Korea. ROK President Moon Jae In was the first party to bring Kim Jong Un and Trump together dating back to his positive response to Kim's 2018 New Year's speech and his diplomatic outreach for the Pyeongchang Winter Olympics. After Moon sent envoys

---

6. "Albright Makes Historic Visit to North Korea." October 23, 2000. *The Guardian*; Robert Einhorn. April 20, 2018. Interview with former missile negotiator and U.S. Special Envoy Robert Einhorn. Interview by Eric Richardson in person, Geneva, Switzerland.

7. Tessa Berenson. March 8, 2018. "Why Trump's Predecessors Did Not Meet with North Korea." *Time*. Former presidents Carter and Clinton did visit North Korea after their time in office had ended. Bill Clinton flew a mission to guarantee the release of journalists who crossed into the DPRK from China (for which I provided support), whereas Carter traveled on humanitarian and food-based missions in his capacity as head of the Carter Center.

8. David Nakamura and Philip Rucker. May 17, 2018. "Trump Offers Reassurance That North Korean Dictator Kim Jong Un Would Remain in Power Under Nuclear Deal." *Washington Post*. https://www.washingtonpost.com/politics/trump-offers-reassurance-that-north-korean-dictator-kim-jong-un-would-remain-in-power-under-nuclear-deal/2018/05/17/901635e0-59ff-11e8-8836-a4a123c359ab_story.html?utm_term=.cacc8dba05f2

to North Korea to engage in shuttle diplomacy to prepare a summit, these envoys reported to Trump at the White House in March 2018 and conveyed the invitation that Kim Jong Un was prepared to meet Trump in a summit. While Trump surprisingly and bravely accepted the invitation, ROK negotiators led by Moon did the leg work. Even after the Singapore Summit took place, the ROK carried out shuttle diplomacy and held three leadership summits in the second half of 2018. Moon's effort was pressing North Korea to make progress on denuclearization and holding out the practical promise of economic benefits by starting reforms such as the linking of roads and railways between North and South.

We have talked in this book about the tactic of working through another party to achieve your goals as part of a multiparty negotiation. Was Trump working through Moon in this case? I think not and in fact it may have been the opposite: Moon was modestly praising Trump and his policy of maximum pressure for driving the DPRK to the table, when in fact it was Moon's involvement that brought in the DPRK and made this largely bilateral negotiation have some of the characteristics of a multiparty one. While Trump was the figure whom the North Koreans desperately wanted to meet in a leadership summit, it was Moon who was the puppet master behind the scenes—prodding, cajoling, and persuading both parties to hold not one but two historic summits. We may be able to learn as much from Moon's negotiating style in this case as we can from either the United States or DPRK. Moon adopted many of the hallmarks of an interested party who also played a mediation role. By carrying letters and messages between Chairman Kim and President Trump, Moon quietly but successfully advanced the process of drawing the United States and DPRK into talks, even though both sides knew he had significant political and economic interests—including those favoring peace and improving ties to the benefit of ROK businesses. Thus Moon's role as an intermediary, as much or more than Trump's negotiating brilliance, pushed Kim to the table. And it was Moon and his envoys who were also working hard to see if he could also persuade Trump to meet Kim. By doing so, Moon was also seeking to advance the ROK's interest and getting President Trump to shift from his 2017 rhetoric about bloody nose strikes and "Fire and Fury" to go along with a North-South rapprochement that would bring the DPRK back into the international community.

Mistakes Were Also Made Ahead of Hanoi: Lessons You Can Learn

So when Trump and Kim agreed to hold a second summit in Hanoi, analysts believed that the outcome would continue the trend of making the world

safer—finding a formula to sequence the complicated steps of denuclearization, an end to the Korean War, and security guarantees that would make
the DPRK feel safer and more comfortable abandoning, in whole or in part,
its nuclear program and so-called deterrent. In fact, that is what the world
expected to hear about in the signing ceremony, before the banquet luncheon in Hanoi was canceled and the parties left with no deal. Analyzing his
behavior more critically, did President Trump make certain mistakes or mis-
calculations that led to the increasingly dangerous situation after the Hanoi
Summit fell through?

Inadequate Preparation

As we have already discussed, the lack of preparation was largely responsible
for the Hanoi Summit breaking down over issues that the parties could and
should have discussed ahead of time. Unlike most summits where "sherpas"
and experts choreograph every move and agree ahead of time on the content
of the agreement to be addressed by the leaders, the Hanoi Summit was no
mere signing ceremony. Key details were kept open for the two-day discussion between President Trump and DPRK leader Kim Jong Un. The North
Koreans bear significant responsibility for this lack of preparation because
they anticipated getting a better deal from the president and they refused to
have their experts work with U.S. experts to preview and prenegotiate all the
fine points of a possible summit agreement.

President Trump's CEO-like negotiating style fed into this mistake. As he
had said many times, he believed that he was the sole person able to strike a
deal with Kim Jong Un and he had little faith in many of the negotiators and
experts working for him. Also Trump's CEO-like desire to simplify the situation was also a significant factor in allowing the leaders to meet in Hanoi
without the content of all elements of their agreement having been arranged
ahead of time. President Trump had little attention or patience for working
through the details, for example of a tedious definition of complete denuclearization of the Korean Peninsula. In Singapore, he had taken Kim's word
that the DPRK leader was committed to this goal without further elabo-
ration. So while President Trump's sense that simplifying the details may
even have facilitated his first meeting with Kim Jong Un, denuclearization
is complicated. The vague Singapore Summit agreement made it difficult
for those who have to implement it to follow-up. By the run-up to Hanoi,
Trump's advisers were insisting that he had to show progress toward denuclearization or he would again be pilloried for having given too much away to

the DPRK. With this general outline agreed, they should have foreseen the need for detailed preparatory work to close the gap on differing views of denuclearization and "corresponding measures" that the DPRK would gain in exchange. In the end, the extent of sanctions relief was the corresponding measure that soured the deal.

But it was not only the U.S. leader who was not fully prepared for the Hanoi meeting in February 2019. According to accounts of the breakdown, the DPRK also appeared unprepared to engage on the issue of complete denuclearization. When U.S. negotiators raised the issue of sites outside of Yongbyon as part of a larger deal of complete denuclearization in exchange for complete sanctions relief, the DPRK did not know how to react. It appears to have been unable to engage significantly on the details of its other facilities and nuclear production programs, not to mention chemical, biological, and other threats. As Condoleezza Rice said in her memoirs, "Only a fool goes to an important meeting in which the President will be involved without an agreed text."[9]

When You Walk Away, Know How to Get Back

Another complicating factor in the abrupt breakdown of talks in Hanoi stems from the intersection of the uniquely public nature of the Hanoi Summit coupled with the cult of personality that surrounds the Kim family regime in DPRK. North Koreans focus all of their efforts on the leader, his reputation, and his near infallibility. For Kim Jong Un to publicly travel to Hanoi to meet with the U.S. president and not return with a deal might be the kind of slight that the country could not get over. If Kim left Hanoi embarrassed or weakened internally, he may be unwilling to again take another risk of letting the United States embarrass him publicly in a future summit. And even if he was willing to take such a risk, the hierarchical nature of the regime and the cult of the leader's perfection may be so threatened by the risk of a future unsuccessful summit that those negotiators further down the North Korean pecking order who would have to engage in the work to repair channels and relationships might be powerless to undertake such efforts.

Nor may it be easy for the United States to get back to the table, even if it wants to offer some concessions. A well-prepared summit creates processes of its own. Negotiations that have a regular framework for meetings make it easier for leaders to meet and work out any issues that may arise and to pre-

9. Rice, *No Higher Honor*, Kindle location 3795 of 12657.

vent leaders from having to address routine questions because the "system" handles most such queries. Unlike the Six-Party Talks or other institutional frameworks, the Singapore and Hanoi Summits were completely isolated one-off events. Linked to the lack of preparation, the summit advance work had no regular system for communication. Restarting talks is relatively easy between parties who have a regular meeting schedule, offices or embassies in each other's capitals, or an established mechanism like the Six-Party Talks that ensures future opportunities for negotiation and interaction. But the U.S.-DPRK relationship and negotiations have no such foundation. Remember, for eight months prior to Hanoi, the U.S. special representative had exactly zero independent meetings with DPRK officials. This suggests that it may be harder to restart any process after the Hanoi Summit failure than at any other time in recent memory. As North Korean Vice Foreign Minister Choe Son Hui threatened on March 15, 2019, the United States may have let a golden opportunity slip through its fingers and the DPRK may never again be willing to negotiate with the United States like it did in Hanoi.[10]

On June 30, 2019, President Trump appeared to have found a creative way to get back to the negotiating table. During a visit to South Korea, he made a trip to the DMZ and announced his willingness to meet Kim Jong Un there. The North accepted and Trump became the first sitting U.S. president to cross into North Korea, with a brief step across the DMZ before holding a forty-five-minute meeting with Kim Jong Un that resulted in an agreement to resume working-level talks on denuclearization in "two or three weeks." As summer turned to fall, no new talks were announced, but the DPRK vocally announced its opposition to renewed U.S.-ROK military exercises and a plan to sell advanced fighter jets to the ROK. It also tested short-range ballistic missiles, in violation of UN Security Council resolutions.[11]

Failure to Empower Others

In general, President Trump has emphasized that he doesn't need regional experts, negotiators, or even the State Department. "I'm the one who mat-

---

10. "We have no intention to make concessions to the U.S. requirements [put forward at the Hanoi Summit] in any form, much less the desire to conduct such negotiations," Choe said in a meeting with foreign ambassadors and press, according to comments carried by Russia's TASS News Agency, warning that the United States risked throwing away "a golden opportunity this time." Colin Zwirko and Oliver Hotham. March 14, 2019. "North Korea Has No Intention to Give U.S. Concessions on Denuclearization." *NK News*.

11. John Hudson. July 26, 2019. "North Korean Saber Rattling Dims Euphoria of Trump's DMZ Meeting." *Washington Post*.

ters," he said when he came into office, suggesting he did not need professional diplomats to deliver messages. In this way, President Trump has hardly ever empowered others to act on his behalf or in support of the United States. This is perhaps the most disempowering approach to a negotiation possible.

Several candidates could have served as proxies and supporters of improved relations with the DPRK, if only Trump would have let them. But rather than empower President Moon in South Korea or the leaders of China or Russia to deliver a message on his behalf, the president tended to go it alone internationally. Ironically, the one successful impact of the president's decision to walk might have been to empower his own subordinates and successors. Prior to the walkout, Biegun had tried unsuccessfully to meet with leading DPRK foreign ministry interlocutors.

Be Sure of Your Own WATNA: What if the DPRK Restarts ICBM Testing?

In walking away, Trump was focused on getting the North Koreans to give more, but he may have failed to consider perhaps the most important negative consequences that walking away might have on U.S. security interests. In considering the United States' Worst Alternative to a Negotiated Agreement (WATNA), Trump should have taken more seriously what might happen if North Korea went back to its more provocative posture as in the past. The United States appears to have taken it for granted that the DPRK was going to come back and continue to propose destruction of its Yongbyon facility and the moratorium on missile and nuclear testing. Following the Singapore Summit, North Korea largely pressed ahead with steps to begin dismantling its main nuclear and missile launch facilities and seemed focused on working with the international community rather than threatening it. The freeze-for-freeze approach by which U.S.-ROK joint military exercises and DPRK nuclear and missile tests were both frozen in 2018 significantly lowered tensions and ushered in a six-month period of intense DPRK-ROK rapprochement and economic cooperation.

President Trump appears to have undervalued an important element of his détente with Kim Jong Un—a North Korean moratorium on missile and nuclear testing—and to have miscalculated how costly it might be for the United States if the DPRK were to reverse this moratorium. According to U.S. and international experts, North Korea's biggest gap in its ability to strike U.S. territory with a nuclear device is its delivery systems—in this case its missiles. Testing is an essential part of refining missile technology and the steps North Korea needs to work on are the miniaturization of a warhead so it can fit on and continue along the proper trajectory of an inflight missile, and the protection of the reentry vehicle so that the warhead will be preserved intact until the missile reaches its desired detonation location on the other end. A moratorium on testing provides an important element of this guarantee. Ongoing missile testing can help refine North Korean technology and make it even more likely that the DPRK could successfully fire a nuclear-tipped Intercontinental Ballistic Missile (ICBM). The more testing the DPRK does, the better its ability to launch such a weapon and strike a target in the mainland United States.

After the summit, North Korea wasted no time in exacerbating U.S. fears and pressing the advantage to make the United States realize the risks of its miscalculation of the U.S. WATNA. North Korea immediately began restarting activity at several missile launching sites. Implications of this effort were not immediately clear: could it be a signal to the United States that the ICBM program was restarting? On March 15, Vice Foreign Minister Choe Son Hui offered a clear shot across the U.S. bow. The United States had thrown away a golden opportunity at the Hanoi Summit and negotiations with the DPRK might no longer be possible, Choe said at a press conference in front of diplomats in Pyongyang.[12]

Moreover, the DPRK ended its moratorium on missile tests. On May 9, the DPRK fired two short-range missiles that some categorized as "projectiles" to leave open the possibility that these launches did not end the missile test moratorium or violate UN sanctions. However, even after the June 20 Trump-Kim meeting at the DMZ, the North continued on this path and left no doubt that the ballistic missile moratorium was over. On July 25, the DPRK launched two new short-range ballistic missiles into the Sea of Japan. It said this launch was a "warning" to South Korean "war mongers." The launch followed Kim Jong Un's highly publicized visit to a new submarine facility, framed as a missile launching option, and the North's public statements threatening to halt future talks with the United States because of resumption of U.S.-ROK military exercises and possible sales of high-tech weaponry, including the F-35 fighter jet. The DPRK has not yet abrogated Chairman Kim's commitments to President Trump not to test another ICBM capable of hitting the United States, but the trend lines even following positive summit statements at the DMZ were not encouraging. For example, in the October 2020 military parade celebrating the seventy-fifth anniver-

---

12. Eric Talmadge. March 15, 2019. "DPRK Chairman Kim Rethinking U.S. Talks, Launch Moratorium." Associated Press.

sary of the Korean Workers Party founding, the DPRK displayed new submarine and mobile ballistic missiles, some of which analysts believed had the enhanced payload space and capacity to launch multiple nuclear warheads deliverable to the U.S. mainland.

Accounting for Time Horizons, as Well as Substantive Goals

Finally, the Americans may have misestimated the relative time horizons of the DPRK and the United States and their relative senses of urgency to strike a deal. To a certain extent, both Kim and Trump focused excessively on the short term, especially the period of their own political viability. But the U.S. election cycle, and scandals taking place in the U.S. political environment, made President Trump particularly focused on a short-term goal of having a North Korea success in his first term in office. For Kim, his lifetime appointment means that his time horizon is longer than Trump's. Compared to most other multiparty negotiations we have analyzed, the two leaders here can afford to make enemies and pursue short-term solutions, while hoping that the negative consequences of their style take effect only later after they leave office.

In fact, this short-term perspective may be an additional reason that the Hanoi walkout should have been anticipated. President Trump's negotiating style is an impatient one of major public posturing, quick wins, and then moving on to the next issue. Such a short-term approach was ill-suited for the longer term, multiparty negotiating process—even after Trump and Kim had established a leader's summit rapport. Building the institutional trust and cooperative mechanisms of a Northeast Asian peace framework to follow up on any denuclearization agreement and support an end to the Korean War is much more complicated than a single summit or closing a real estate deal. This may be why the illusion of a quick, top-down win from DPRK summitry is not likely to bring sustained change on the Korean Peninsula and the parties' best next step is to create the kind of institutional connections that might be advanced by the establishment of liaison offices and an ongoing negotiations framework.

Conclusion: Mistakes Made All Around

Perhaps the Hanoi Summit was a missed opportunity. Alternatively, perhaps Kim Jong Un never really intended to denuclearize and was just trying to "milk" the United States and the international community for greater concessions and economic benefits in the Singapore and Hanoi summits. If so, no deal with North Korea and its current leader is ever likely to stick, and President Trump was correct to walk away. However, Trump's failure to consider the U.S. WATNA also left the United States more vulnerable. Instead of maintaining a win-win environment where negotiations could resume at an important, but lower, working level, President Trump focused more on his image as the only one who could resolve the North Korean nuclear issue, which probably led him to miscalculate. Some speculate that Trump's motivation for entering into negotiations with North Korea in the first place was a vain desire to pursue the Nobel Peace Prize, something he wanted so badly that his officials asked the Japanese prime minister to nominate him.[13] Much as the Kim family regime cult of personality may make it hard for the North Korean leader to return to his offer at the Hanoi Summit, the president's narrative that only he could negotiate peace with North Korea and that he should win the Nobel Prize if he achieved it, made it difficult for President Trump to convincingly walk away from the process as well. The DPRK believed Trump will always want to come back and it engaged in activities to adjust his BATNA/WATNA calculation by reestablishing some of its dismantled capabilities and resuming missile launches to remind the United States and the region of the threat that it can pose.

As the United States headed into the Biden administration, North Korea appeared to be the party most prepared to exercise strategic patience. North Korea has refrained from any discussion with the United States since October 2019, even before the COVID-19 pandemic resulted in closing of the country's borders. Stephen Biegun, President Trump's Special Representative for North Korea Policy, said that Trump's surprise June 30, 2019 visit to Panmunjom when he stepped across into North Korea was the Trump administration's last chance to break the logjam. Likening negotiations about Trump's visit to DPRK as a discussion in a *souk* (Middle Eastern marketplace), Biegun noted that Trump's proposal to meet Chairman Kim at Panmunjom was issued on Twitter and that North Korea responded with a press statement saying the idea was "interesting" but no substantive discussions followed the brief visit.[14] On

---

13. House Republicans, Japanese prime minister Shinzo Abe, and ROK president Moon Jae-In have made public calls for Trump to be nominated for the Nobel Peace Prize, to which Trump has responded by saying "Everybody thinks so (that he should win the prize)" but all he wants is peace for the world. See Emily Cochrane. May 9, 2018. "President Trump a Nobel Laureate? It's a Possibility." *New York Times*; Jason Lemon. February 9, 2019. "Trump's Government Asked Japan's Prime Minister to Nominate Him for Nobel Peace Prize." *Newsweek*.

14. NK News Podcast, Episode 191, July 14, 2021 at 92 minutes to 94 minutes, 30 sec-

October 5, 2019, DPRK and U.S. negotiators met in "working-level talks" in Stockholm, Sweden, for a final bid at restarting talks. In only a few hours, it became clear that DPRK negotiators attended only to see if the United States was bringing any new approaches to the negotiating table.[15] Seeing that it had nothing new to offer, the DPRK negotiators were the ones to walk away. They described the talks as "sickening" and unlikely to produce an outcome. DPRK officials told me this was an intentional "insult" to the United States, as a reciprocal payback for the insult they felt in having their leader travel all the way to Hanoi and not walk away with a deal. After Stockholm, DPRK officials threatened a year-end deadline for the United States to produce a new offer, after which time they said the DPRK would pursue a "new path" to negotiations, widely believed to indicate new military tests and provocations, coupled with a policy of economic self-reliance and not depending on negotiations with the United States.

The DPRK appears to have made good on its promise to abandon negotiations with the United States made after the Stockholm talks. After the failed Stockholm talks, it had no further contact with the Trump administration or its negotiators and had no early contacts with the Biden administration. The Biden administration's North Korea policy review suggests that it is similarly in no hurry to talk to the DPRK. For instance, President Biden has appointed as his lead negotiator the U.S. ambassador to Indonesia, who has said he will remain at his post in Jakarta until the North Koreans "pick up the phone" or otherwise show interest in talks with the United States.[16] But the DPRK also refrained from a major military provocation in the form of a new nuclear or ICBM test. What had been expected as a December 2019 "Christmas gift" never materialized. Why didn't the DPRK make such a test? Was this not a way to up the ante for the Trump administration and change the U.S. BATNA? Perhaps the DPRK exercised restraint because it realized that, as much as it was embarrassed and angry after Hanoi, it had few alternatives. Perhaps China discouraged it from following through. Like

onds discussion. https://www.nknews.org/category/north-korea-news-podcast/latest/an-inte
rview-with-stephen-biegun-nknews-podcast-ep-191/902590

15. David Sanger. October 5, 2019. "U.S. Nuclear Talks with North Korea Break Down in Hours." *New York Times*; Jung Pak. October 18, 2019. "Why North Korea Walked Away from Negotiations in Sweden." Brookings Institution. https://www.brookings.edu/blog/order-from-chaos/2019/10/18/why-north-korea-walked-away-from-negotiations-in-sweden/

16. White House Press Briefing, May 21, 2021, Remarks by President Biden and H. E. Moon Jae In, President of the Republic of Korea. https://www.whitehouse.gov/briefing-room/speeches-remarks/2021/05/21/remarks-by-president-biden-and-h-e-moon-jae-in-president-of-the-republic-of-korea-at-press-conference/

it or not, the path to improved relations, an end to the Korean War, security guarantees, and a brighter economic future for Pyongyang inevitably must lead through Washington. As a result, I assess that at the time of publication, the DPRK is waiting to see what happens with the Biden administration. If it pursues negotiations, the DPRK will listen. If not, DPRK officials have said, they gained time to increase and perfect their military technologies after the Hanoi Summit. In terms of a BATNA, they are no worse off by waiting out the U.S. decision, and they may have gained progress and practice in advancing their military technology in the interim.

CHAPTER 14

Conclusion

You Can Get More Back . . . Without Giving Up Your Core Interests

In the preceding chapters, we analyzed a range of frameworks, tactics, and strategies for Getting More Back in multiparty international negotiations. Awareness of key frameworks—such as the roles of direct and indirect parties, mediators, guarantors, and observers—can help you to communicate effectively and situationally with the relevant players and to focus your negotiation approaches and outreach. Understanding the tactics and strategies in your toolbox—and those that may be used against you—prepares you to get the most for your country or client in any negotiation and not to be fooled by tactics deployed by your counterpart. In this concluding chapter, we will review the case studies we have analyzed to illustrate these frameworks, tactics, and strategies and consider one additional case—the ongoing discussion shaping global leadership roles between the United States and China. In part a bilateral dispute and in part a multiparty discussion, the question whether a multiparty international negotiation develops over the United States' and China's future leadership roles in world affairs is likely to be part of one of the most important international negotiations of power in our lifetimes. We will also explore how the lens of negotiation theory can help you better understand the underlying political elements of conflicts being negotiated and how power is exercised in a negotiation, whether or not you subscribe to the businessman's negotiating style.

U.S.-China Tensions in 2020 and the Missed Opportunity of COVID

As the coronavirus pandemic struck the world early in 2020, Chinese and American leaders entered into a negotiation of sorts, but one with many challenging characteristics. The outbreak of the pandemic asserted strong pressure initially on Beijing and later on Washington to come up with a response to this nontraditional security threat amid loss of life and economic strength. It also took place under an intense spotlight of domestic pressure and international scrutiny. As we have seen in previous case studies, face-to-face discussion among diplomats meeting privately and seeking to identify common interests and goals in a neutral setting with time to have multiple rounds of discussion is the preferred setting for a multiparty international negotiation. By contrast, discussion about how the United States and China might work together to organize a global response to the pandemic took place in the worst possible conditions. In person, quiet, face-to-face negotiations were impossible in an era of travel bans and under a spotlight with the whole world wondering how its superpowers would respond.

Moreover, the power dynamics between China and the United States created a breeding ground for mistrust and mutual suspicion. For the world at large, the coronavirus crisis could not have come at a worse time for getting Beijing and Washington to work together. Brewing conflicts over trade, technology, economic espionage, human rights, rule of law, and global projection of economic, political, and military power had been ramping up since Trump arrived in office. In trade negotiations, Trump heralded his success in standing up to the Chinese, encouraging greater purchases of soybeans and other agricultural products and tamping down on Chinese technology companies' access to U.S. and global markets where Chinese surveillance practices may violate rule of law standards. For its part, China's rising power and confidence under President Xi Jinping had made it more willing to stand up to U.S. tactics and to use some elements of its rising global power to push back. On the global stage and especially in the United Nations, China has claimed that it has played by the rules of the international system . . . and is winning. In this environment, many Chinese felt the United States was trying to change the rules of the game once China learned them. From this perspective, Chinese officials felt the Trump administration unfairly labeled China a cheater, especially when the Trump administration found China's trade practices unfair and initiated new tariffs, bans on Chinese companies like Huawei, and even threatened to limit access to the United States by Chinese students. With actors on both sides of the Pacific eager to find opportunities to blame the other and press advantage against a weakened adversary, any exploration of positions and interests to find mutual gain or create value would be challenging.

To make matters worse, preexisting frameworks and established dialogues where negotiators might have privately worked to find a global solution in an atmosphere of trust had all been closed down. More than thirty thematic bilateral dialogues between the United States and China had taken place to flesh out details of the Bush and Obama administration relationships with China under Hu Jintao. The dialogues were even organized under an overarching framework known as the Strategic and Economic Dialogue. But those dialogues were closed down during the Trump and Xi administrations, replaced by trade wars and increasing political and military competition. When contacts did occur, they were either summits between the two leaders or cabinet-level negotiations to resolve the trade tensions. Again, this left little space for professional negotiators. In short, the status of the bilateral relationship and underlying political dynamics into which the coronavirus pandemic emerged created a difficult environment to get any negotiation off the ground involving these two mutually suspicious powers.

As the pandemic spread and public pressure mounted, U.S. and Chinese leaders traded increasingly confrontational public allegations of fault. In January and early February 2020 when China and South Korea were the main locations of the virus, Asia mostly battled the virus alone and its governments took strong measures in response. The United Nations played a limited role in organizing what could have been a more conducive environment for constructive negotiation, but the world mostly watched. In terms of negotiation roles, the world outside the United States and China was an interested observer but at most an indirect participant in the crisis. It seems clear in retrospect that an opportunity for better U.S.-China coordination in better conditions was missed. As the disease spread to Europe in February and the WHO declared a global pandemic on March 11, attention shifted briefly to a global response. The United States and China worked together for a short time in March, especially on issues of the global supply chain and distribution of mostly Chinese-made protective equipment and pharmaceuticals. But without any party creating organizing principles or a framework for talks on how assistance could be spread equitably around the world, the competitive bilateral power dynamics and recriminations of recent trade and technology wars quickly turned a possible global negotiation into a bilateral free for all. U.S. attention became focused on getting a sufficient supply of masks and medicines for its cities and major impacted areas, with little or no attention to the global nature of the pandemic. China, as the manufacturer of most of the suddenly scarce medical supplies, had greater leverage to organize a global discussion. But it also failed to use this leverage and instead appears to have followed a transactional model of individual companies distributing supplies for financial gain without broad consultation or principles aimed at benefitting the global environment. As the disease spread in the United States, public pressure and antagonistic rhetoric against China mounted, especially coming from the White House and Secretary of State Pompeo. Any opportunity for holding a constructive negotiation between Beijing and Washington about how best to defend the international community from the common threat the virus posed to the health of all had been lost.

By mid-March, the United States was clear in blaming China for causing the virus. President Trump frequently insulted China on Twitter for its handling of the virus response, repeatedly labeling the disease the "China virus." Secretary of State Pompeo went so far as to destroy consensus at the March 2020 G7 leaders' summit on a statement of global response because the United States insisted on labeling COVID-19 the "Wuhan virus," which European, Canadian, and Japanese leaders rejected. For its part, China's "wolf warrior" spokesman at the foreign ministry, Zhao Lijian, suggested that it might have been the U.S. army who brought COVID to Wuhan when it participated in military sporting games there in 2019. On March 20, he told those who criticize China's handling of the virus to "stop wearing Chinese-made masks and protective gowns." The uproar caused a rare public split between positions of Chinese diplomats, with China's ambassador in Washington saying in a televised interview that it is "crazy" to spread conspiracy theories that the United States caused the coronavirus and rather acknowledging that the virus regrettably originated in China. After failing to resolve the dispute through a "war of words," the United States took the dispute to the United Nations, where the Trump administration criticized, conditioned, and ultimately threatened to withdraw from participation in and financial support of the World Health Organization, the global body tasked with advising the world on pandemics and other emerging health issues. The prospect of the two superpowers leading a multiparty international negotiation to address the virus was essentially dead, along with hundreds of thousands of COVID victims.

In this context, let us quickly review the primary tactics and strategies we have discussed in this book and see how they might apply to the U.S.–China dynamic. As a negotiator, you are likely to get more back if you can successfully deploy the following tactics outlined in the previous chapters:

- Explore Interests to Better Understand Your and Your Counterpart's Positions and Options
- Invent Options for Mutual Gain or Creating Value
- Test Positions Articulated by Counterpart for Seriousness and Sincerity
- Be Nice While Disagreeing, Unless You Have a Good Reason to be Nasty
- Avoid Leaving Money, or a Better Deal, on the Table
- Be Careful Not to Overplay Your Hand
- Avoid Falling for Typical Arguments, and Know When or When Not to Deploy These Arguments around Wording
  - We Know You Are Our Friend
  - We Have No Such Word in Our Language
  - Just a Little Streamlining/Updating
  - Focus Internationally to Distract from Domestic Situation
  - Credibility of Institution Requires It
  - Know When to Obfuscate Using Lawyers or Experts
- Avoid Moving the Goal Posts
- Know When to Walk Away, and How to Get Back if You Do Walk
- Give Respect, Which Often Costs Nothing and Can Earn a Lot
- Negotiate Mostly in Private, Unless You Need to Use the Media
- Use Objective Criteria Rather than Dwelling on Difficult Rhetoric
- Understand Each Party's Timeframe
- Understand Your Best and Worst Alternatives to a Negotiated Agreement (BATNA and WATNA) and Learn How to Influence Your Counterpart's Perception of His BATNA and WATNA

Among these tools and tactics, we spent significant time thinking about the BATNA and other alternatives that a negotiator will have. The sense of whether or not the United States or China have alternatives to dealing with each other is one of the more central issues in their ongoing power dynamic. President Trump has frequently proposed that the United States does not need China and can "go it alone" in the world, achieving its objectives without interconnectedness to this second-largest but rising global power. President Trump may be trying to use negotiator tactics to press China to reconsider its alternatives and offer concessions to the United States. Initially, this appears to have enjoyed some success, as China and President Xi came forward with additional purchases and offered other concessions in order to reach a Phase 1 trade deal on January 15, 2020. Pursuant to that deal, China agreed to purchase $200 billion more of U.S. goods than it had in 2017, encompassing four sectors (manufacturing, services, agriculture, and energy). The discussion ended months of tariffs and recriminating trade restrictions between the two countries ongoing since March 2018, when the United States published findings that China was distorting trade under Section 301 of the Trade Act and began taking retaliatory measures.

What would be the alternatives to an economically interconnected China and the United States? If the U.S. threat of a trade war carried on to a stronger conclusion, how would global growth suffer? Chinese manufacturers need a U.S. market to sell their wares and U.S. consumers have become accustomed to the low cost and broad range of options for consumer goods that Chinese manufacturing affords. Some entire sectors of new and modern products—including solar panels and, as the world realized during the coronavirus, medical supplies and pharmaceuticals—are produced almost entirely and exclusively in China. Would each country truly decouple and produce only for its own market? Not to mention how decoupling would affect our increasingly interconnected online economy, where Chinese restrictions on content and free expression in what it considers sensitive areas like human rights, Taiwan, Hong Kong, and Xinjiang threaten to produce two different World Wide Webs of Internet information, one accessible behind China's great firewall and another one beyond. And how would the United States respond if China called in the over $1 trillion in U.S. debt it holds? Could a separate and isolated China survive U.S. threats to default on such a large sum given the already shaky nature of its banking system?

But unlike other adversaries who have sometimes been cowed or intimidated by threatening efforts to change their view of alternatives, China has a long-term view of its alternatives, or its own BATNA. As a rising power, with a huge population of low-cost labor, China's timeline is vastly different from that of the United States. It has viewed itself able to wait out the United States, and specifically wait for President Trump's first term to end, because of this rising power, elements of which include economic, military, and diplomatic strength.

The majority of this book's focus on multiparty international negotiations has emphasized that bullying tactics of a businessman-turned-international negotiator may not work because of the need to come back to the same international participants time and again. But the other context in which bullying tactics may also suffer is when a negotiating adversary has the strength and long-term time horizon to wait and outlast bullying tactics. This may be the case with the U.S.-China relationship in 2020.

Second, we have seen the importance of analyzing your own country's or client's positions within a negotiation. Are you among the most directly interested parties, indispensable to a resolution of the agreement? Or, such as China in the Six-Party Talks on North Korea, or Egypt in the Libyan conflict, are you an interested party who can use tactics such as hosting, mediating, or even political and military pressure to gain what you want without participating in every part of the negotiation? Can you use other players in the negotiation as proxies—as all sides did in Libya's postindependence struggle—or should you get more involved as a mediator or guarantor of a certain outcome? And are parties in a negotiation sometimes preforming just for the purposes of the observer or the media—as with Israeli and Palestinian negotiators during the efforts to implement the Oslo Accords? When you are not representing one of the most directly involved parties, we discussed how a party can still gain leverage and influence by acting as a host, mediator, or guarantor of the behavior of other parties. Hosts and mediators often wield outsized influence by controlling the agenda for talks, regulating the pace and setting of ice-breakers and informal negotiations, and by holding the pen for documenting outcomes and agreements. We saw how convening power carries with it not only benefits but also expectations, and observed how a host can also be blamed for the breakdown of negotiations, even though the host often lacks control of all elements that caused the talks to fail. Most of the tools a host or other mediator can use remain available with the recent shift to online negotiations, although in-person meetings remain a preferable format for addressing multiparty political disputes and ensuring that all viewpoints, emotions, and interests relevant to resolving such disputes are thoroughly aired before crafting an agreement.

For the United States and China today, much of their conflict is bilateral. But the process by which they address the coronavirus crisis or other global issues is a form of multiparty international political negotiation. In the discussion of how to address coronavirus, the United States and China are both direct participants, as each is clearly a country strongly impacted by the virus, albeit on different time scales with China facing the first major outbreak and the United States among the most impacted beginning in the summer of 2020. In responding to the crisis—such as with the provision of drugs, protective equipment, and a potential vaccine—both are also directly and closely involved. Beijing and Washington could play important additional roles as facilitators, conveners, and hosts of an international process to guide and direct a global response to the pandemic. But largely because of their bilateral conflict and the hardline negotiating styles and attitudes learned as a result of their trade war, they have so far chosen not to play a constructive role in leading or shaping a global response to coronavirus. And at least the United States has chosen to weaken international institutions, like the WHO, which might have stepped up to lead a global response in the absence of leadership from Beijing and Washington. In this way, both power dynamics and domestic politics have prevented the consensus necessary for a multiparty international negotiation to take place and become mature enough to help resolve the coronavirus crisis. If an international negotiation to address COVID does take place in the future, using the lenses of negotiation theory and power may help us understand the changes that facilitate such a discussion. The power-based perceptions of both China and the United States with respect to their alternatives and options in what, up to 2020, had been an increasingly interconnected world, will also play a key role in shaping how they decide to respond.

Third, we discussed the importance of having broad support for one's positions in multiparty negotiations, especially in the formation of cross-regional "core groups." We saw how states in the UN often follow their regional group, unless one state breaks consensus, after which each state must make its own judgement. For example, Ghana broke consensus of the African Group in 2015 and called for criticism of Burundi's human rights when its president sought an unconstitutional third term in office. This willingness to criticize a fellow African country opened the door for each country to make its own assessment, rather than the African group reflexively defending Burundi's actions. We also saw how states often make mistakes when they do not try to bring other participants into a negotiation and "go it alone" based on parochial concerns. This could be true in the Trumpian approach to North Korea or in Germany and Brazil's excessive focus on digital privacy and the perceived political slight caused when "Five Eyes" countries intercepted their leaders' communications, rather than following their national interests to find a balance between counterterror, privacy, free expression, and human rights concerns. Sometimes leading from behind is also the most powerful approach in international multiparty negotiations. Rather than having a large country or former colonial power take the lead as a public champion of a critical position, it can be much more effective for those within the region or from the developing world to lead efforts to resolve an issue. U.S. negotiators could have been more successful by taking a backseat in the effort to encourage Latin American states to take the lead on LGBTI rights, or in a modern example, to let Latin America lead in the handling of the Maduro regime in Venezuela, rather than having the United States as the public face of such efforts. Leading from behind takes confidence and a belief that getting a good outcome is more important than getting public credit for the outcome.

For the U.S.-China competition in the decade of the 2020s, power dynamics and absence of those preconditions makes working through others or leading from behind more challenging. The two countries have become very outspoken and competitive with one another on most global questions, making it a challenge for international institutions or regional powers to lead in problem solving if Washington and Beijing do not take part. But both states do have allies, proxies, and partners that can help to advance their points of view in a global discussion, even if not in a formal negotiation. In the United States, those allies have traditionally included the free market and democratic states of Europe, Canada, Mexico, Japan, South Korea, and Australia. China's allies have traditionally included other states with a similar worldview historically embedded in communism. More recently, however, the worldview China takes with its allies has coalesced around common interests in calling for "noninterference in internal affairs." This has given China a broader, more diverse group of authoritarian-leaning allies and proxies with like-minded views including Russia and Pakistan, plus others like Iran, Egypt, Tanzania, Burundi, Venezuela, and Sri Lanka. China's growing wealth has also changed its economic rhetoric in a decidedly non-Marxist direction. Traditionally, Beijing sought to lead the international coalition of developing states known as the G77 in efforts to demand greater wealth and assistance to the developing world. But China's growth and need for markets and natural resources has shifted its economic partnerships. Programs like its Belt and Road Initiative seek to weave networks of economic interdependence with potential partners beginning in China's Central and Southeast Asian neighbors and extending into Africa, the Indian subcontinent, and even Europe.

In the domain of economics and power, the United States and China have already deployed proxies and allies in their competition over 5G technology, and in particular, the Chinese company Huawei's role in developing 5G networks. The United States has consistently, and often successfully, persuaded traditional allies to ban Huawei and other Chinese-produced components from modern telecommunications systems in the name of national security.[1] The United States and its allies see a risk that sensitive information, including intellectual property and political information, might be taken by China through these Huawei-produced components and used to benefit the

---

1. See Lindsay Maizland and Andrew Chatzky. August 6, 2020. "Huawei: China's Controversial Tech Giant." CFR Backgrounder. Council on Foreign Relations. https://www.cfr.org/backgrounder/huawei-chinas-controversial-tech-giant; Justin Sherman. August 12, 2020. "Is the U.S. Winning Its Campaign Against Huawei?" *Lawfare*. https://www.lawfareblog.com/us-winning-its-campaign-against-huawei

Chinese state and the Communist Party. India, Singapore, and some others have also been persuaded of these risks and blocked Huawei-made components, albeit in more of a unilateral action than as part of a negotiation. China, for its part, is waging an aggressive campaign in support of Huawei, which has persuaded Russia, Hungary, Thailand, and the Philippines, among others, to use Huawei components. China has expressed frustration that Huawei is "playing by the rules of free market competition," and that Huawei is winning by providing quality components at lower prices. But experts say Huawei bids are sometimes so far below market rates—as in the Netherlands—that they are only possible due to Chinese government subsidies.[2] In both Washington and Beijing, the intensity of their competition has led both to lead from the front, rather than from behind. Most allies and potential proxies on either side are playing a secondary role as customers, although the U.S. campaign against Huawei technology has more recently led some NATO allies of the United States to publicly condemn Huawei as a security threat.

Fourth, we analyzed negotiations where words are the currency of a negotiation, as when the outcome is a resolution in the United Nations. In such negotiations, wording may allow significant opportunity for creative thinking. In such negotiations, the true interests of the parties can be less evident than in a peace negotiation or an agreement over military forces or arms control. Thus in negotiations over wording it is important to penetrate beyond the articulated positions of the parties and press to comprehend underlying interests. By so doing, numerous opportunities for creative win-win solutions can be found. For example, did certain African and Middle Eastern states have an unchangeable cultural objection to the support for LGBTI rights? Alternatively, could all parties agree that violence and attacks against any citizen, gay or straight, are unacceptable?

In discussing negotiations over wording, we have also analyzed when it is important that words convey stark meaning of condemnation—to highlight brutal practices, such as war crimes or mass atrocities in Burundi, South Sudan, and Syria, for example. Similarly, we found that when talking about delicate subjects—like the security services' responsibility for human rights abuses in Sudan—it might be necessary to address the cause and responsibility for violations in reference to other documents in order to find an agreement. Slogans and catch phrases can also sometimes take on larger-than-life meaning. The idea that citizens in the digital age "should enjoy the same rights online that they have offline," for example, was deployed to hoist the

---

2. See Maizland and Chatzky.

United States on its own petard in discussions of the right to privacy in the digital age. Further, in other negotiations in the UN Human Rights Council, we also observed how the responsibility of being members of the UN's foremost body to promote and protect human rights motivated states that might not be thought of as progressive to speak out in favor of the rights of other citizens and victims. Examples I witnessed of African diplomats from Ghana, Somalia, Ethiopia, and non-African El Salvador taking such stands were especially compelling. States can sometimes be motivated by the call that the "credibility of the institution" requires action, particularly action that protects the rights and lives of innocent civilians.

Neither China nor the United States appears to be deploying these tactics in their negotiations over dominance of global institutions and standards. President Trump's Twitter feed, Secretary of State Pompeo's public pronouncements, and the "Wolf Warrior" tone of Chinese public diplomacy have left little space for such nuanced uses of language. These tactics remain more appropriately deployed in technical negotiations over contracts, agreements, and UN resolutions.

Fifth, we looked at several examples of best and worst practices to inform your negotiating style. In addition to providing tools for the toolkit, these offered illustrations of what *not* to do. For example, American negotiators handling human rights with China knew that the Chinese preferred private discussion of human rights challenges to the kind of Twitter diplomacy more popular today. In negotiating over the release of human rights prisoners, Americans learned the hard way not to overplay their hands and the costs of making China feel inured to public criticism. We also looked at cases where negotiators accepted stated positions of their counterparts without putting them to the test. In the context of the UN Human Rights Council, this may have meant that action on LGBTI rights was delayed longer than necessary because of the desire of some leaders of the developing world to maintain regional or political solidarity.

Sixth, we have looked at several case studies that refine the concepts of BATNA and WATNA. I believe this tool is so powerful that its deployment should not just be limited to negotiations, but that it can be used to help analyze and improve conflict prevention in a range of potential political crises and scenarios. When a dictator is considering unleashing atrocity on his own people—as in South Sudan or Burundi, for example—making clear to him the consequences and alternatives to his action can be essential in preventing such a horror. Similarly, it is sometimes necessary to offer a negotiating counterpart an off-ramp to strike a deal. Thus we saw that deploying respect in the real world of diplomacy is almost always a cost-free way to create value and find win-win solutions. Using the BATNA/WATNA calculation can help to sharpen the choices not only for a dictator but also for those parties seeking to prevent violent behavior. Is it truly the best alternative to acquiesce to a campaign of murder like Asad waged in Syria—especially if you factor in the human cost of sustained internal conflict and the post-conflict cost of dealing with a rogue state like Syria that now believes it can survive any conflict or pressure placed on it from the outside world?

Finally, former President Trump has come in for particularly close scrutiny of the strengths and weaknesses of his CEO approach to negotiation, stereotyped by the *Art of the Deal*. President Trump's approach shows how to deploy many tactics of a good negotiator: don't leave money on the table, never be afraid to walk away, test the position of your counterpart. But the weakness of such a zero-sum approach has also been demonstrated, and in particular how destructive it can be in the domain of international multi-party negotiations. We highlighted how, in a recurring context of multiparty negotiations, a party cannot afford sharp tactics aimed at short-term gain because one will have to come back to the same parties time and again for future negotiations. Unlike a real estate deal, the costs of brinksmanship are just too high, as they threaten not only the outcome of the deal at hand but the relationships and systems that are important for reaching agreement on the next deal and future topics that may be far more significant than the issue at hand. As the United States struggles with the aftermath of Trump's decision to walk away from a partial deal at the Hanoi Summit with North Korean leader Kim Jong Un, will we find a path that makes the region and the world safer? Or will we continue to face the greatest nuclear threat to the world since the Cuban Missile Crisis as a result of the mercurial personalities who one day exchange "love letters" and engage in summitry, but the next day threaten rhetoric that could engulf the world's most prosperous region in a nuclear conflict?

Negotiations are a chance to have a unique view into the domain of foreign policy where power is exercised. My experience has been that negotiation theory and the quest by a good negotiator to find win-win solutions leads a diplomat to consider all sources of power and all issues of interest to his counterpart or counterparts. Sometimes these are obvious sources of hard power, such as the military resources at issue on the Korean Peninsula. But in many cases a counterpart has multiple interests, some of which are easier for a superpower like the United States to satisfy than for many other actors in the international arena. To do so, it requires deftly using the different negotiating styles, tools, and positions in a multiparty negotiation. And often good negotiation requires using the tools of soft power. For the

United States, it has often gained benefit, and sometimes increased its own soft power, through the use of such tools in negotiation. Giving a counterpart respect or prestige, offering to host a meeting in the United States, taking advantage of the cultural popularity of U.S. music and cinema, offering trade access to popularize Coca-Cola or Levis, or even giving the credibility that comes with a meeting with the leader of the free world are all tools of diplomacy uniquely available to the United States and American negotiators. Unfortunately, my concern is that the Trump administration too often disregarded these soft power benefits for the win-lose viewpoint embodied in *The Art of the Deal*. Far from making America great again, this shortsighted negotiation style may be accelerating American decline. By unnecessarily pressing the advantage and turning allies into enemies, this style has given competitors like a rising China the upper hand across the world, be it in soft power, political relationships, or even in President Trump's supposed specialty of commerce and trade negotiations.

Bibliography

"Albright Makes Historic Visit To North Korea." 2000. *Guardian*. October 23.

Albright, Madeleine Korbel. 2003. *Madam Secretary*. New York: Miramax Books.

ARC International. 2016. "Action On No-Action Motion On SOGI Resolution." http://arc-international.net/global-advocacy/human-rights-council/32nd-session -of-the-human-rights-council/appointing-an-independent-expert-on-sexual-orie ntation-and-gender-identity-an-analysis-of-process-results-and-implications/ann ex-ii-description-of-the-vote-on-the-sogi-resolution/action-on-no-action-motion/

Berenson, Tessa. 2018. "Why Trump's Predecessors Did Not Meet with North Korea." *Time*. March 8.

Bolton, John R. 2020. *The Room Where It Happened*. New York: Simon & Schuster.

Borger, Julian. 2019. "Vietnam Summit: North Korea and US Offer Differing Reasons for Failure of Talks." *Guardian*. https://www.theguardian.com/world/2019 /feb/28/vietnam-summittrump-and-kim-play-down-hopes-of-quick-results-nucle ar-talks

Bouhane, Yacine. 2014. "Op/Ed: Algeria's Role in Solving the Libya Crisis." https:// www.washingtoninstitute.org/policy-analysis/view/algerias-role-in-solving-the-lib ya-crisis

Browne, Ryan. 2019. "Trump Praises Libyan General as His Troops March on US Backed Government in Tripoli." CNN.com. https://edition.cnn.com/2019/04/19 /politics/us-libya-praise-haftar/index.html

Canineu, Maria Laura. 2019. "For Brazil at the UN, Rights Values Begin at Home." Human Rights Watch. https://www.hrw.org/news/2019/03/08/brazil-un-rights -values-begin-home

Centre for Humanitarian Dialogue. 2007. "A Guide to Mediation: Enabling Peace Processes in Violent Conflict." http://www.hdcentre.org/wp-content/uploads/20 16/08/83Guidedelamediation-February-2008.pdf

Cheney, Richard B., and Liz Cheney. 2011. *In My Time*. New York: Simon & Schuster.

Cheong, Young-rok. 2009. "Presentation by Seoul National University Professor Cheong Young-Rok." KEIA Conference on Dynamic Forces on the Korean Peninsula. http://keia.org/sites/default/files/publications/09.Cheong.pdf

Chestnut Greitens, Sheena, Myunghee Lee, and Emir Yazici. 2020. "Counterterrorism and Preventive Repression: China's Changing Strategy in Xinjiang." *International Security* 44 (3). https://www.mitpressjournals.org/doi/pdf/10.1162/isec_a_00368

"China Releases Political Prisoner Ahead of Visit by Rice." (Published 2005). 2020. Nytimes.com. https://www.nytimes.com/2005/03/17/international/asia/china-rel eases-political-prisoner-ahead-of-visit-by-rice.html

Christenfeld, Nicholas. 1995. "Choices from Identical Options." *SAGE Journals.* http://journals.sagepub.com/doi/abs/10.1111/j.1467-9280.1995.tb00304.x

Clinton, Hillary Rodham. 2017. *What Happened.* New York: Simon & Schuster.

Cochrane, Emily. 2018. "President Trump a Nobel Laureate? It's a Possibility." *New York Times.* May 9.

Craner, Lorne. 2004. "Remarks by U.S. Assistant Secretary for Democracy and Human Rights Lorne Craner, 'A Comprehensive Human Rights Strategy for China,' Delivered at the Carnegie Endowment for International Peace, January 29, 2004." https://2001-2009.state.gov/g/drl/rls/rm/28693.htm

Denyer, Simon. 2019. "North Korea's Yongbyon Nuclear Complex at the Heart of Trump-Kim Summit." *Washington Post.* February 22.

"East Libya Strongman Visits Russian Aircraft Carrier in Mediterranean: RIA." 2017. Reuters. January 11.

Einhorn, Robert. 2018. Interview by Eric Richardson with former U.S. Special Envoy and Missile Negotiator. In person. Geneva.

Elgot, Jessica. 2015. "Burundi: 87 Killed in Worst Violence since April Coup Attempt." *Guardian.* December 12.

"Emmanuel Macron Plans Crunch Summit to Push for Libyan Elections." 2018. *Guardian.* May 23.

Fasanotti, Frederica Saini, and Ben Fishman. 2018. "How France and Italy's Rivalry Is Hurting Libya." *Foreign Affairs.* October 31.

Feder, J. Lester. 2014. "South Africa, Which Once Led on Promoting LGBT Rights Abroad, Could Become a Roadblock." *Buzzfeed News.* http://ps://www.buzzfeed .com/lesterfeder/south-africa-which-once-led-on-promoting-lgbt-rights-abroad ?utm_term=.qrLb0n0YZ#.gnmmkwkjB

Getahun, Minelik. 2017. Interview with Former Ethiopian Ambassador Minelik Getahun by Eric Richardson. September. In person. Geneva.

Glendon, A. Ian, and Larry Crump. 2003. "Towards a Paradigm of Multiparty Negotiation." *International Negotiation* 8 (2): 197–234. doi:10.1163/1571806033225 76112

Glenn, Cameron. 2017. "Libya's Islamists: Who They Are and What They Want." Wilson Center. https://www.wilsoncenter.org/article/libyas-islamists-who-they -are-and-what-they-want

Goodenough, Patrick. 2019. "China Thanks 36 Countries, Half of Them Islamic States, for Praising Its Uighur Policies." CNS News. July 15. https://www.hrw .org/news/2019/07/10/un-unprecedented-joint-call-china-end-xinjiang-abuses. https://www.cnsnews.com/news/article/patrick-goodenough/china-thanks-37-co untries-including-islamic-states-praising-its

Grimes, William. 2005. "Ben Franklin Took on France with Insouciant Diplomacy." *New York Times.* April 6. E6.

Gstalter, Morgan. 2019. "Brazil's New President Removes LGBT Concerns from Human Rights Ministry." *The Hill.* https://thehill.com/policy/international/human-rights/423594-brazils-new-president-removes-lgbt-concerns-from-human

Hartzell, Caroline, and Matthew Hoddie. 2003. "Institutionalizing Peace: Power Sharing and Post-Civil War Conflict Management." *American Journal of Political Science* 47 (2): 318–32.

Hecker, Sigfried. 2010. "Lessons Learned from the North Korea Nuclear Crisis." *Daedalus.* Winter.

Howard, Adam. 2014. "UN Passes Resolution on Behalf of LGBT Citizens Around the Globe." MSNBC.com. October. http://www.msnbc.com/msnbc/un-passes-resolution-behalf-lgbt-citizens-around-the-globe

Hudson, John. 2019. "North Korean Saber Rattling Dims Euphoria of Trump's DMZ Meeting." *Washington Post.* July 26.

International Criminal Court. n.d. Al Bashir Case. https://www.icc-cpi.int/darfur/al bashir

"Interviews—Madeleine Albright | Kim's Nuclear Gamble | FRONTLINE | PBS." 2003. PBS.Org. http://www.pbs.org/wgbh/pages/frontline/shows/kim/interviews/albright.html

Israeli Ministry of Foreign Affairs. 1999. "The Israeli-Palestinian Interim Agreement on the West Bank and the Gaza Strip." http://www.mfa.gov.il/MFA/ForeignPolicy/Peace/Guide/Pages/THE%20ISRAELI-PALEST

Japanese Ministry of Foreign Affairs. 2006. "Japan-China Relations, Basic Data." https://www.mofa.go.jp/region/asia-paci/china/data.html

Kamm, John. 2009. "Remarks to the Commonwealth Club of San Francisco, 'How Tiananmen Changed China.'" Dui Hua Foundation. http://duihua.org/wp/?page_id=2520

Kessler, Glenn. 2011. "Colin Powell versus Dick Cheney." *Washington Post.* August 30.

"Khalifa Haftar: The Libyan General With Big Ambitions." 2019. BBC News. April 8.

"Khalifa Haftar, Libya's Strongest Warlord, Makes a Push for Tripoli." 2019. *Economist.* April 20.

Labott, Elise. 2005. "U.S. Drops China Rights Censure." 2005. CNN.com. March 18. http://edition.cnn.com/2005/WORLD/asiapcf/03/17/china.humanrights

Landler, Mark. 2018. "Trump Pulls Out of North Korea Summit Meeting with Kim Jong Un." *New York Times.* May 24.

Launspach, Fleur. 2016. "ÚN: Tens of Thousands Killed in South Sudan War." *Al Jazeera.* March 3.

Lazaroff, Tovah. 2014. "UNHRC Delays Appointing New Special Rapporteur to Replace Falk." *Jerusalem Post.* March 29.

Lemon, Jason. 2019. "Trump's Government Asked Japan's Prime Minister to Nominate Him for Nobel Peace Prize." *Newsweek.* February 9.

"Libyan Factions Agree to Hold Elections on 10 December." 2018. *Guardian.* May 29.

"Libyan Officials Meet in London in Hopes of Economic Stabilization." 2016. *Libya Gazette.*

Maizland, Lindsay, and Andrew Chatzky. 2020. "Huawei: China's Controversial Tech

Giant." CFR Backgrounder. Council on Foreign Relations. https://www.cfr.org/ba
ckgrounder/huawei-chinas-controversial-tech-giant

Malsin, Jared. 2017. "U.S.-Made Airplanes Deployed in Libya's Civil War, in Defiance
of U.N." *Time*. http://time.com/4746914/libya-civil-war-airplanes-haftar-uae/

Mitra, Devirupa. 2019. "Despite SC Ruling, India Abstains Again on Vote on LGBT
Rights at UN." *The Wire*. https://thewire.in/diplomacy/india-abstains-again-on-vo
te-expert-lgbt-rights-at-un

Morello, Carol. 2016. "UN Council Creates Watchdog for LGBT Rights." *Washington Post*. June 30.

Nakamura, David, and Philip Rucker. 2018. "Trump Offers Reassurance That North
Korean Dictator Kim Jong Un Would Remain in Power Under Nuclear Deal."
Washington Post. https://www.washingtonpost.com/politics/trump-offers-reassura
nce-that-north-korean-dictator-kim-jong-un-would-remain-in-power-under-nuc
lear-deal/2018/05/17/901635e0-59ff-11e8-8836-a4a123c359ab_story.html?utm
_term=.cacc8dba05f2

Natsios, Andrew. 2012. "U.S. Food Aid to North Korea Sends the Wrong Message."
Washington Post. March 7.

NK News, 2021. "An Interview With Steve Biegun," *NK News Podcast Episode* 191,
July 14. https://www.nknews.org/category/north-korea-news-podcast/latest/an-
interview-with-stephen-biegun-nknews-podcast-ep-191/902590/

OECD. 2011. "China's Emergence as a Market Economy: Achievements and Challenges." OECD Contribution to the China Development Forum 20–21 March
2011, Beijing. http://www.oecd.org/governance/public-finance/47408845.pdf

O'Grady, Siobhain. 2019. "A Shared Dinner, a Canceled Lunch: What Trump and
Kim Did—And Didn't—Eat in Vietnam." *New York Times*. February 28.

Olson, Elizabeth. 1999. "China Escapes Censure in Vote by UN Human Rights Agency." *New York Times*. April 24.

"Oslo Accords Fast Facts." 2013. CNN.com. https://edition.cnn.com/2013/09/03
/world/meast/oslo-accords-fast-facts/index.html

Pagano Dritto, Alessandro. 2017. "Libya's HOR's Ageela Saleh and State Council's
Abdul Rahman Sewehli Met in Rome, Italy, for the First Time." *Between Libya And
Italy*. https://betweenlibyaanditaly.wordpress.com/2017/04/23/6950/

Pak, Jung. 2019. "Why North Korea Walked Away from Negotiations in Sweden."
Order from Chaos. Washington, DC: Brookings Institution. https://www.brooki
ngs.edu/blog/order-from-chaos/2019/10/18/why-north-korea-walked-away-from
-negotiations-in-sweden/

Park, Ju-min, and James Pearson. 2019. "Inside the Dying Moments of the Trump-
Kim Summit at a Hanoi Hotel." Reuters. February 28.

"People Prefer the Middle Option." 2012. *British Psychological Society's Research Digest*.
April 30.

Pigman, Lincoln, and Kyle Orton. 2017. "Inside Putin's Libyan Power Play." *Foreign
Policy*. September 14.

Ploughshares Fund. 2019. "Begun Is Half Done." https://www.ploughshares.org/sites
/default/files/resources/Begun-is-Half-Done-2019.pdf

Quinney, Nigel, and Richard Solomon. 2010. *American Negotiating Behavior: Wheeler-
Dealers, Legal Eagles, Bullies, and Preachers*. Washington, DC: U.S. Institute of Peace.

"Rebiya Kadeer's Release Part of China's Hostage Diplomacy." 2005. Radio Free Asia. March 18.

Rice, Condoleezza. 2011. *No Higher Honor*. New York: Broadway Books.

Salacuse, Jeswald W. 2003. *The Global Negotiator*. New York: St. Martin's Press.

Sanger, David. 2002. "North Korea Says It Has a Program on Nuclear Arms." *New York Times*. October 17.

Sanger, David. 2019. "U.S. Nuclear Talks with North Korea Break Down in Hours." *New York Times*. October 5.

Sasaki, Hitoshi, and Yuko Koga. 2003. "Trade Between Japan and China: Dramatic Expansion and Structural Changes." Bank of Japan Research and Statistics Department. August. https://www.boj.or.jp/en/research/wps_rev/ec/data/rkt03e03.pdf

Schiff, Stacy. 2005. *A Great Improvisation: Franklin, France and the Birth of America*. New York: Henry Holt and Co.

Schriver, Randall. 2009. "Testimony Before House Foreign Affairs Committee, Subcommittee on Oversight, June 16, 2009." http://project2049.net/documents/uigh er_testimony_of_randall_schriver.pdf

Sherman, Justin. 2020. "Is the U.S. Winning Its Campaign Against Huawei?" *Lawfare*. August 12. https://www.lawfareblog.com/us-winning-its-campaign-against-huawei

Smale, Alison. 2013. "Anger Growing Among Allies on U.S. Spying." *New York Times*. October 23.

Spiegel, Mickey. 2003. "China's Game with Political Prisoners, Op/Ed." *International Herald Tribune*. December 6.

"Strike Hard Campaigns in Xinjiang." 2013. *China Daily*. December 28.

"Stung by the NSA's Reach, Brazil and Germany Prepare for Closer Ties." 2015. *Deutsche Welle*. August 13.

Talmadge, Eric. 2019. "DPRK Chairman Kim Rethinking U.S. Talks, Launch Moratorium." Associated Press. March 15.

Thrush, Glenn. 2017. "No U.S. Military Role in Libya, Trump Says, Rejecting Italy's Pleas." *New York Times*. April 20.

Tiezi, Shannon. 2015. "It's Official: China, South Korea Sign Free Trade Agreement." *The Diplomat*. https://thediplomat.com/2015/06/its-official-china-south-korea-si gn-free-trade-agreement/

Tossell, Jonathan. 2020. "Libya's Haftar and the Fezzan: One Year On." CRU Policy Brief. Clingandael Institute. January. https://www.clingendael.org/sites/default/fil es/2020-01/Policy_Brief_Libyas_Haftar_and_the_Fezzan_Jan_2020.pdf

"Trump Praises Libyan General as His Troops March on U.S. Backed Government in Tripoli." 2019. CNN News. April 19.

"UAE Provided Military Aid for Haftar, Says Libyan Politician." 2017. *Middle East Eye*. April 27.

UNICEF. 2015. "Unspeakable Violence Against Children in South Sudan—UNICEF Chief." https://www.unicef.org/media/media_82319.html

United Nations. 1999. "Commission on Human Rights Adopts Resolutions on Situation of Human Rights in Nigeria, Lebanon, Iran, Iraq, Sudan." Press Release HR/CN/931. April 26. https://www.un.org/press/en/1999/19990426.HRCN9 31.html

United Nations. 2017. "Report of the Commission on Human Rights in South

Sudan." UN Document A/HRC/34/63, March 6, 2017. https://ap.ohchr.org/doc uments/dpage_e.aspx?si=A/HRC/34/63

United Nations. 2020. "Security Council Backs Long-Delayed Call to Support SG Call for Humanitarian Ceasefires." https://news.un.org/en/story/2020/07/106 7552

United Nations. 2020. "UN Secretary General Reiterates Call for Global Ceasefires." https://www.un.org/press/en/2020/sgsm20032.doc.htm

United Nations General Assembly. 2013. "The Right to Privacy in the Digital Age." Resolution 68/137 (adopted December 18, 2013). https://www.un.org/en/ga/sear ch/view_doc.asp?symbol=A/RES/68/167

United Nations General Assembly. 2019. "Report of the Independent Expert on Violence and Discrimination on the Basis of Sexual Orientation and Gender Identity." July 17. https://undocs.org/A/74/181

United Nations Human Rights Council. 2011. "Human Rights, Sexual Orientation and Gender Identity (SOGI)." HRC Resolution 17/19 (adopted June 17, 2011). https://documents-dds-ny.un.org/doc/UNDOC/GEN/G11/148/76/PDF/G111 4876.pdf?OpenElement

United Nations Human Rights Council. 2012. "The Promotion, Protection and Enjoyment of Human Rights on the Internet." HRC Resolution 20/8 (adopted July 5, 2012). https://undocs.org/A/HRC/RES/20/8

United Nations Human Rights Council. 2014. "Human Rights, Sexual Orientation and Gender Identity Resolution." HRC Resolution 27/32 (adopted September 26, 2014). https://documents-dds-ny.un.org/doc/UNDOC/GEN/G14/177/32/PDF /G1417732.pdf?OpenElement

United Nations Human Rights Council. 2015. "Technical Assistance and Capacity-Building to Improve Human Rights in the Sudan." HRC Resolution 30/22 (adopted October 2, 2015). https://documents-dds-ny.un.org/doc/UNDOC /GEN/G15/233/12/PDF/G1523312.pdf?OpenElement

United Nations Human Rights Council.2016. "March 10, 2016, Item 2 Joint Statement On Human Rights Situation In China." https://geneva.usmission.gov/2016 /03/10/item-2-joint-statement-human-rights-situation-in-china/.

United Nations Human Rights Council. 2016. "The Promotion, Protection and Enjoyment of Human Rights on the Internet." HRC Resolution 20/16 (adopted July 1, 2016). https://undocs.org/A/HRC/RES/32/13

United Nations Human Rights Council. 2016. "Protection Against Violence and Discrimination Based on Sexual Orientation and Gender Identity." HRC Resolution 32/2 (adopted June 30, 2016). https://documents-dds-ny.un.org/doc/UNDOC /GEN/G16/154/15/PDF/G1615415.pdf?OpenElement

United Nations Human Rights Council. 2016. "The Situation of Human Rights in South Sudan." HRC Resolution 31/20 (adopted March 23, 2016). UN General Assembly. https://documents-dds-ny.un.org/doc/UNDOC/GEN/G16/086/91 /PDF/G1608691.pdf?OpenElement

United Nations Human Rights Council. 2019. "Mandate of the Independent Expert on Protection Against Violence and Discrimination Based on Sexual Orientation and Gender Identity." HRC Resolution 41/18 (adopted July 12, 2019). https://do cuments-dds-ny.un.org/doc/UNDOC/GEN/G19/221/62/PDF/G1922162.pdf ?OpenElement

United Nations Human Rights Council. 2020. "Report of the Independent Expert on Protection Against Violence and Discrimination Based on Sexual Orientation and Gender Identity." May 1. https://undocs.org/A/HRC/44/53

United Nations Human Rights Council Webcast Archives. 2015. Video. Geneva: October 2, 2015, under Item 10, Sudan, including statements by the European Union and the United Kingdom.

"UN News Press Release, UN Issues First Report on Human Rights of Gay and Lesbian People." 2011. December 15.

"UN: Unprecedented Joint Call for China to End Xinjiang Abuses, 22 Countries Decry Mass Detention, Seek Monitoring." 2019. Human Rights Watch. https://www.hrw.org/news/2019/07/10/un-unprecedented-joint-call-china-end-xinjiang-abuses

United Nations Office of the High Commissioner for Human Rights. "Special Procedures of the UN Human Rights Council." n.d. https://www.ohchr.org/EN/HRBodies/SP/Pages/Welcomepage.aspx

Ury, William L., and Roger Fisher. 2011. *Getting To Yes*. 2nd ed. New York: Penguin Books.

"U.S. Mission Geneva, March 11, 2016 Side Event of the UN Human Rights Council." 2016. Facebook.com. https://www.facebook.com/usmissiongeneva/photos/his-holiness-the-dalai-lama-participates-in-a-side-event-of-the-un-human-rights-/10153728017638876/

The White House. 2018. "Singapore Summit Communique." https://www.whitehouse.gov/briefings-statements/joint-statement-president-donald-j-trump-united-states-america-chairman-kim-jong-un-democratic-peoples-republic-korea-singapore-summit/

The White House, 2021. "Remarks by President Biden and H.E. Moon Jae In, President of the Republic of Korea at Press Conference," May 21. https://www.whitehouse.gov/briefing-room/speeches-remarks/2021/05/21/remarks-by-president-biden-and-h-e-moon-jae-in-president-of-the-republic-of-korea-at-press-conference

Whitfield, Theresa. 2010. "External Actors in Mediation." Center for Humanitarian Dialogue Practice Series. Geneva. https://www.hdcentre.org/wp-content/uploads/2016/08/35Externalactorsinmediation-MPS-February-2010.pdf

Zoellick, Robert. 2005. "Whither China: From Membership to Responsibility? Remarks of the U.S. Deputy Secretary of State to National Committee on U.S.-China Relations, Sept. 21, 2005, New York City." https://2001-2009.state.gov/s/d/former/zoellick/rem/53682.htm

Zwirko, Colin, and Oliver Hotham. 2019. "North Korea Has No Intention to Give U.S. Concessions on Denuclearization." *NK News*. March 14.

Index